Computer Network Security and Cyber Ethics

FOURTH EDITION

Computer Network Security and Cyber Ethics

FOURTH EDITION

Joseph Migga Kizza

McFarland & Company, Inc., Publishers

Jefferson, North Carolina

ISBN 978-0-7864-9392-0 (softcover : acid free paper) ∞
ISBN 978-1-4766-1560-8 (ebook)

LIBRARY OF CONGRESS CATALOGUING DATA ARE AVAILABLE

BRITISH LIBRARY CATALOGUING DATA ARE AVAILABLE

Front cover: Firewall lock on mainboard (© iStock/Thinkstock)

Manufactured in the United States of America

*McFarland & Company, Inc., Publishers
Box 611, Jefferson, North Carolina 28640
www.mcfarlandpub.com*

Celebrating what is good within us all.
Keep the fire burning!

Acknowledgments

I am very grateful to all colleagues for the ideas, suggestions, and criticisms they freely gave to me.

I am indebted to my daughters, Josephine and Florence, and to my dear wife, Omumbejja Immaculate, for her input and support. She was instrumental in many ways.

Finally, to all those who, in one way or another, contributed to this project, but whose names do not appear, thanks!

Contents

Preface

Since the publication of the third edition of this book in 2011, a lot has changed. Dramatic advances in mobile technology have resulted in the unprecedented growth of social networks. This fast-changing technology landscape has forced me to make considerable changes to the contents of the book to bring my faithful readers and students of information technology up to date.

We have updated most of the contents in a good number of chapters, added chapters with new contents and removed chapters with outdated content. With all these alterations, additions and removals, we have kept the core theme of the text the same but brought new light, and new discussion points, to the table. Although the book has been in production since 2002, when it was selected as a **Choice** *Outstanding Academic Title*, the core theme of the book has endured. This is a testimony not only to the quality of the book but also to the persistence and growing relevancy of the issues discussed.

The growing relevancy of the issues in the book have confirmed and solidified my belief over the years that the security of cyberspace, as it evolves and engulfs all of us, is and will always be based on secure, reliable software and hardware protocols and best practices and a strong ethical framework for all its users. If a morally astute and ethically trained user is missing from the equation, cyberspace will never be secure and, therefore, the information infrastructure we have come to depend on so much will likewise never be secure. We focus on these core issues throughout the book.

Because of the central role of this ethical framework, we devote the first four chapters to morality, ethics, and technology and value. In these, we demonstrate the central role of morality and ethics in the decision-making process of an information professional, and indeed all humans handling information technology. We also discuss in depth the value that technology adds and the role it plays in our deliberations before we make decisions. We ponder the question of whether technology makes decisions for us or whether we depend on and use it to make wise decisions of our own.

1

In all, the security of information in general and of computer networks in particular, on which our national critical infrastructure and, indeed, our lives is increasingly depending, is based squarely on the individuals who build the hardware and design and develop the software that run the networks that store our vital information.

To address security issues in the rapidly changing technology and in the growing ecosystem of online social networks, we have added two new chapters, "Security in Mobile Systems" and "Security in the Cloud." To continue the discussion of the ever-changing nature of security protocols and best practices, we have reworked and kept Chapter 8 as "Information Security Protocols and Best Practices." The last chapter has been updated and renamed "Security and Compliance" to update the debate in the changing business information security landscape.

Although we seem to be making efforts toward mitigating computer security incidents, the progress we are achieving seems insignificant. Indeed, data from incident reporting centers shows no let-up in activity from the time of this book's first edition to today. In fact, data shows that digital crime incidents are mutating, unrelenting, always on the rise, which begs the question—are we doing the right thing?

Maybe not. After more than 10 years of efforts to rein in the growing and indeed mutating information infrastructure security problems, we still do not seem to be doing the right thing. Maybe we need to change course. The rise in such incidents has been and still is an indication of the poor state of our cyberspace infrastructure security policies and the vulnerability of all cyberspace resources. We have been pointing out over the years that we are yet not doing enough. Toward this end, several private and public initiatives and partnerships have been have been established and are discussed throughout the book.

Finally, as has been the case in the last three editions, we are still keeping the fire burning, for public awareness of the magnitude of cyber security and cybercrimes, the weaknesses and loopholes inherent in the cyberspace infrastructure, and the ways to protect ourselves and our society. We also must have more debate on the need for a strong ethical framework as a way to safeguard cyberspace.

Chapter 1

The Changing Landscape of Cybercrime

LEARNING OBJECTIVES:

After reading this chapter, the reader should be able to:
- Describe trends in computer crimes and protection against viruses and other cybercrimes.
- Discuss the history of computer crimes.
- Describe several different cyber-attacker approaches and motivations.
- Identify the professional's role in security and the tradeoffs involved.

In the last two decades, we have witnessed the rapid growth of the Internet, mobile technology and the correspondingly rapid growth of online crimes, or cybercrimes. With this growth, there has been a spike in the rate of cybercrimes committed over the Internet. This has resulted into some people condemning the Internet and partner technologies as responsible for creating new crimes and the root causes of these crimes. However, there is hardly any new crime resulting from these new technologies. What has changed, as a result of these new technologies, is the enabling environment. Technology is helping in the initiation and propagation of most known crimes. As we get rapid changes in technological advances, we are correspondingly witnessing waves of cybercrimes evolving. Figure 1.1 shows the changing nature of the cyber-crime landscape since 1980.

The period before 1980 was an experimental period. Then, the Internet was new and required sophisticated and specialized knowledge that very few people back then had. There was very little valuable information and data stored in online databases as there is today, and there were no free online hacking tools available. If one wanted to hack, one had to develop the tools to do the job— a daunting task that required expertise. The easiest way to do it was to join hacking groups. Ganglike groups like the Legions of Doom, the Chaos Computer

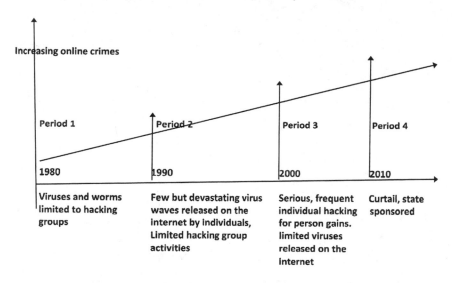

Figure 1.1 The Changing Nature of Cybercrimes

Club, NuPrometheus League, and the Atlanta Three were formed. Most of these groups were led by notorious individuals like Kevin Mitnick ("The Condor"), Ian Murphy ("Captain Zap"), and Patrick K. Kroupa ("Lord Digital").

At the tail end of the 1980s, computers had become smaller. The personal computer (PC) had been introduced and was becoming very successful. Businesses were buying these computers at a rapid pace. Schools of varying standards were opening up and filling with students interested in becoming computer programmers. More computers started getting into the hands of young people through their schools, libraries, and homes as it was becoming more and more possible for affluent families to afford a home PC. Curious young people got involved with the new tools in large numbers. As their numbers rose, so did cybercrimes.

A profile of a cyber criminal soon emerged—a privately schooled, suburban, highly intelligent, soccer-playing but lonely wolf in thrill-seeking escapades that would lead to bragging rights. We called them computer whiz kids. Their operations were more or less predictable and, with exception of a few cases, there was a complete lack of organizational structure, something that is significantly noticeable in later generations of attacks. These whiz kids led the second generation of cybercrimes.

The second generation of cybercrimes probably started at the tail end of the first generation, around 1990, and lasted through 2000. This period was characterized by serious, often devastating, and widespread virus attacks on global computer networks. This period saw an unprecedented growth in computer networks around the globe. These interconnected and interdependent networks became a very good conduit for these virus attacks. As the world became a mesh of thousands of interdependent computer networks, more individuals, businesses, organizations, and nations became more dependent on them. Because of this high dependence, which continues, the mere mention of a virus attack, whether real or not, caused panic in company boardrooms, classrooms, and family living rooms.

The sources of these attacks (mostly viruses) were often the whiz kids of the 1980s. The period experienced monstrous attacks including "Melissa," "The Goodtimes," "Distributed Denial of Service," "Love Bug," and "Code Red," to name a few. The inputs fuelling the rise and destructive power of the attacks were the large volume of free hacker tools available on the Internet, the widespread use of computers in homes, organizations and businesses, large numbers of young people growing up with computers in their bedrooms, the growing interest in computers, the anonymity of users of the Internet, and the ever-growing dependence on computers and computer networks. All these put together contributed to the wild, wild cyberspace of the 1990s.

The third generation of cybercrimes began around the turn of the century. As the Computer Science Institute and Federal Bureau of Investigation's (CSI/FBI) 2005 survey results indicate, virus attacks continued as the source of the greatest financial losses. Closely behind viruses were unauthorized access, which showed a dramatic cost increase and replaced denial of service as the second most significant contributor to computer crime losses during that period, unauthorized use of computer systems, and Web site incidents in that order.[1]

Overall, the period saw a gradual move away from the huge devastating virus attacks released by lonely wolves who expected no reward beyond proof of their prowess and the corresponding infamous notoriety. This period was, so far, characterized by small, less powerful, sometimes specialized but selective and targeted attacks. The targets were preselected to maximize personal gains, usually financial. Attacks so far in this period were overwhelmingly targeted at financial institutions. The list of victims was long and included the following examples:

- In February 2005, Bank of America Corp. reported computer tapes containing credit card records of U.S. senators and more than a million U.S. government employees went missing, putting customers at increased risk of identity theft.
- In February 2005, ChoicePoint Inc., a Georgia-based credit reporting company, had a breach of its computer databases, rendering nearly 145,000 people vulnerable to identity theft.

- In April 2005, data wholesaler LexisNexis, a division of Reed Elsevier, admitted having personal information from about 310,000 customers stolen.

Because of strict reporting laws in California, more and more companies and institutions were reporting losses of personal accounts. Among the companies and institutions were PayMaxx, health care heavyweight San Jose Medical Group, California State University at Chico, Boston College, and the University of California at Berkeley.[2] These made headlines, but many more did not.

A decade later since the beginning of the thrird generation, around 2010, probably the fourth generation started. This was driven by a dramatic change in communication technologies and the nature of the information infrastructure. First, there is a fast rate of convergence of computing and telecommunication coming a lot earlier than has been predicted. Second, there is a developing trend in computing and communication devices' miniaturization, leading us faster to the long-awaited and often talked-about ubiquitous computing driven by faster, more powerful machines and with a rich application repertoire that makes the technology of a decade earlier look prehistoric. The result of these combined forces are the exceptionally fast growing infrastructure of social networks that are leading us into a new unplanned, unpredictable, and more threatening computing environment. This changing nature of information technology against the changing background of user demographics is creating a dynamic mosaic of security threats and problems. Plenty of IT administrators are tossing and turning at night over the security risks that may threaten their servers, networks and client computers. According to the 2010 survey of 353 network administrators conducted by Amplitude Research on behalf of VanDyk Software (2010) and the Australian Cyber Crime and Security Survey Report 2012,[3] historically and traditionally leading threats are no longer in the lead as indicated in Tables 1.1 and 1.2. Most traditional cybercrimes witnessed in the previous two generations are in decline. This can be attributed to the continuously changing landscape of cybercrimes.

Currently there are two major trends in this generation of cyber attacks. First, the cyber criminals are organizing themselves more into criminal enterprise cartels, and two, we are seeing more state-sponsored hacking activities than ever before. This seems to be a more troubling trend. New threats, according to the U.S. Department of Homeland Security's ICS-CERT, include[4]:

- National governments—where we see government-sponsored programs developing capabilities with the future prospect of causing widespread, long-duration damage to critical national infrastructures of adversarial nations.

Table 1.1 Changing System Threat Landscape, 2010

Threat Management Technique	Percentage of Admins Who Identified
Securing remote access	52
Keeping virus definitions up to date	44
Patching systems	36
Monitoring intrusions	33
Secure file transfer	30
Network use monitoring	28
User awareness	26
Password management	16
Managing logs	11
Replacing non-secure protocols	11

Data Source: http://www.channelinsider.com/c/a/Security/10-Security-Risks-That-Keep-Customers-Up-at-Night–893339/

Table 1.2 Change in Types of Attack and Misuse, 1999–2012

Type of attack	(yr/perc.)	(yr/perc.)	(yr/perc.)	(Down/Up)
Inside abuse of info access	1999/99	2005/50	2012/55	Down
Virus	2000/95	2005/75	2012/30	Down
Theft of computing devices	1999/70	2005/50	2012/33	Down
Unauthorized access	2000/70	2005/35	2012/18	Down
Denial of service	2002/40	2005/35	2012/15	Down
System penetration	2002/40	2005/18	2012/ 9	Down
Theft of proprietary info	2001/30	2005/10	2012/34	Up
Telecom fraud	1999/18	2005/10	2012/ 4	Down
Financial fraud	2003/18	2005/ 4	2012/ 9	Down
Sabotage/degradation of networks	2003/20	2005/ 2	2012/ 9	Up
Abuse of wireless network	2005/18	2003/ 0	2012/18	Up
Web site defacement	2004/ 5	2005/ 3	2012/ 6	Down
Trajon/Rootkit	N/A	N/A	2012/20	Up
None of the above	N/A	N/A	2012/35	not enough info

Data Source: (1) CSI/FBI Computer Crime and Security Survey—http://i.cmpnet.com/gocsi/db_area/pdfs/fbi/FBI2005.pdf. (2) CYBER CRIME & SECURITY SURVEY REPORT 2012, http://www.canberra.edu.au/cis/storage/Cyber%20Crime%20and%20Security%20Survey%20Report%202012.pdf.

- Terrorists—where terrorists are starting to acquire skill to direct cyber threats to individuals and increasingly critical national infrastructures.

- Industrial spies and organized crime groups—with profit motivation, international corporate spies and organized crime organizations are slowly mounting cyber threats to individuals and critical national infrastructures.
- Hacktivism—an old type of cybercrime that has not abetted with changes in technology. In fact, hacktists have been presented, thanks to new technologies, with new ways of increasing their political activism. This legion of hackers includes individuals and groups.
- Hackers—like hactivists, are also as old as computer crimes themselves.

Efforts to Combat and Curtail Old and New Cybercrimes

Against this background, efforts need to be and are being taken to protect online data and information. Throughout this book, we are going to look at methods, tools and best practices to combat these increasing and evolving crimes. We summarize below, but we will detail in the coming chapters the global efforts by governments, civil society and individuals that include:

- **Security awareness**. Data from PricewaterhouseCoopers (PwC)'s Breaches Survey (ISBS) report (2012) shows that an organization with a quality end-user security awareness program is less likely to suffer a security breach.[5] The report further shows that security awareness through enterprise security policies is very effective. For example, data in the report show that organizations with a clearly understood security policy are less likely to be breached.
- **Formation of public-private partnerships**. Public private partnerships are going to bear good results. Some of these partnerships include:
  o The United Kingdom's Cyber Crime Reduction Partnership (CCRP). This effort is to provide a forum in which government, law enforcement, industry and academia can regularly come together to tackle cybercrime more than before.[6] During National Cyber Security Awareness Month 2012, the U.S. Department of Homeland Security (DHS) and its partners from the public and private sector highlighted the importance of protecting against cybercrime.[7]
  o DHS collaborates with financial and other critical infrastructure sectors to improve network security. Additionally, DHS components, such as the U.S. Secret Service and U.S. Immigrations and Customs Enforcement (ICE), have special divisions dedicated to fighting cybercrime.
  o The FBI has the following cybercrime partnerships and initiatives[8]:
    ▪ National Cyber Investigative Joint Task Force—as the focal point for

all U.S. government agencies to coordinate, integrate, and share information related to all domestic cyber threat investigations.

- Cyber Task Forces (CTF)—a group of all key law enforcement agencies in all 56 field offices at the state and local levels.
- InfraGard: Protecting Infrastructure—an information sharing and analysis effort serving the interests and combining the knowledge base of a wide range of members. At its most basic level, InfraGard is a partnership between the FBI and the private sector.
- National Cyber-Forensics & Training Alliance—an early-warning system based on the exchange of strategic and threat among members.
- Strategic Alliance Cyber Crime Working Group—a global alliance of law enforcement community sharing and steadily building operational partnerships for joint investigations of cybercrimes.
- Cyber Action Teams—small but highly trained teams of FBI agents, analysts, and computer forensics and malicious code experts who travel around the world on a moment's notice to respond to cyber intrusions.

- Setting up publicly funded agencies to go after cyber criminals. Representative examples include:
  - o The Secret Service maintains Electronic Crimes Task Forces (ECTFs), which focus on identifying and locating international cyber criminals connected to cyber intrusions, bank fraud, data breaches, and other computer-related crimes. The Secret Service's Cyber Intelligence Section has directly contributed to the arrest of transnational cyber criminals responsible for the theft of hundreds of millions of credit card numbers and the loss of approximately $600 million to financial and retail institutions. The Secret Service also runs the National Computer Forensic Institute, which provides law enforcement officers, prosecutors, and judges with cyber training and information to combat cybercrime.
  - o ICE's Cyber Crimes Center (C3) works to prevent cybercrime and solve cyber incidents. From the C3 Cyber Crime Section, ICE identifies sources for fraudulent identity and immigration documents on the Internet. C3's Child Exploitation Section investigates large-scale producers and distributors of child pornography, as well as individuals who travel abroad for the purpose of engaging in sex with minors.
- Security Information Sharing Partnership (CSISP) with long-term plans to establish a National Computer Emergency Response Team (CERT). These CERT teams are now in several countries including the United States, Australia, the United Kingdom and others.
- In addition to sustained awareness programs, legislation is also beginning to pay off. In the CSI Computer Crime and Security Survey 2009, in which

responses were from 443 information security and information technology professionals in United States corporations, government agencies, financial institutions, educational institutions, medical institutions and other organizations, respondents generally said that regulatory compliance efforts have had a positive effect on their organization's security programs.
- You and I. Cybersecurity is a shared responsibility, and each of us has a role to play in making it safer, more secure and resilient.

Although investment in public awareness, especially through moral and ethical education, is long-term, these are encouraging signs that there might be light at the end of the tunnel if we intensify our training programs. So, we need to concurrently educate the user as well as develop security tools and best practices as we look for the essential solutions to the ills of cyberspace. We focus on them in the rest of the book and we begin by looking at morality and ethics.

Chapter 2

Morality

LEARNING OBJECTIVES:

After reading this chapter, the reader should be able to:
- Understand how to make sound moral reasoning.
- Discuss moral values and ideals in a person's life.
- Understand the relationship between morality and religion.
- Understand what it means to have moral principles, the nature of conscience, and the relationship between morality and self-interest.

Human beings do not live randomly. We follow a complex script, a life script, a script based on cultural, religious, and philosophical concepts and beliefs. Using the guidelines in that script, individuals then determine whether their actions are right or wrong. The concepts and beliefs making up the guidelines are formulated, generalized, and codified by individual cultures or groups over long periods of time. The main purpose of such guidelines is to regulate the behavior of the members of that culture or group to create happiness for all members of the culture or group. We define the concept of morality as the conformity to such guidelines.

Morality

Morality is a set of rules of right conduct, a system used to modify and regulate our behavior. It is a quality system by which we judge human acts right or wrong, good or bad. This system creates moral persons who possess virtues like love for others, compassion, and a desire for justice; thus, it builds character traits in people. Morality is a lived set of shared rules, principles, and duties, independent from religion which is practiced, applicable to all in a group or society, and having no reference to the will or power of any one individual whatever his or her status in that group or society. Every time we interact in a society or group, we act the moral subscript. Because morality is territorial and culturally based, as long as we live in a society, we are bound to live the society's moral script. The actions of individuals in a society only have moral values if taken within the context of this very society and the culture of the individual.

Although moral values are generally lived and shared values in a society, the degree of living and sharing of these values varies greatly. We may agree more on values like truth, justice, and loyalty than on others. A number of factors influence the context of morality, including time and place.

Moral Theories

If morality is a set of shared values among people in a specific society, why do we have to worry about justifying those values to people who are not members of that society? To justify an action or a principle requires showing good reason for its existence and why there are no better alternatives. Justifying morality is not a simple thing since morality, by its own definition, is not simply justifiable especially to an outsider. Moral reasons require more justification than social reasons because moral reasons are much stronger than aesthetic ones; for example, murder is not immoral just because most people find it revolting; it is much more than that. To justify more reasons, therefore, we need something strong and plausible to anchor our reasoning on. That something cannot be religion, for example, because one's religion is not everyone's religion. We need something that demonstrates that the balance of good in an action is favorable to other people, not only to one's interests and desires. Moral theories do satisfy this purpose. According to Chris MacDonald, moral theories "seek to introduce a degree of rationality and rigor into our moral deliberations."[1] They give our deliberations plausibility and help us better understand those values and the contradictions therein. Because many philosophers and others use the words *moral* and *ethical* synonymously, we delay the discussion of moral theories until we discuss ethics.

Moral Codes

For one to be morally good, one must practice the qualities of being good. To live these qualities, one must practice and live within the guidelines of these qualities. These guidelines are moral codes. The *Internet Encyclopedia of Philosophy* defines moral codes as rules or norms within a group for what is proper behavior for the members of that group.[2] The norm itself is a rule, standard, or measure for us to compare something else whose qualities we doubt. In a way, moral codes are shared behavioral patterns of a group. These patterns have been with us since the first human beings inhabited the Earth and have evolved mainly for survival of the group or society. Societies and cultures survive and thrive because of the moral code they observe. Societies and cultures throughout history like the once mighty Babylonians, Romans, and Byzantines probably failed because their codes failed to cope with the changing times.

We have established that morality and cultures are different in different societies. This does not, however, exclude the existence of the commonality of humanity with timeless moral code. These codes are many and they come in different forms including:

- The Golden Rule: "Do unto others as you would have them do unto you."
- The Bronze Rule: "Repay kindness with kindness." This rule is widely observed because of its many varying interpretations.

There is a commonality of good in these rules which equate to Carl Sagan's culture-free and timeless universal set of moral codes[3]:

- Be friendly at first meeting.
- Do not envy.
- Be generous; forgive your enemy if he or she forgives you.
- Be neither a tyrant nor a patsy.
- Retaliate proportionately to an intentional injury (within the constraints of the rule of the law).
- Make your behavior fairly (although not perfectly) clear and consistent.

The purpose of moral codes in a society is to exert control over the actions of the society's members that result from emotions. Observance of moral codes in most societies is almost involuntary mostly because members of such societies grow up with these codes so they tend to follow them religiously without question. In some societies, observance is enforced through superstition, and in others through folklore and custom.

The Need for a Moral Code

When you ask people what kind of life they like most, the most popular answer is always going to be a life full of freedoms. They want to be free. Democratic societies always claim to be free. The citizens have freedom. When you ask anyone what they mean by freedom, they will say that freedom is doing what they want to do, when they want to do it, and in the way that they want to do it. What they are actually talking about is a life without restraints.

But can we live in a society where an individual can do anything that he or she wants? Popular culture dictates this kind of freedom. One would therefore say that in a world or society like this, where everyone enjoys full freedoms, there would be anarchy. Well, not so. God created humans, probably the only creatures on earth who can reason. God endowed us with the capacity to reason, to create guidelines for life so that everyone can enjoy freedom with reason. Freedom with reason is the bedrock of morality. True, morality cannot exist without freedom. Because humans have the capacity to reason, they can attain the freedom they want by keeping a moral code. The moral code, therefore, is essential for humanity to attain and keep the freedoms humans need. By neglecting the moral code in search of more freedoms, human beings can lose the essential freedoms they need to live. Lee Bohannon calls it a moral paradox: by wrongly using your freedom, you lose your freedom.[4] Humanity must realize the need for freedom within reasonable restraints—with the moral code, because without the code, absolute freedoms result in no freedom at all.

Moral Standards

A moral standard is a moral norm, a standard to which we compare human actions to determine their goodness or badness. This standard guides and enforces policy. Morality is a system that, in addition to setting standards of virtuous conduct for people, also consists of mechanisms to self-regulate through enforcement of the moral code and to self-judge through guilt, which is an internal discomfort resulting from disappointment self-mediated by conscience.

Guilt and Conscience

Moral guilt is a result of self-judging and punishing oneself for not living up to the moral standards set for oneself or for the group. If individuals judge that they have not done "good" according to moral standards, they activate the guilt response, which usually makes them feel bad, hide their actions from both self and others, and find a fitting punishment for themselves, sometimes a very severe punishment. This internal judgment system is brought about because human beings have no sure way of telling whether an action is good or bad based independently on their own standards. Individual standards are usually judged based on group standards. So individuals judge themselves based on group standards, and self-judgment sets in whenever one's actions fall short of the group's standards.

The problem with guilt is that it can be cumulative. If individuals commit acts repeatedly that they judge to be below moral standards, they tend to become more and more withdrawn. This isolation often leads individuals to become more comfortable with the guilt. As they become comfortable living with the guilt, their previous actions, which were previously judged below standards, begin to look not so bad after all. Individuals become more and more complacent about the guilt and begin to look at the whole moral system as amoral.

Guilt can be eased by encouraging people to focus on the intentions behind the actions. Sometimes the intentions may be good but the resulting action is bad. In such a case the individual should not feel so guilty about the action. Besides looking for intent, one should also have the will and ability to forgive oneself. Self-forgiveness limits the cumulative nature of guilt and hence helps an individual to keep within the group.

Our moral code, and many times the law, lay out the general principles that we *ought* not do because it is wrong to do it. The law also tells us not to do this or that because it is illegal to do so. However, both systems do not specifically tell us whether a particular human action is an immoral or illegal act. The link must be made by the individual—a self-realization. It is this inner judgment that tells us if the act just committed is right or wrong, lawful or unlawful. This inner judgment is what we call *conscience*. Additionally, conscience is the capacity and ability to judge our actions ourselves based on what we set as our moral standards. The word *conscience* comes from the Latin word *conscientia* which means *knowing with*. It is an "inner voice" telling us what to do or not to do. This kind of self-judgment is based on the responsibility and control we have over our actions. Conscience is motivated by good feelings within us such as pride, compassion, empathy, love, and personal identification. Conscience evolves as individuals grow. The childhood conscience is far different from the adult conscience because the perception of evil evolves with age. The benefits of conscience are that the actions taken with good conscience, even if the results are bad, do not make one guilty of the actions.

Fr. Austin Fagothey[5] writes that conscience applies to three things:

(i) the intellect as a faculty of forming judgments about right and wrong individual acts,
(ii) the process of reasoning that the intellect goes through to reach such judgment, and
(iii) the judgment itself which is the conclusion of this reasoning process.

We have seen in this section that morality does not belong to any individual, nor does it belong to any society or group of people. Thus, it cannot be localized. However, those parts of the moral code that can be localized become law.

The Purpose of Morality—The Good Life

According to Michael Miller, the ancients identified the purpose of morality with the *chief good*. Because morality is territorial, whatever chief good they proposed—happiness for Aristotle, no pain for Epicurus, apathy for the Stoics, heavenly afterlife for Christians—they took that chief good to be the moral purpose.[6] In general, the chief good is not to suffer and die, but to enjoy and live.

Chapter 3

Ethics

LEARNING OBJECTIVES:

After reading this chapter, the reader should be able to:
- Analyze an argument to identify premises and conclusion using ethical theories.
- Understand the use of ethical theories in ethical arguments.
- Detect basic logical fallacies in an argument.
- Articulate the ethical tradeoffs in a technical decision.
- Understand the role of professional codes of ethics.

"The unexamined life is not worth living." This is a statement made by Socrates before the Athenian court. The jury gave him a death sentence for his menacing practice of going around Athens asking its citizens the ultimate questions of human existence.[1] Socrates agreed to drink hemlock and kill himself for his belief in a science that represents a rational inquiry into the meaning of life. Socrates's pursuit was a result of the Greeks' curiosity and their desire to learn about themselves, human life and society. This led to the examination of all human life, to which Socrates devoted his life. Philosophers call this *ethics*. Ethics is, therefore, the study of right and wrong in human conduct. Ethics can also be defined as a theoretical examination of morality or "theory of morals." Other philosophers have defined ethics in a variety of ways.

Robert C. Solomon, in *Morality and the Good Life*,[2] defines ethics as a set of "theories of value, virtue, or of right (valuable) action." O.J. Johnson, on the other hand, defines ethics as a set of theories "that provide general rules or principles to be used in making moral decisions and, unlike ordinary intuitions, provides a justification for those rules."[3] The word *ethics* comes from the ancient Greek word *eché*,[4] which means character. Every human society practices ethics in some way because every society attaches a value on a continuum of good to bad, right to wrong, to an individual's actions according to where that individual's actions fall within the domain of that society's rules and canons.

The role of ethics is to help societies distinguish between right and wrong and to give each society a basis for justifying the judgment of human actions. Ethics is, therefore, a field of inquiry whose subject is human actions, collectively called *human conduct,* that are taken consciously, willfully, and for which one can be held responsible. According to Fr. Austin Fagothey,[5] such acts must have knowledge, which signifies the presence of a motive, be voluntary, and have freedom to signify the presence of free choice to act or not to act.

The purpose of ethics is to interpret human conduct, acknowledging and distinguishing between right and wrong. The interpretation is based on a system which uses a mixture of induction and deduction. In most cases, these arguments are based on historical schools of thought called ethical theories. There are many different kinds of ethical theories, and within each theory there may be different versions of that theory. Let us discuss these next.

Ethical Theories

Since the dawn of humanity, human actions have been judged good or bad, right or wrong based on theories or systems of justice developed, tested, revised, and debated by philosophers and elders in each society. Such theories are commonly known as *ethical theories.* An ethical theory determines if an action or set of actions is morally right or wrong. Codes of ethics have been drawn up based on these ethical theories. The processes of reasoning, explanation, and justification used in ethics are based on these theories. Ethical theories fall into two categories: those based on one choosing his or her action based on the expected maximum value or values as a consequence of the action and those based on one choosing his or her action based on one's obligation or requirements of duty. The Greeks called the first category of theories *telos,* meaning purpose or aim. We now call these *teleological* or *consequentialist* theories. The Greeks called the second category of theories *deon,* meaning binding or necessary. Today, we call them *deontological* theories.[6]

Consequentialist Theories

We think of the right action as that which produces good consequences. If an act produces good consequences, then it is the right thing to do. Those who subscribe to this position are called *consequentialists.* Consequentialist theories judge human actions as good or bad, right or wrong, based on the best attainable results of such actions—a desirable result denotes a good action, and vice versa. According to Richard T. Hull, consequentialist theories "have three parts: a theory of value, a principle of utility, and a decision procedure."[7]

Within these are further theories. For example, in the theory of value there are several other theories held by consequentialists including[8]:

- Hedonism, which equates good with pleasure, bad or evil with pain.
- Eudamonism, which equates good with happiness, bad or evil with unhappiness.
- Agathism, which views good as an indefinable, intrinsic feature of various situations and states. Evil is seen as either an indefinable, intrinsic feature of other situations and states, or simply as the absence of good.
- Agapeism, which equates good with live, bad with hate.
- Values pluralism, which holds that there are many kinds of good, including pleasure and happiness, but also knowledge, friendship, love, and so forth. These may or may not be viewed as differing in importance or priority.

There are three commonly discussed types of consequentialist theory[9]:

(i) Egoism puts an individual's interests and happiness above everything else. With egoism, any action is good as long as it maximizes an individual's overall happiness. There are two kinds of egoism: ethical egoism, which states how people ought to behave as they pursue their own interests, and psychological egoism, which describes how people actually behave.

(ii) Utilitarianism, unlike egoism, puts a group's interest and happiness above those of an individual, for the good of many. Thus, an action is good if it benefits the maximum number of people. Among the forms of utilitarianism are the following:
- Act utilitarianism tells one to consider seriously the consequences of all actions before choosing that with the best overall advantage, happiness in this case, for the maximum number of people.[10]
- Rule utilitarianism tells one to obey those rules that bring the maximum happiness to the greatest number of people. Rule utilitarianism maintains that a behavioral code or rule is good if the consequences of adopting that rule are favorable to the greatest number of people.[11]

(iii) Altruism states that an action is right if the consequences of that action are favorable to all except the actor.

Deontological Theories

The theory of deontological reason does not concern itself with the consequences of the action but rather with the will of the action. An action is good or bad depending on the will inherent in it. According to deontological theory, an act is considered good if the individual committing it had a good reason to do so. This theory has a duty attached to it. For example, we know that killing is bad, but if an armed intruder enters your house and you kill him, your action is good, according to deontologists. You did it because you had a duty to protect your family and property. Deontologists fall into two categories: act deontologists and rule deontologists.

- Act deontologists consider every judgment of moral obligation to be based on its own merit. We decide separately in each particular situation what is the right thing to do.
- Rule deontologists consider that one's duty in any situation is to act within rules.

All other contemporary ethical theories, as Richard T. Hull contends, are hybrids of utilitarianist and deontologist theories.

The process of ethical reasoning takes several steps, which we refer to as *layers of reasoning*, before one can justify to someone else the goodness or badness, rightness or wrongness of one's action. For example, if someone wants to convince you to own a concealed gun, he or she needs to explain to you why it is good to have a concealed gun. In such an exercise, the person may start by explaining to you that we are living in difficult times and that no one is safe. You may then ask why no one is safe, to which the person might reply that there are many bad people out there in possession of high-powered guns waiting to fire them for various and very often unbelievable reasons. So owning a gun will level the playing field. Then you may ask why owning a gun levels the playing field, to which the answer would be that if the bad guys suspect that you own a gun just like theirs, they will think twice before attacking you. You may further ask why this is so; the answer may be that if they attack you, they themselves can get killed in the action. Therefore, because of this fear, you are not likely to be attacked. Hence, owning a gun may save your life and enable you to continue pursuing the ultimate concept of the good life: happiness.

On the other hand, to convince somebody not to own a concealed gun also needs a plausible explanation and several layers of reasoning to demonstrate why owning a gun is bad. Why is it a bad thing, you would ask, and the answer would be because bad guys will always get guns. And if they do, the possibility of everyone having a concealed gun may make those bad guys trigger-happy to get you fast before you get them. It also evokes an imageof the Wild West filled with gun-toting people daring everyone in order to get a kick out of what may be a boring life. You would then ask why is this situation dangerous if no one fires? The reply might be because it creates a situation in which innocent people may get hurt, denying them happiness and the good life. The explanation and reasoning process can go on and on for several more layers before one is convinced that owning a gun is good or bad. The act of owning a gun is a human act that can be judged as either good or bad, right or wrong depending on the moral and ethical principles used.

The spectrum of human actions on which ethical judgments can be based is wide-ranging, from simple, traditional and easy to understand actions like killing and stealing, to complex and abstract ones like hacking, cellular telephone scanning, and subliminal human brain alterations. On one side of this spectrum, the inputs have straight output value judgments of right and wrong or good and evil. The other end of the spectrum, however, has inputs that cannot be easily mapped into the same output value judgments of right and wrong or good and evil. It is on this side of the input spectrum that most new human actions, created as a result of computer technology, are found. It is at this end, therefore, that we need an updated definition of ethics—a functional definition.

Codes of Ethics

The main domains in which ethics is defined are governed by a particular and definitive regiment of guidelines and rules of thumb called *codes of ethics*. These rules, guidelines, canons, advisories, or whatever you want to call them, are usually followed by members of the respective domains. For example, your family has an ethical set of rules that every member of the family must observe. Your school has a set of conduct rules that all students, staff and faculty must observe. And, your college has a set of rules that govern the use of college computers. So depending on the domain, ethical codes can take any of the following forms:

- principles, which may act as guidelines, references, or bases for some document;
- public policies, which may include aspects of acceptable behavior, norms, and practices of a society or group;
- codes of conduct, which may include ethical principles; and
- legal instruments, which enforce good conduct through courts.

Although the use of ethical codes is still limited to professions and high visibility institutions and businesses, there is a growing movement toward widespread use. The wording, content, and target of codes can differ greatly.

Some codes are written purposely for the public, others target employees, and yet others are for professionals only. The reader is referred to the codes of the Association of Computing Machinery (ACM) and the Institute of Electric and Electronics Engineers' Computer Society (IEEE Computer), both professional organizations. Codes for the ACM can be found at and those for IEEE Computer at www.ieee.org.

Objectives of Codes of Ethics

Different domains and groups of people formulate different codes of ethics, but they all have the following objectives:

- Disciplinary: By instilling discipline, the group or profession ensures professionalism and integrity of its members.
- Advisory: Codes are usually a good source of tips for members, offering advice and guidance in areas where moral issues are fuzzy.
- Educational: Ethical codes are good educational tools for members of the domain, especially new members who have to learn the dos and don'ts of the profession. The codes are also a good resource for existing members needing to refresh and polish their possibly waning morals.
- Inspirational: Besides being disciplinary, advisory, and educational, codes should also carry subliminal messages to those using them to inspire them to be good.
- Publicity: One way for professions to create a good clientele is to show that they have a strong code of ethics and, therefore, their members are committed to basic values and are responsible.

The Relevancy of Ethics to Modern Life

When Socrates made the statement, "the unexamined life is not worth living" before the Athens court in 399 BC, human life was the same as it is today in almost every aspect except quality. Not much has changed in the essence of life since Socrates's time and now. We still struggle for the meaning of life, we work to improve the quality of life and we do not rest unless we have love, justice and happiness for all. Socrates spent time questioning the people of Athens so that they, together with him, could examine their individual lives to find "What I Individually *Ought* to Do" and "To Improve the Lot of Humankind." Many philosophers and those not so schooled believe that this is the purpose of ethics.

The difficulty in finding "What I Individually *Ought* to Do" has always been, and continues to be for a modern life, a myriad of decisions that must be made quickly, with overwhelming and quickly changing information, and must be done reasonably well. This is not a simple statement that can be quickly overlooked. We face these decision-making dilemmas every minute of every day. Under these circumstances, when we are faced with the need to make such decisions, do we really have enough information to make a sound decision? When the information at hand is not complete and when the necessary knowledge and understanding of reality is lacking, the ability to identify the consequences of a decision may often lead to a bad decision. For a number of people, when the ingredients of a good decision-making process are missing, they rely on habits. Decisions based on habits are not always sound ethical decisions, and they are not always good.

The purpose of ethics has been and continues to be, especially for us in a modern and technologically driven society, the establishment of basic guidelines and rules of thumb for determining which behaviors are most likely to promote the achievement of the "The Best," over the long-term.[12] These guidelines and rules of thumb are the codes of ethics.

Chapter 4

Morality, Technology and Value

LEARNING OBJECTIVES:

After reading this chapter, the reader should be able to:
- Identify assumptions and values embedded in a particular computer product design including those of a cultural nature.
- Understand the moral value of technology.
- Understand the role morality plays in decision making.
- Describe positive and negative ways in which computing alters the way decisions are made by different people.
- Explain why computing/network access is restricted in some countries.
- Analyze the role and risks of computing in the implementation of public policy and government.
- Articulate the impact of the input deficit from diverse populations in the computing profession.

Every time I am onboard an aircraft, I reflect on how technology has drastically changed our lives. Great things have happened during my life to make our lives easier. Planes, trains and automobiles have all been invented to ease our daily needs and necessity of movement. Near miraculous drugs and difficult-to-believe medical procedures have been made possible because of technology. The advent of computer technology has opened a new chapter in technological advances, all to make our lives easier so that we all can live good lives.

Ken Funk defines technology as a rational process of creating a means to order and transform matter, energy, and information to realize certain valued ends.[1] Technology is not a value. Its value depends on how we use it. Indeed, technology is a utility tool like a device, system, or method that represents the process to the good life. Technological processes have three components:

inputs, an engine, and outputs. For technology to be novel and useful to us as a utility, the engine must be new and the outputs must have *value* to us. We derive usefulness out of this utility based on the quality of that value in relation to our value system. If the outputs of the processes have relevancy and contribute to the knowledge base that we routinely use to create other utilities that ease our lives, then, the new technology *has* value. Otherwise, it is not a good technology. We have seen and probably used many technologies that we judge to be of no use to us.

What we call good and bad technologies are scaled on our value system. If the process outputs are judged as having contributed to good knowledge in our value system (moral values), then that technology is judged good and useful. We have seen many such technologies. However, we have also seen a myriad of technologies that come nowhere near our value systems. These we call bad technologies. So all judgments of technology are based on a set of value standards, our moral values.

There are many who will disagree with me in the way I define value, as it is derived from technology. In fact, some argue that this value is subjective. Others define it as objective. Many say it is intrinsic yet others call it instrumental. We are saying that this value is personal, hence, moral. In the end, when we use technology, the value we derive from the technology and the value we use in decision making while using the technology is based on one's beliefs and moral value system. This value scaling problem in the use of technology haunts all of us in the day-to-day use of technology and even more so in decision making.

Moral Dilemmas, Decision Making, and Technology

Dilemmas in decision making are quite common in our everyday activities. The process of decision making is complex: It resembles a mathematical mapping of input parameters into output decisions. The input parameters in the decision-making process are premises. Each premise has an attached value. The mapping uses these values along with the premises to create an output, which is the decision. For example, if I have to make the decision whether to walk to church or take the car, the set of premises might include time, parking, exercise, and gas. If I take the car, the values attached to the premises are saving time, needing a parking space, not getting any exercise, and buying gas. However, if I decide to walk, my decision might be based on another set of premises like: Walking to church one day a week is good exercise, and I will save money by not buying gas. The mapping function takes these premises together with the values and outputs a "logical" decision. Dilemmas in decision making are caused by one questioning the *values* attached to one's premises as inputs to the decision being made. One's scaling of values to the inputs may be influenced by a number of factors such as advances in technology and incomplete or misleading information.

Advances in Technology

Dilemmas are usually caused by advances in technology. Computer technology in particular has created more muddles in the decision-making process than in any other technology. Advances in computer technology create a multitude of possibilities that never existed before. Such possibilities present professionals with myriad temptations.[2]

Incomplete or Misleading Information

Not having all the information one needs before making a decision can be problematic. Consider the famous prisoners' dilemma. Two people are caught committing a crime, and they are taken to different interrogation rooms before they have a chance to coordinate their stories. During the interrogation, each prisoner is told that the other prisoner has agreed to plead guilty on all charges. Authorities inform each prisoner that agreeing to plead guilty on all charges as the other prisoner has done will bring him or her a reduced sentence. Rejecting the plea will mean that the prisoner refuses to cooperate with the investigation and may result in he or she receiving the maximum punishment. Each prisoner has four recourses:

(i)   plead guilty without the friend pleading guilty, which means deserting a friend;
(ii) refuse to plead guilty while the friend pleads guilty, which means betrayal and probably a maximum sentence;
(iii) plead guilty while the friend pleads guilty, which means light sentences for both of them; or
(iv) both refuse to plead guilty and each receives either a light sentence or a maximum sentence.

Whichever option the prisoners take is risky because they do not have enough information to enable them to make a wise decision. There are similar situations in professional life when a decision has to be made quickly and not enough information is available. In such a situation, the professional must take extra care to weigh all possibilities in the input set of premises with their corresponding values.

Making Good Use of Technology

How can we use technology in a nondestructive way to advance human society? Technology has placed at our disposal a multitude of possibilities, many of which we never had before, that are shrouding our daily value-based decision making in confusion and doubt. Doubt of our own value system, the system we grew up with. Doubts are created because gaps in reasoning between right and wrong has been muddled up because of the many possibilities, many of which are new and we are no longer sure! An appropriate response to this confusion of reasoning is multifaceted and may include the following solutions:

- Formulate new laws to strengthen our basic set of values, which are being rendered irrelevant by technology.
- Construct a new moral and ethical conceptual framework in which the new laws can be applied successfully.
- Launch a massive education campaign to make society aware of the changing environment and the impact such an environment is having on our basic values.

Nations and communities must have a regulated technology policy. Technology without a policy is dangerous technology. We are not calling for a burdensome policy. We are calling for a guided technology policy that is based on a basket of values. In formulating a policy like this, societies must be guided by the critical needs of their society based on a sound value system. Scientists and researchers must also be guided by a system of values.

Strengthening the Legal System

In many countries and local governing systems, technology has outpaced the legal system. Many laws on the books are in serious need of review and revision. Lawyers and judges seriously need retraining to cope with the new realities of information technology and its rapidly changing landscape. Legal books and statutes need to be updated. The technology in many courtrooms in many countries needs to be updated in order to handle the new breed of criminal.

Updating the legal system to meet new technology demands cannot be done overnight. It is complex. It needs a training component that will involve judges, lawyers, court clerks, and every other personnel of the court. It also needs an implementation component that involves acquiring the new technologies for the courtrooms. This will involve software and hardware and the training of the people to use such facilities. Lastly, and probably the most difficult, is the legislative component. A thorough review of current law is needed to update the relevant laws and to draw up new ones to meet current needs. Also, since technology is stretching the legal garment and constantly causing tears in the seams, there is a need for a policy to allow quick and effective reaction to new technologies so relevant and needed laws are created quickly.

A New Conceptual Moral Framework

New technologies in communication have resulted in demographical tidal waves for the global societies. Only primitive societies (which themselves are disappearing) have not been touched. The movement of people and goods between nations and societies and the Internet are slowly creating a new global society with serious social and moral characteristics. With this new society, however, no corresponding moral and ethical framework has been created. This has resulted in a rise in crime in the new nonmonolithic societies. The future of monolithic societies is uncertain because of the rapid globalization of cultures and languages. This globalization, along with the plummeting prices of computers and other Internet-accessing devices, had ignited a growing realization and fear, especially among religious and civic leaders, moralists, and parents, that society is becoming morally loose and citizens are forgetting what it is to be human. Of immediate concern to these groups and many others is that a common morality is needed. However, they also realize that morality is not easily definable. As societies become diverse, the need for a common moral framework as a standard for preserving decency and effectively reversing the trend of skyrocketing moral decadence and combating crimes becomes most urgent.

Moral and Ethics Education

It is not easy to teach morality. In many countries this has been accomplished through the teaching of character. Character education in public schools has raised many controversies between civil libertarians and the religious right. Each believes they have a God-given right to character education. So while it is good to teach, we will focus on ethics education for now. Ethics education can take many forms. We will discuss formal education and advocacy.

Formal Education

The formal education of ethics should start in elementary schools. As students are introduced to information technology in elementary school, they should be told not to use machines to destroy other people's property or to hurt others. This should be explained in age-appropriate language. For example, children should be taught to use computers and the Internet responsibly. They should be told not to visit certain Web pages, to avoid getting involved in relationships online, not to give out personal or family information online, and not to arrange to meet anyone offline. In addition, they should be told to respect the work and property of others whether they are online or off. There are already reported cases of children as young as 14 years old breaking into computer systems and destroying records. In fact, many of the computer network attacks and a good number of the headline-making computer attacks have been perpetrated by young people, sometimes as young as ten years old. For example, in a certain county in Tennessee, several ninth graders broke into their school's computer system and infected it with a virus that wiped out most of the school's records. It is believed the students got the virus off the Internet.[3] The educational content must be relevant and sensitive to different age groups and professionals.

As students go through high school, content should become progressively more sophisticated. The message on the responsible use of computers should be stressed more. The teen years are years of curiosity and discovery and a lot of young people find themselves spending long hours on computers. Those long hours should be spent responsibly. While a good portion of the message should come from parents, schools should also play a part by offering courses in responsible use of computers. The teaching should focus on ethics; students should be given reasons why they should not create and distribute viruses, download copyrighted materials off the Internet, or use the Internet to send bad messages to others. These are ethical reasons that go beyond the "do it and you will be expelled from school" type of threats.

In college, of course, the message should be more direct. There are several approaches to deliver the message:

- Students take formal courses in professional ethics in a number of professional programs in their respective colleges.
- Instead of taking formal ethics courses, students are taught the information sprinkled throughout their courses, either in general education or in their major.
- Include an ethics course in the general education requirements or add ethics content to an existing course. For example, many colleges now require computer literacy as a graduation requirement. Adding ethics content to the already required class is an option.
- Require a one-hour online information ethics course.

Once students join the workplace environment, they should be required to attend informal refresher courses, upgrading sessions, seminars, in-service courses or short workshops periodically.

Advocacy

Advocacy is a mass education strategy which has been used for generations. Advocacy groups work with the public, corporations and governments to enhance public education through awareness. A mass education campaign involves distributing a message in magazines, and electronic publications, by supporting public events and by communicating through the mass media like television, radio, and now the Internet.

Advocacy is intended to make people part of the message. For example, during the struggles for voting rights in the United States, women's groups and minorities designed and carried out massive advocacy campaigns that were meant to involve all women who eventually became part of the movement. Similarly, in the minority voting rights struggles, the goal was to involve all minorities whose rights had been trampled. The purpose of advocacy is to organize, build, and train so there is a permanent and vibrant structure people can be a part of. By involving as many people as possible, including the intended audience in the campaigns, the advocacy strategy brings awareness which leads to more pressure on lawmakers and everyone else responsible. The pressure brought about by mass awareness usually results in some form of action, usually the desired action.

The expansion and growth of cyberspace has made fertile ground for advocacy groups, because now they can reach virtually every society around the globe. Advocacy groups rally their troops around issues of concern. So far, online issues include individual privacy and security, better encryption standards and the blocking of pornographic materials and any other materials deemed unsuitable or offensive to certain audiences. The list of issues grows every day as cyberspace gets more exposure.

Not only is the list of issues getting longer, but the number of advocacy groups is also getting larger as more groups form in reaction to new issues. Renowned advocacy groups for moral issues include[4]:

- The Family Research Council (FRC) works to promote and defend common morality through traditional family values in all media outlets. It develops and advocates legislative and public policy initiatives that promote and strengthen family and traditional values, and it established and maintains a database for family value research.

- Enough Is Enough (EE) is dedicated to preserving common morality in cyberspace through fighting pornography on the Internet.
- The Christian Coalition (CC) represents some Christian churches in the United States. It works on legislative issues and on strengthening families and family values.

Chapter 5

Cyberspace Infrastructure

LEARNING OBJECTIVES:

After reading this chapter, the reader should be able to:
- Describe the evolution of and types of computer networks.
- Understand networking fundamentals, including network services and transmission media.
- Understand network software and hardware, including media access control, network topologies, and protocols, as well as connectivity hardware for both local area and wide area networks.
- Understand how and why the computer network infrastructure is the bedrock that enables and offers a medium of computer crimes

---

In his science-fiction novel *Neuromancer*, William Gibson first coined the term "cyberspace" to describe his vision of a three-dimensional space of pure information, moving between computer and computer clusters that make up this vast landscape. This infrastructure, as envisioned by Gibson, links computers as both computing and transmitting elements, people as generators and users of information, and pure information moving at high speed between highly independent transmitting elements. The transmitting elements are linked by conducting media, and the information moving from the sourcing element to the receiving element via intermediary transmitting elements is handled by software rules called *protocols*. The cyberspace infrastructure, therefore, consists of hardware nodes as sourcing, transmitting, and receiving elements; software as protocols; humanware as users of information; and finally pure information that is either in a state of rest at a node or a state of motion in the linking media.

Computer Communication Networks

A computer communication network system consists of hardware, software, and humanware. The hardware and software allow the humanware—

the users—to create, exchange, and use information. The hardware consists of a collection of nodes that include the end systems, commonly called *hosts*, and intermediate switching elements that include hubs, bridges, routers and gateways. We will collectively call all of these *network* or *computing elements*, or sometimes without loss of generality, just *network elements*. The software, all application programs and network protocols, synchronize and coordinate the sharing and exchange of data among the network elements and the sharing of expensive resources in the network. Network elements, network software, and users, all work together so that individual users get to exchange messages and share resources on other systems that are not readily available locally. The network elements may be of diverse hardware technologies and the software may be different, but the whole combo must work together in unison. This concept that allows multiple, diverse underlying hardware technologies and different software regimes to interconnect heterogeneous networks and bring them to communicate is called *internetworking* technology. Internetworking technology makes Gibson's vision a reality; it makes possible the movement and exchange of data and the sharing of resources among the network elements. This is achieved through the low-level mechanisms provided by the network elements and the high-level communication facilities provided by the software running on the communicating elements. Let us see how this infrastructure works by looking at the hardware and software components and how they produce a working computer communication network. We will start with the hardware components, consisting of network types and network topology. Later, we will discuss the software components consisting of the transmission control system.

Network Types

The connected computer network elements may be each independently connected on the network or connected in small clusters, which are in turn connected together to form bigger networks via connecting devices. The size of the clusters determines the network type. There are, in general, two network types: a local area network (LAN) and a wide area network (WAN). A LAN consists of network elements in a small geographical area such as a building floor, a building, or a few adjacent buildings. The advantage of a LAN is that all network elements are close together so the communication links maintain a higher speed data movement. Also, because of the proximity of the communicating elements, high-cost and quality communicating elements can be used to deliver better service and higher reliability. Figure 5.1 shows a LAN network.

WANs cover large geographical areas. Some advantages of a WAN

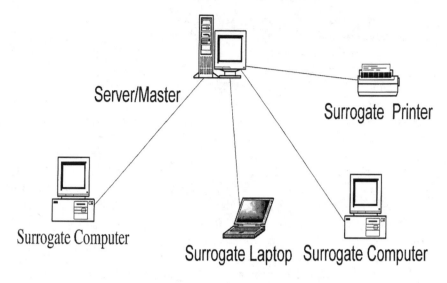

Figure 5.1 A LAN Network

include the ability to distribute services to a wider community and the availability of a wide array of both hardware and software resources that may not be available in a LAN. However, because of the large geographical areas covered by WANs, communication media are slow and often unreliable. Figure 5.2 shows a WAN network.

Network Topology

WAN networks are typically found in two topologies: mesh and tree. WANs using a mesh topology provide multiple access links between network elements. The multiplicity of access links offers an advantage in network reliability because whenever a network element failure occurs, the network can always find a bypass to the failed element and the network continues to function. Figure 5.3 shows a mesh network.

A WAN using a tree topology uses a hierarchical structure in which the most predominant element is the root of the tree and all other elements in the network share a child-parent relationship. The tree topology is a generalization of the bus topology. As in ordinary trees, there are no closed loops, so dealing with failures can be tricky, especially in deeply rooted trees. Transmission from any element in the network propagates through the network and is received by all elements in the network. Figure 5.4 shows a WAN using a tree topology.

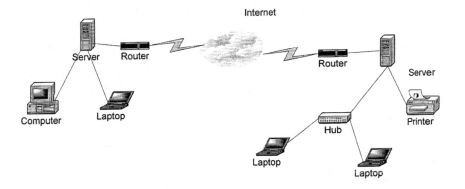

Figure 5.2 A WAN Network

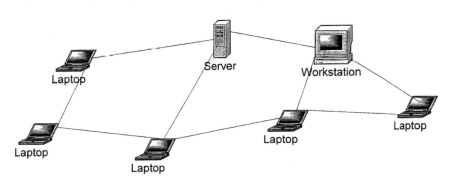

Figure 5.3 A Mesh Network

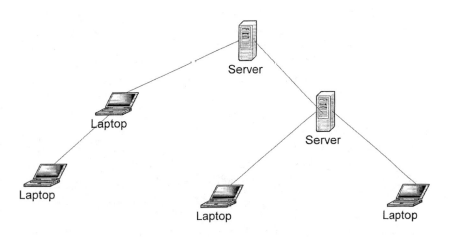

Figure 5.4 A Tree Topology

A LAN can be a bus, a star, or a ring topology. Elements in a bus topology, as seen in Figure 5.5, are on a shared bus and, therefore, have equal access to all LAN resources. All network elements have full-duplex connections to the transmitting medium which allow them to send and receive data. Because each computing element is directly attached to the transmitting medium, a transmission from any one element propagates the whole length of the medium in either direction and, therefore, can be received by all elements in the network. Because of this, precautions need to be taken to make sure that transmissions intended for one element can only be gotten by that element and no one else.

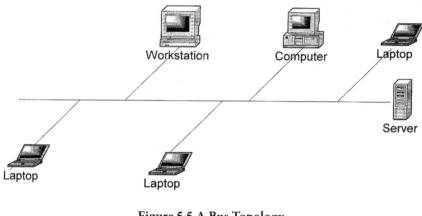

Figure 5.5 A Bus Topology

Also, if two or more elements try to transmit at the same time, there is a mechanism to deal with the likely collision of signals and to bring a quick recovery from such a collision. It is also necessary to create fairness in the network so that all other elements can transmit when they need to do so.

To improve efficiency in LANs that use a bus topology, only one element in the network can have control of the bus at any one time. This requirement prevents collisions from occurring in the network as elements in the network try to seize the bus at the same time.

In a star topology setting, all elements in the network are connected to a central element. However, elements are interconnected as pairs in a point-to-point manner through this central element, and communication between any pair of elements must go through this central element. The central element, or node, can operate either in a broadcast fashion, in which case information from one element is broadcast to all connected elements, or it can transmit as a switching device in which the incoming data are transmitted to only one element, the nearest element en route to the destination. The biggest disad-

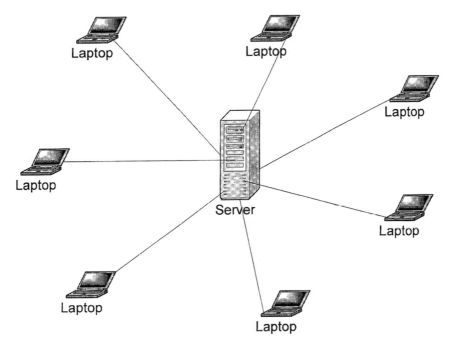

Figure 5.6 A Star Topology

vantage to the star topology in networks is that the failure of the central element results in the failure of the entire network. Figure 5.6 shows a star topology.

In networks using a ring topology, each computing element is directly connected to the transmitting medium via a unidirectional connection so that information put on the transmission medium is able to reach all computing elements in the network through a system of taking turns in sending information around the ring. Figure 5.7 shows a ring topology network. The taking of turns in passing information is managed through a token system. An element currently sending information has control of the token and it passes it downstream to its nearest neighbor after its turn. The token system is a good management system of collision and fairness.

There are variations of a ring topology collectively called *hub* hybrids. They can be a combination of either a star with a bus as shown in Figure 5.8 or a stretched star as shown in Figure 5.9.

Although network topologies are important in LANs, the choice of a topology depends on a number of other factors including the type of transmission medium, reliability of the network, the size of the network and the

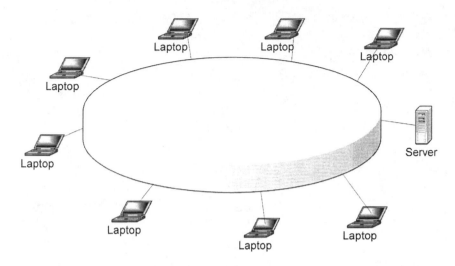

Figure 5.7 A Ring Topology

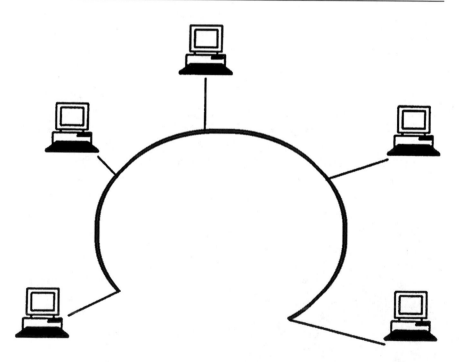

Figure 5.8 A Bus and Star Topology Hub

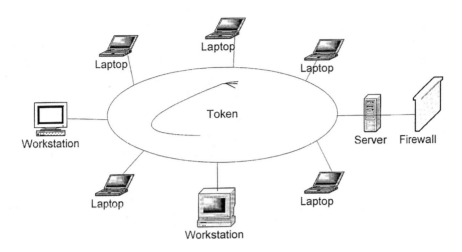

Figure 5.9 A Token Ring Hub

anticipated future growth of the network. Recently, the most popular LAN topologies have been the bus, star, and ring topologies. The most popular bus- and star-based LAN topology is the Ethernet and the most popular ring-based LAN topology is the Token Ring.

Ethernet as a LAN technology started in the mid–1970s. Since then, it has grown at a rapid rate to capture a far larger LAN technology market share than its rivals, which include Asynchronous Transfer Mode (ATM), Fiber Distributed Data Interface (FDDI), and Token Ring technologies. Its rapid growth is partly historical. It has been on the market for the longest period and it is simple. Many variations of Ethernet use either a bus or a star topology and can run over any of the following transmission media: coaxial cable, twisted pair, and optical fiber. We will discuss transmission media in the coming sections.

Ethernet can transmit data at different speeds, varying from a few Mbps to higher numbers Gbps. The basic Ethernet transmission structure is a frame and it is shown in Figure 5.10.

The source and destination fields contain six byte LAN addresses of the form xx-xx-xx-xx-xx-xx, where X is a hexadecimal integer. The error detection field is four bytes of bits used for error detection, usually using Cyclic Redundancy Check (CRC) algorithm, in which the source and destination elements synchronize the values of these bits.

Ethernet LANs broadcast data to all network elements. Because of this, Ethernet uses a collision and fairness control protocol commonly known as *Carrier Sense Multiple Access (CSMA) and Collision Detection (CD)*, combined

Other control headers	Destination address	Source address	Type	Data	Error detection (CRC)

Figure 5.10 Ethernet Frame Data Structure

as CSMA/CD. CSMA/CD makes sure that an element never transmits a data frame when it senses that some other element on the network is transmitting.

Table 5.1 Popular Ethernet Technologies

Technology	Transmission medium	Topology	Speed
10Base2	Coaxial	Bus	10Mbps
10Base-T	Twisted	Star	10Mbps
100Base-T	Copper wire	Star	100Mbps
Gigabit	Optical fiber	Star	Gigabps

In this case it is carrier sensitive. If an element detects another element on the network transmitting, the detecting element immediately aborts its efforts. It then tries to retransmit later after a random amount of time. Table 5.1 shows some popular Ethernet technologies.

Token Ring LAN technology is based on a token concept which involves passing the token around the network so that all network elements have equal access to it. The token concept is very similar to a worshipping house collection basket. If and when an attendee wants to donate money during the service, they wait until the basket makes its way to where they are sitting. At that point the donor grabs the basket and puts in money. Precisely, when the network element wants to transmit, it waits for the token on the ring to make its way to the element's connection point on the ring. When the token arrives at this point, the element grabs it and changes one bit of the token, which becomes the start bit in the data frame the element will be transmitting. The element then inserts data and releases the payload onto the ring. It then waits for the token to make a round and come back. Upon return, the element withdraws the token and a new token is put on the ring for another network element that may need to transmit.

Because of its round-robin nature, the Token Ring technique gives each network element a fair chance of transmitting if it wants to. However, if the token ever gets lost, the network business halts. Figure 5.11 shows the structure of a Token Ring data frame.

Like Ethernet, Token Ring has a variety of technologies based on transmission rates. Table 5.2 shows some of these topologies.[1]

Start field	Access control	Source address	Destination address	Data	Ending field

Figure 5.11 Token Ring Data Frame

Rival LAN technologies such as FDDI uses a Token Ring scheme with many similarities to the original Token Ring technology. ATM transports real-time voice and video, text, e-mail, and graphic data and offers a full array of network services that make it a rival of the Internet network.

Table 5.2 Token Ring Topologies

Technology	Transmission medium	Topology	Speed
1	Twisted pair	Ring	4Mbps
2	Twisted	Ring	16Mbps
3	Twisted pair	Ring	100Mbps
4	Optical fiber	Ring	100Mbps

Transmission Control Systems

The performance of a network type depends greatly on the transmission control system (TCS) the network uses. Network transmission control systems have five components: transmission technology, transmission media, connecting devices, communication services, and transmission protocols.

Transmission Technology

Data movement in a computer network is either analog or digital. In an analog format, data is sent as continuous electromagnetic waves on an interval representing things like voice and video. In a digital format, data is sent as a digital signal, a sequence of voltage pulses which can be represented as a stream of binary bits. Transmission itself is the propagation and processing of data signals between network elements. The concept of representation of data for transmission, either as an analog or a digital signal, is called an *encoding scheme*. Encoded data is then transmitted over a suitable transmission medium that connects all network elements. There are two encoding schemes: analog and digital. Analog encoding propagates analog signals representing analog data. Digital encoding, on the other hand, propagates digital signals representing either an analog or a digital signal representing digital data of binary streams. Because our interest in this book is in digital networks, we will focus on the encoding of digital data.

In an analog encoding of digital data, the encoding scheme uses a continuous oscillating wave, usually a sine wave, with a constant frequency signal called a *carrier signal*. Carrier signals have three characteristics: amplitude, frequency, and phase shift. The scheme then uses a modem, a modulation-demodulation pair to modulate and demodulate any one of the three carrier characteristics. Figure 5.12 shows the three carrier characteristic modulations.[2] Amplitude modulation represents each binary value by a different amplitude of the carrier frequency. For example, as Figure 5.12 (a) shows, the absence of a low carrier frequency may be represented by a 0 and any other frequency then represents a 1. Frequency modulation also represents the two binary values by two different frequencies close to the frequency of the underlying carrier. Higher frequency represents a 1 and low frequency then represents a 0. Frequency modulation is represented in Figure 5.12 (b). Phase shift modulation changes the timing of the carrier wave, shifting the carrier phase to encode the data. One type of shifting may represent a 0 and another type a 1. For example, as Figure 5.12 (c) shows, a 0 may represent a forward shift and a 1 may represent a backward shift.

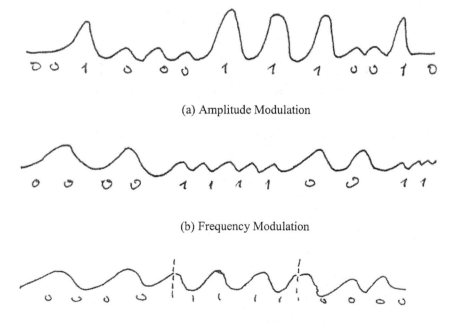

(a) Amplitude Modulation

(b) Frequency Modulation

(c) Phase Shift Modulation

Figure 5.12 Carrier Characteristic Modulations

Quite often during transmission of data over a network medium, the volume of transmitted data may far exceed the capacity of the medium. When this happens, it may be possible to make multiple signal carriers share a transmission medium. This is referred to as *multiplexing*. There are two ways multiplexing can be achieved: time-division multiplexing (TDM) and frequency-division multiplexing (FDM).

The second encoding scheme is the digital encoding of digital data. Before information is transmitted, it is converted into bits (zeros and ones). The bits are then sent to a receiver as electrical or optical signals. The scheme uses two different voltages to represent the two binary states (digits). For example, a negative voltage may be used to represent a 1 and a positive voltage to represent a 0. Figure 5.13 shows the encoding of digital data using this scheme.

To ensure a uniform standard for using electrical signals to represent data, the Electrical Industries Association (EIA) developed a standard widely known as *RS-232*. RS-232 is a serial, asynchronous communication standard: serial, because during transmission, bits follow one another, and asynchronous, because it is irregular in the transfer rate of data bits. The bits are put in the form of a packet and the packets are transmitted. RS-232 works in full duplex between the two transmitting elements. This means that the two elements can both send and receive data simultaneously. RS-232 has a number of limitations including the idealizing of voltages, which never exists, and limits on both bandwidth and distances.

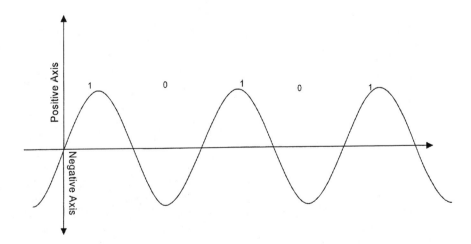

Figure 5.13 Encoding Electrical Signal and Showing of Zeros and Ones

Transmission Media

The transmission medium is the physical medium between network elements. The characteristic quality, dependability, and overall performance of a network depends heavily on its transmission medium. Transmission medium determines a network's key criteria, the distance covered, and the transmission rate. Computer network transmission media fall into two categories: wired and wireless transmission.[3]

Wired transmission consists of different types of physical media. A very common medium, for example, is optical fiber, a small medium made up of glass and plastics that conducts an optical ray. As shown in Figure 5.14 (b), a simple optical fiber has a central core made up of thin fibers of glass or plastics. The fibers are protected by a glass or plastic coating called a *cladding*. The cladding, though made up of the same materials as the core, has different properties that give it the capacity to reflect back to the core rays that tangentially hit on it. The cladding itself is encased in a plastic jacket. The jacket is meant to protect the inner fiber from external abuses like bending and abrasions.

The transmitted light is emitted at the source either from a light emitting diode (LED) or an injection laser diode (ILD). At the receiving end, the emitted rays are received by a photo detector.

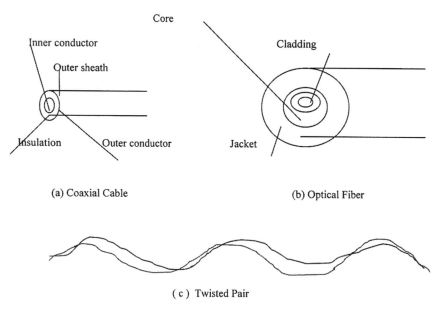

(a) Coaxial Cable   (b) Optical Fiber

(c) Twisted Pair

Figure 5.14 Types of Physical Media

Another physical medium is the twisted pair, two insulated copper wires wrapped around each other forming frequent and numerous twists. Together, the twisted, insulated copper wires act as a full-duplex communication link. To increase the capacity of the transmitting medium, more than one pair of the twisted wires may be bundled together in a protective coating. Twisted pairs are far less expensive than optical fibers, and indeed other media, and they are, therefore, widely used in telephone and computer networks. However, they are limited in transmission rate, distance, and bandwidth. Figure 5.14 (c) shows a twisted pair.

Coaxial cables are dual conductor cables with an inner conductor in the core of the cable protected by an insulation layer and the outer conductor surrounding the insulation. The outer conductor is itself protected by yet another outer coating called the *sheath*. Figure 5.14 (a) shows a coaxial cable. Coaxial cables are commonly used in television transmissions. Unlike twisted pairs, coaxial cables can be used over long distances.

A traditional medium for wired communication are copper wires, which have been used in communication because of their low resistance to electrical currents which allow signals to travel even further. But copper wires suffer from interference from electromagnetic energy in the environment, including from themselves. Because of this, copper wires are insulated.

Wireless communication involves basic media like radio wave communication, satellite communication, laser beam, microwave, and infrared.[4] Radio, of course, is familiar to us all as radio broadcasting. Networks using radio communications use electromagnetic radio waves or radio frequencies commonly referred to as *RF transmissions*. RF transmissions are very good for long distances when combined with satellites to refract the radio waves.

Microwave, infrared, and laser are other communication types that can be used in computer networks. Microwaves are a higher frequency version of radio waves but whose transmissions, unlike radio, can be focused in a single direction. Infrared is best used effectively in a small confined area, for example, in a room as you use your television remote, which uses infrared signals. Laser light transmissions can be used to carry data through air and optical fibers, but like microwaves, they must be refracted when used over large distances.

Cell-based communication technology of cellular telephones and personal communication devices are boosting this wireless communication. Wireless communication is also being boosted by the development in broadband multimedia services that use satellite communication.

Connecting Devices

Computing elements in either LAN or WAN clusters are brought together by and can communicate through connecting devices commonly referred to as network *nodes*. Nodes in a network are either at the ends as end systems, commonly known as clients, or in the middle of the network as transmitting elements. Among the most common connecting devices are: hubs, bridges, switches, routers, and gateways. Let us briefly look at each one of these devices.

A hub is the simplest in the family of network connecting devices because it connects LAN components with identical protocols. It takes in imports and retransmits them verbatim. It can be used to switch both digital and analog data. In each node, presetting must be done to prepare for the formatting of the incoming data. For example, if the incoming data is in digital format, the hub must pass it on as packets; however, if the incoming data is analog, then the hub passes it on in a signal form. There are two types of hubs: simple and multiple port. Figure 5.15 shows both types of hubs in a LAN.

Bridges are like hubs in every respect including the fact that they connect LAN components with identical protocols. However, bridges filter incoming data packets, known as *frames*, for addresses before they are forwarded. As it filters the data packets, the bridge makes no modifications to the format or content of the incoming data. A bridge filters frames to determine whether a frame should be forwarded or dropped. It works like a postal sorting machine which checks the mail for complete postal addresses and drops a piece of mail if the address is incomplete or illegible. The bridge filters and forwards frames on the network with the help of a

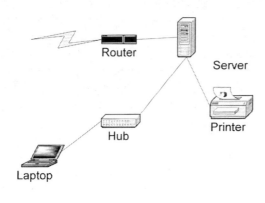

A Simple Port Hub

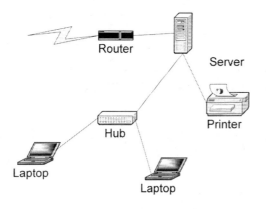

Figure 5.15 Types of Hubs in a LAN

dynamic bridge table. The bridge table, which is initially empty, maintains the LAN addresses for each computer in the LAN and the addresses of each bridge interface that connects the LAN to other LANs. Bridges, like hubs, can be either simple or multiple port. Figure 5.16 shows the position of a simple bridge in a network cluster. Figure 5.17 shows a multiple port bridge.

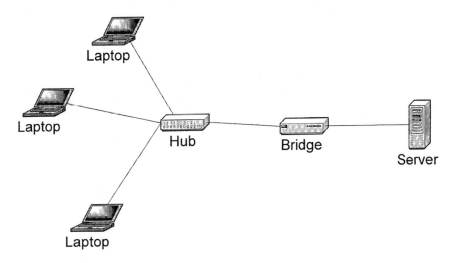

Figure 5.16 A Simple Bridge

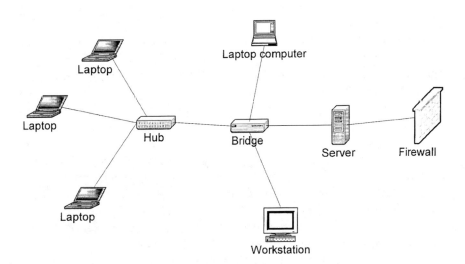

Figure 5.17 A Multiple Port Bridge

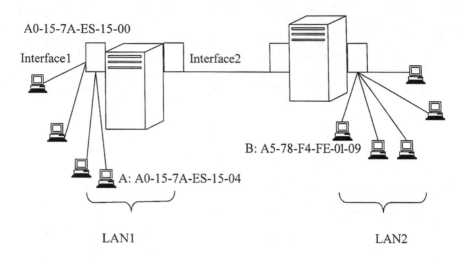

Figure 5.18 LAN with Two Interfaces

LAN addresses on each frame in the bridge table are of the form cc-cc-cc-cc-cc-cc-cc-cc, where cc are hexadecimal integers. Each LAN address in the cluster uniquely connects a computer on a bridge. LAN addresses for each machine in a cluster are actually network identification card (NIC) numbers that are unique for every network card ever manufactured. The bridge table, which initially is empty, has a turnaround time slice of n seconds, and node addresses and their corresponding interfaces enter and leave the table after n seconds.[5] For example, suppose in Figure 5.18 we begin with an empty bridge table and node A in cluster 1 with the address A0-15-7A-ES-15-00 sending a frame to the bridge via interface 1 at time 00:50. This address becomes the first entry in the bridge table, Table 5.3, and it will be purged from the table after n seconds. The bridge uses these node addresses in the table to filter and then forwards LAN frames onto the rest of the network.

Switches are newer network intercommunication devices that are nothing more than high-performance bridges. Besides providing high performance, switches accommodate a high number of interfaces. They can, therefore, interconnect a relatively high number of hosts and clusters. Like their cousins the bridges, the switches filter and then forward frames.

Routers are general purpose devices that interconnect two or more heterogeneous networks. They are usually dedicated to special purposes computers with separate input and output interfaces for each connected network. Each network addresses the router as a member computer in that network. Because routers and gateways are the backbone of large computer networks

Table 5.3 Changes in the Bridge Table

Address	Interface	Time
A0-14-7A-ES-15-08	1	00:50

like the Internet, they have special features that give them the flexibility and the ability to cope with varying network addressing schemes and frame sizes through segmentation of big packets into smaller sizes that fit the new network components. They can also cope with both software and hardware interfaces and are very reliable. Since each router can connect two or more heterogeneous networks, each router is a member of each network it connects to. It, therefore, has a network host address for that network and an interface address for each network it is connected to. Because of this rather strange characteristic, each router interface has its own Address Resolution Protocol (ARP) module, its own LAN address (network card address), and its own Internet Protocol (IP) address.

The router, with the use of a router table, has some knowledge of possible routes a packet could take from its source to its destination. The routing table, like in the bridge and switch, grows dynamically as activities in the network develop. Upon receipt of a packet, the router removes the packet headers and trailers and analyzes the IP header by determining the source and destination addresses, data type, and noting the arrival time. It also updates the router table with new addresses if not already in the table. The IP header and arrival time information is entered in the routing table. Let us explain the working of a router by using Figure 5.19.

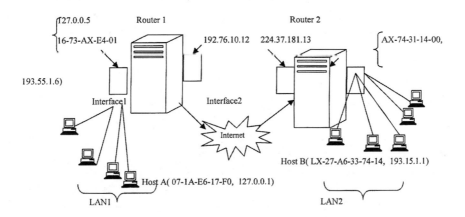

Figure 5.19 Routers in Action

In Figure 5.19, suppose Host A tries to send a packet to Host B. Host A is in network 1 and host B is in network 2. Both Host A and Host B have two addresses, the LAN (host) address and the IP address. Notice also that the router has two network interfaces: Interface1 for LAN1 and Interface2 for LAN2 (for the connection to a bigger network like the Internet). Each interface has a LAN (host) address for the network the interface connects on and a corresponding IP address. As we will see later in this chapter, Host A sends a packet to Router 1 at time 10:01 that includes, among other things, both its addresses, message type, and destination IP address of Host B. The packet is received at Interface1 of the router; the router reads the packet and builds row 1 of the routing table.

The router notices that the packet is to go to network 193.55.1.***, where *** are digits 0–9, and it has knowledge that this network is connected on Interface2. It forwards the packet to Interface2. Now Interface2 with its own ARP may know Host B. If it does, then it forwards the packet on and updates the routing table with inclusion of row 2. What happens when the ARP at the router Interface1 cannot determine the next network? That is, if it has no knowledge of the presence of network 193.55.1.***, then it will ask for help from a gateway.

Gateways are more versatile devices that provide translation between networking technologies such as Open System Interconnection and Transmission Control Protocol/Internet Protocol. (We will discuss these technologies shortly.) Because of this, gateways connect two or more autonomous networks each with its own routing algorithms, protocols, domain name service, and network administration procedures and policies. Gateways perform all of the functions of routers and more. In fact, a router with added translation functionality is a gateway. The function that does the translation between different network technologies is called a *protocol converter*. Figure 5.20 shows the position of a gateway in a network.

Communication Services

Now that we have a network infrastructure in place, how do we get the network transmitting elements to exchange data over the network? The communication control system provides services to meet specific network reliability and efficiency requirements. Two services are provided by most digital networks: connection-oriented and connectionless services.

With a connection-oriented service, before a client can send packets with real data to the server, there must be a three-way handshake. We will discuss the three-way handshake in detail in Chapter 6. For our purpose now, let us

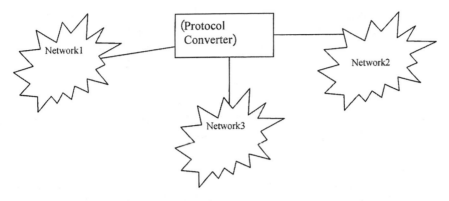

Figure 5.20 Position of a Gateway

just give the general outline. The three-way handshake includes a client initi-ating a communication by sending the first control packet, the SYN (short for synchronization), with a "hello" to the server's welcoming port. The server creates (opens) a communication socket for further communication with a client and sends a "hello, I am ready" SYN-ACK (short for synchronization-acknowledgment) control packet to the client. Upon receipt of this packet, the client then starts to communicate with the server by sending the ACK (short for acknowledgment) control packet usually piggybacked on other data packets. From this point on, either the client or the server can send an onslaught of packets. The connection just established, however, is very loose, and we call this type of connection, a *connection-oriented* service. Figure 5.21 shows a connection-oriented three-way handshake process.

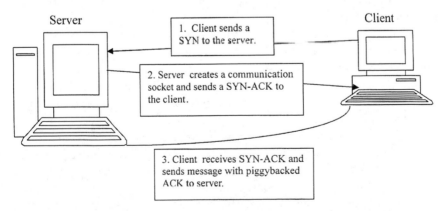

Figure 5.21 A Connection-Oriented Three-Way Handshake

In a connectionless service there is no handshaking. This means that a client can start to communicate with a server, without warning or inquiry for readiness; it simply sends streams of packets from its sending port to the server's connection port. There are advantages and, of course, disadvantages to this type of connection service as we discuss in the next section. Briefly, the connection is faster because there is no handshaking which sometimes can be time consuming. However, this service offers no safeguards or guarantees to the sender because there is no prior control information and no acknowledgment.

Before we discuss communication protocols, let us take a detour and briefly discuss data transfer by a switching element. This is a technique by which data is moved from host to host across the length and width of the network mesh of hosts, hubs, bridges, routers, and gateways. This technique is referred to as *data switching*. The type of data switching technique a network uses determines how messages are transmitted between two communicating elements and across that network. There are two types of data switching techniques: circuit switching and packet switching.

Circuit switching networks reserve the resources needed for the communication session before the session begins. The network establishes a circuit by reserving a constant transmission rate for the duration of transmission. For example, in a telephone communication network a connected line is reserved between the two points before the users can start using the service. One issue of debate on circuit switching is the perceived waste of resources during the so-called silent periods, when the connection is fully in force but not being used by the parties. This situation happens when, for example, during a telephone network session, a telephone receiver is not hung up after use, leaving the connection established. During this period while no one is utilizing the session, the session line is still open.

Packet switching networks, on the other hand, do not require any resources to be reserved before a communication session begins. Packet switching networks, however, require the sending host to send the message as a packet. If a message is large, it is broken into smaller packets. Then, each of the packets is sent on the communication links and across packet switches (routers). Each router, between the sender and receiver, passes the packet on until it reaches the destination server. The destination server reassembles the packets into the final message. Figure 5.22 shows the role of routers in packet switching networks.

Packet switches are considered to be store-and-forward transmitters, meaning they must receive the entire packet before the packet is retransmitted to the next switch. Before we proceed let us make three observations:

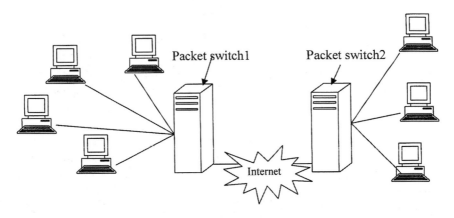

Figure 5.22 A Packet Switching Network

(i)   The transmission rate of a packet between two switching elements depends on the maximum rate of transmission of the link joining them and on the switches themselves.

(ii) There are always momentary delays introduced whenever the switch is waiting for a full packet. The longer the packet, the longer the delay.

(iii) Each switching element has a finite buffer for the packets. So it is possible for a packet to arrive only to find the buffer full with other packets. Whenever this happens, the newly arrived packet is not stored but gets lost, a process called *packet drop*. So in peak times, servers may drop a lot of packets. Congestion control techniques use the rate of packet drop as one of the measures of traffic congestion in a network.

Transmission Protocols

Packet switching networks are commonly referred to as packet networks for obvious reasons. These networks are also called *asynchronous* networks and in such networks packets are ideal because the bandwidth is shared and, of course, there is no hassle of making reservations for any anticipated transmission. There are two types of packet switching networks. One is the virtual circuit network, in which a packet route is planned and becomes a logical connection before a packet is released. The other is the datagram network, which is the focus of this book.

Because the packet network is very similar to the postal system we discussed earlier in this chapter, let us draw parallels between the protocols of the postal communication system and those of the packet network or computer network communication system. You may recall that in the postal system, messages were also moved in packets, like envelopes, cards, and boxes. The protocols in the process of moving a letter from your hands to your aunt's hands were in a stack. In fact, we had two corresponding stacks, one on the sending (you) node and the other on the receiving (your aunt) node. Also recall that the tasks in each protocol in the stack were based on a set of guidelines.

Now consider the same communication in a computer communication network. Suppose now that your aunt has a computer and an e-mail account and instead of writing a letter you want to be modern and e-mail. The process, from the start on your side to the finish on your aunt's side, would go as follows.

You would start your computer, load your e-mail program, type your message and include mail your aunt's e-mail address, something like aunt Kay@something.tk. When you send your e-mail, your e-mail software will try to talk to your server as it tries to send your e-mail to the server that will deliver it to your aunt, just like taking a letter to a mailbox in the postal system. Upon acceptance of your e-mail, your server will try to locate your aunt's server in domain .tk. We have left out lots of details which we will come back to later. After locating your aunt's server, your server will then forward your e-mail to it. Your aunt's server will then store the e-mail in your aunt's e-mail folder waiting for her computer to fetch it for her. The trail of this e-mail from the time it left your computer to the time it arrived in your aunt's e-mail folder consists of sets of activity groups we called stations in the postal system. We will call the electronic version of these stations *layers*. Again, like in the postal communication system, activities in each layer are performed based on a set of operational procedures we will also call *protocols*. In networking, protocols are like algorithms in mathematical computations. Algorithms spell out logical sequences of instructions for the computations and, of course, hide the details. Protocols do a similar thing in networking, providing hidden (from the user) logical sequences of detailed instructions. Broadly, these instructions make the source element initiate a communication, providing the identity of the destination and providing assurances that the intended destination will accept the message before any further communication is called for, and provide agreed on schemes to the destination element for translating and file management once the message is received. These instructions call for a dual layered set of instructions we have called *protocol stacks*.

To streamline network communication, the International Standards Organization (ISO) developed the Open System Interconnection (OSI) model. The OSI is an open architecture model that functions as the network communication protocol standard, although it is not the most widely used. The Transmission Control Protocol/Internet Protocol (TCI/IP) protocol suite is the most widely used. Both OSI and TCP/IP models, like the postal system, use two protocol stacks, one at the source element and the other at the destination element.

The development of the OSI model was based on the secure premise, like the postal communication system, that different layers of protocol provide different services and that each layer can communicate with only its own neighboring layers. That is, the protocols in each layer are based on the protocols of the previous layers. Figure 5.23 shows an OSI model consisting of seven layers and the descriptions of the services provided in each layer.

Although the development of the OSI model was intended to offer a standard for all other proprietary models and it was as encompassing of all existing models as possible, it never really replaced many of those rival models it was intended to replace. In fact, it is this "all in one" concept that caused its failure on the market because it became too complex. And, its late arrival on

Layer	Description
Application	The interface between the user and all network application software.
Presentation	Responsible for message syntax, conversions, compression, and encryption.
Session	Responsible for the organization and synchronization of source and destination during a communication session
Transport	Determines the class of service necessary for communication over the network. Among the classes are the connection-oriented and the connectionless.
Network	This is responsible for mainly routing messages in the network from source to destination.
Data link	Responsible for acknowledging and retransmitting frames as an error control. It also controls the amount and speed of transmission on the network.
Physical	Responsible for placing bits on the transmission medium and has protocols that make all connectors and adaptors work.

Figure 5.23 OSI Protocol Layers and Corresponding Services

Layer	Delivery Unit	Protocols
Application	Message	File Transfer Protocol (FTP), Name Server Protocol (NSP), Simple Mail Transfer Protocol (SMTP), Simple Network Management Protocol (SNMP), HTTP, Remote file access (telnet), Remote file server (NFS), Name Resolution (DNS)
Transport	Segment	Transmission Control Protocol (TCP), User Datagram Protocol (UDP)
Network	Datagram	Internet Protocol (IP), Internet Control Message Protocol (ICMP), Internet Group Management Protocol (IGMP)
Data Link	Frame	CSMA/CD for Ethernet and Token Ring
Physical	Bit Stream	All network card drivers

Figure 5.24 TCP/IP Protocol Stack

the market also prevented its much anticipated interoperability across networks. Among OSI rivals was the TCP/IP which was far less complex and more historically established by the time the OSI came on the market. Let us now focus on the TCP/IP model.

An Example of a Computer Communication Network Using TCP/IP: The Internet

The Internet is a network of communicating computing elements that uses a TCP/IP interoperability network model which is far less complex than the OSI model. The TCP/IP model is an evolving model that changes requirements as the Internet grows.

The Internet had its humble beginning in the research to develop a packet switching network funded by the Advanced Research Projects Agency (ARPA) of the Department of Defense (DOD). The resulting network was of course named ARPANET. TCP/IP is a protocol suite consisting of details of how computers in a network should intercommunicate, convey and route traffic on the computer networks. Like the OSI model, TCP/IP uses layered protocol stacks. These layers are application, transport, network, data link, and physical. Figure 5.24 shows an Internet protocol stack of these layers.

However, whereas the OSI model uses seven layers as shown in Figure 5.23, the TCP/IP model uses five. Figure 5.25 shows the differences in layering between the OSI and TCP/IP models.

OSI - Layer	TCP/IP Layer	Protocols
Application	Application	File Transfer Protocol (FTP), Name Server Protocol (NSP), Simple Mail Transfer Protocol (SMTP), Simple Network Management Protocol (SNMP), HTTP, Remote file access (telnet), Remote file server (NFS), Name Resolution (DNS)
Presentation		-
Session		-
Transport	Transport	Transmission Control Protocol (TCP), User Datagram Protocol (UDP)
Network	Network	Internet Protocol (IP), Internet Control Message Protocol (ICMP), Internet Group Management Protocol (IGMP)
Data Link	Data Link	CSMA/CD for Ethernet and Token Ring
Physical	Physical	All network card drivers

Figure 5.25 OSI and TCP/IP Protocol Stack

Application header protocols	Bit stream

Figure 5.26 Application Layer Data Frame

Application Layer

The Application Layer provides the user interface with resources rich in application functions. It supports all network applications and includes many protocols such as HTTP for Web page access, SMTP for electronic mail, telnet for remote login, and FTP for file transfers. In addition, it provides Name Server Protocol (NSP) and Simple Network Management Protocol (SNMP), remote file server (telnet), and Domain Name Resolution Protocol (DNRP). Figure 5.26 shows an Application Layer data frame.

Transport Layer

The Transport Layer is a little bit removed from the user and it is hidden from the user. Its main purpose is to transport Application Layer messages that include Application Layer protocols in their headers between the host and the server. For the Internet network, the Transport Layer has two standard protocols: Transport Control Protocol (TCP) and User Datagram Protocol (UDP). TCP provides a connection-oriented service and it guarantees delivery of all Application Layer packets to their destinations. This guarantee is based on two mechanisms: congestion control, which throttles the transmission rate of the source element when there is traffic congestion in the network and the

Source address	Destination address
Sequence number	Acknowledgment number
Other control information	
Data	

Figure 5.27 The TCP Packet Structure

flow control mechanism, which tries to match sender and receiver speeds to synchronize the flow rate and reduce the packet drop rate. While TCP offers guarantees of delivery of the Application Layer packets, UDP on the other hand offers no such guarantees. It provides a no frills connectionless service with just delivery and no acknowledgments. But it is much more efficient and the protocol of choice for real-time data like streaming video and music. Transport Layer delivers Transport Layer packets and protocols to the Network Layer. Figure 5.27 shows the TCP data structure and Figure 5.28 shows the UDP data structure.

Network Layer

The Network Layer moves packets, now called datagrams, from router to router along the path from a source host to a destination host. It supports a number of protocols including the Internet Protocol (IP), Internet Control Message Protocol (ICMP) and Internet Group Management Protocol (IGMP). The IP is the most widely used Network Layer protocol. IP uses header information from the Transport Layer protocols that include datagram

Source address	Destination address
Other header control information	UDP Checksum
Data	

Figure 5.28 The UDP Data Structure

Other header control information	Source port number	Destination port number	Data

Figure 5.29 IP Datagram Structure

source and destination port numbers from IP addresses, and other TCP header and IP information, to move datagrams from router to router through the network. The Best routes are found in the network by using routing algorithms. Figure 5.29 shows an IP datagram structure.

The standard IP address has been the so-called IPv4, a 32-bit addressing scheme. But with the rapid growth of the Internet, there was fear of running out of addresses, so a new IPv6, a 64-bit addressing scheme, was created. The Network Layer conveys the network layer protocols to the Data Link Layer.

Data Link Layer

The Data Link Layer provides the network with services that move packets from one packet switch, like a router, to the next over connecting links. This layer also offers reliable delivery of Network Layer packets over links. It is at the lowest level of communication and it includes the network interface card (NIC) and operating system (OS) protocols. The list of protocols in this layer include: Ethernet, ATM, and others like frame relay. The Data Link Layer protocol unit, the frame, may be moved over links from source to destination by different link layer protocols at different links along the way.

Physical Layer

The Physical Layer is responsible for literally moving Data Link datagrams bit by bit over the links and between network elements. The protocols here depend on and use the characteristics of the link medium and the signals on the medium. For the remainder of this book, we will use TCP/IP model used by the Internet.

Chapter 6

Anatomy of the Problem

You have to do something to raise their level of awareness that they cannot be victims. — Kevin Mitnick

---

LEARNING OBJECTIVES:

After reading this chapter, the reader should be able to:
- Understand computer network infrastructure weaknesses and vulnerabilities.
- Learn the major computer network attacks.
- Articulate the daily problems faced by computer network system administrators.
- Articulate the enormous problems faced by the security community in protecting the information infrastructure.
- Understand the role of computer users in protecting cyberspace.

The computer security breaches that included the much-debated distributed denial of service (DDoS) attacks, some of which were attributed to a Canadian teen masquerading in cyberspace as "Mafiaboy," the Philippine-generated "Love Bug," and the "Killer Resume" e-mail attacks that wreaked havoc on world computer networks, were, in addition to being attention-grabbing headlines, loud wake-up bells. Not only did these incidents expose law enforcement agencies' lack of expertise in digital forensics, they also alerted a complacent society to the weaknesses in the computer network infrastructure, the poor state of the nation's computer security preparedness, the little knowledge many of us have about computer security and the lack of efforts to secure computer system infrastructure at that time.[1] They also highlighted the vulnerability of cyberspace businesses including critical national infrastructures like power grids, water systems, financial institutions, communication systems, energy, public safety, and all other systems run by computers that foreign governments or cyber terrorists could attack via the Internet.

In fact, the "Love Bug's" near-lightning strike of global computers, its capacity to penetrate the world's powerful government institutions with impunity, though by its very origin very unsophisticated, and the easy and rapid spread of the "Killer Resume" virus, although it attacked during off-peak hours, showed how easy it was and still is to bring the world's computer infrastructure and all that depend on it to a screeching stop. They also demonstrated how the world's computer networks are at the mercy of not only affluent pre-teens and teens, as in the case of Mafiaboy, but also of the not so affluent, as in the case of the Philippine "Love Bug" creator. With national critical systems on the line, sabotage should no longer be expected to come from only known high-tech and rich countries but from anywhere, the ghettos of Manila and the jungles of the Amazon included.

As computer know-how and use spreads around the world, so do the dangers of computer attacks. How on earth did we come to this point? We are a smart people that designed the computer, constructed the computer communication network, and developed the protocols to support computer communication, yet we cannot safeguard any of these jewels from attacks, misuse, and abuse. One explanation might be rooted in the security flaws that exist in the computer communication network infrastructures, especially the Internet. Additional explanations might be: users' and system administrators' limited knowledge of the infrastructure, society's increasing dependence on a system whose infrastructure and technology it least understands, lack of long-term plans and mechanisms in place to educate the public, a highly complacent society which still accords a "whiz kid" status to cyber vandals, inadequate security mechanisms and solutions often involving no more than patching loopholes after an attack has occurred, lack of knowledge concerning the price of this escalating problem, the absence of mechanisms to enforce reporting of computer crimes (which is as of now voluntary, sporadic, and haphazard), and the fact that the nation has yet to understand the seriousness of cyber vandalism. A detailed discussion of these explanations follows.

Computer Network Infrastructure Weaknesses and Vulnerabilities

The cyberspace infrastructure, as we studied in Chapter 1, was developed without a well-conceived or understood plan with clear blueprints, but in reaction to the changing needs of developing communication between computing elements. The hardware infrastructure and corresponding underlying protocols suffer from weak points and sometimes gaping loopholes partly as a result of the infrastructure's open architecture protocol policy. This policy, coupled with the spirit of individualism and adventurism, gave birth to the computer industry and underscored the rapid, and sometimes motivated, growth of the Internet. However, the same policy acted as a magnet, attracting all sorts of people to the challenge, adventurism, and fun of exploiting the network's vulnerable and weak points.

Compounding the problem of open architecture is the nature and processes of the communication protocols. The Internet, as a packet network, works by breaking data to be transmitted into small individually addressed packets that are downloaded on the network's mesh of switching elements. Each individual packet finds its way through the network with no predetermined route and is used in the reassembling of the message by the receiving element. Packet networks need a strong trust relationship among the transmitting elements. Such a relationship is actually supported by the communication protocols. Let us see how this is done.

Computer communicating elements have almost the same etiquette as us. For example, if you want a service performed for you by a stranger, you first establish a relationship with the stranger. This can be done in a number of ways. Some people start with a formal "Hello, I'm..." then, "I need..." upon which the stranger says "Hello, I'm..." then, "Sure I can...." Others carry it further to hugs, kisses, and all other techniques people use to break the ice. If the stranger is ready to do business with you, then he passes this information to you in the form of an acknowledgment to your first inquiry. However, if the stranger is not ready to talk to you, you will not receive an acknowledgment and no further communication may follow until the stranger is ready. At this point, the stranger puts out a welcome mat and leaves the door open for you to come in and start business. Now it is up to the initiator of the communication to start full communication.

When computers are communicating, they follow these etiquette patterns and protocols and we call this procedure a handshake. In fact, for computers it is called a three-way handshake. A three-way handshake, briefly discussed in Chapter 5, starts with the client sending a packet called a SYN which contains both the client and server addresses together with some initial information for introductions. Upon receipt of this packet by the server's open door, called a *port*, the server creates a communication socket with the same port number through which future communication will pass. After creating the communication socket, the server puts the socket in queue and informs the client by sending an acknowledgment called a SYN-ACK. The server's communication socket will remain open and in queue waiting for an ACK from the client and data packets thereafter. As long as the communication socket remains open and as long as the client remains silent, not sending in an ACK, the communication socket is half open and it remains in the queue in the server memory. During this time, however, the server can welcome many more clients that want to communicate, and communication sockets will be opened for each. If any of their corresponding clients do not send in the ACK, their sockets will remain half open and also queued. Queued half-open sockets can stay in the queue for a specific time interval after which they are purged.

The three-way handshake establishes a trust relationship between the sending and receiving elements. However, network security exploits that go after infrastructure and protocol loopholes do so by attempting to undermine this trust relationship created by the three-way handshake. A discussion of the infrastructure protocol exploits and other operating system specific attacks follows.

IP-Spoofing

Internet Protocol spoofing (IP-spoofing) is a technique used to set up an attack on computer network communicating elements by altering the IP addresses of the source element in the data packets by replacing them with bogus addresses. IP-spoofing creates a situation that breaks down the normal trust relationship that should exist between two communicating elements. IP, as we saw in Chapter 5, is the connectionless, unreliable network protocol in the TCP/IP suite charged with routing packets around the network. In doing its job, IP simply sends out datagrams (data packets) with the hope that, with luck, the datagrams will make it to the destination intact. If the datagrams do not make it all the way to the destination, IP sends an error message back to the sending element to inform it of the loss. However, IP does not even guarantee that the error message will arrive to the sending element. In fact, IP does not have any knowledge of the connection state of any of the datagrams it has been entrusted with to route through the network. In addition, IP's datagrams are quite easy to open, look at and modify allowing an arbitrarily chosen IP address to be inserted in a datagram as a legitimate source address.

These conditions set the stage for IP-spoofing by allowing a small number of true IP addresses to be used bogusly by a large number of communicating elements. The process works as follows: one communicating element intercepts IP datagrams, opens them and modifies their source IP addresses and forwards them on. Any other switching element in the network that gets any of these datagrams maps these addresses in its table as legal source IP addresses, and uses them for further correspondence with the "source" elements with those bogus addresses. IP-spoofing, as we will soon see, is a basic ingredient in many types of network attacks.

SYN Flooding

SYN flooding is an attack that utilizes the breakdown in the trust relationship between two or more communicating elements to overwhelm the resources of the targeted element by sending huge volumes of spoofed packets. SYN flooding works as follows. Recall that when a client attempts to establish a TCP connection to a server, the client and server first exchange packets of data in a three-way handshake. The three-way handshake creates a half-open connection while the server is waiting for an ACK packet from the client. See Figure 6.1 for a TCP SYN and ACK-SYN exchange in a three-way handshake. During this time, however, other communicating elements may start their own three-way handshakes. If none of the clients send in their respective ACKs, the server queue of half-open connection sockets may grow beyond the server system memory capacity and thus create a memory overflow. When a server memory overflow occurs, a couple of things happen to the server. In the first instance, the server table grows huge and for each new SYN request, it takes

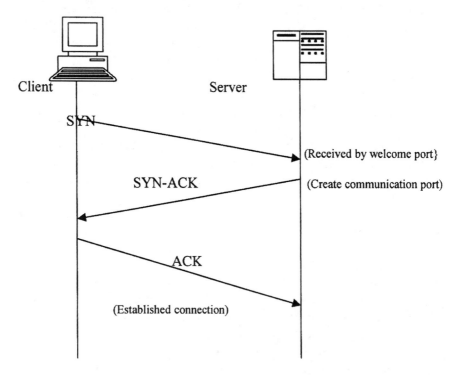

Figure 6.1 TCP SYN and ACK-SYN Exchanges in a Three-way Handshake

a lot of time for the server to search the table, thus increasing the system response time. Also, as the response time grows and the buffer fills up, the server starts to drop all new packets directed to it. This server state can be maliciously brought about intentionally by selecting a victim server and bombarding it with thousands of SYN packets each with what appears to be legitimate source IP addresses. However, these are usually bogus IP addresses with no existing client to respond to the server with an ACK. Although the queued half-open connections have a time slice quantum limit beyond which they are automatically removed from the queue, if the rate at which new incoming SYN connections are made is higher than the rate that the half-open connections are removed from the queue, then the server may start to limp. If the attacking clients simply continue sending IP-spoofed packets, the victim server will succumb to the avalanche and crash. Figure 6.2 shows a TCP SYN flood-

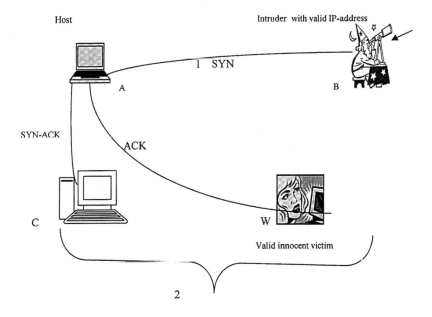

1. B sends A streams SYN with randomly
   changing source addresses from valid IP addresses.
2. A sends a stream of SYN-ACK to each valid addressed
   SYN - these are sent to hosts with no knowledge of what
   is going on and have no involvement in the attack.
   These victims have no addresses in the global Internet
   routing tables, therefore, they are not reachable.

Figure 6.2 TCP SYN Flooding

ing. SYN flooding does not only affect one victim's server. It may also ripple through the network creating secondary and subsequent victims.

Secondary and subsequent victims are created by making source IP addresses appear to come from legitimate domains whose addresses are in the global routing tables. Those legitimate machines with forged IP addresses become secondary victims because the first victim server unknowingly sends them SYN-ACKs. The victims may reply to the unsolicited SYN-ACKs by themselves sending an ACK to the victim server, therefore, becoming victims themselves.

Sequence Numbers Attack

Two of the most important fields of a TCP datagram, shown in Figure 6.4, are the sequence number field and the acknowledgment field. The fields are filled in by the sending and receiving elements during a communication session. Let us see how this is done. Suppose client A wants to send 200 bytes of data to server B using 2-byte TCP packets. The packets A will send to B are shown in Figure 6.3.

The first packet A will send to B will have two bytes, byte 0 and byte 1, and will have a sequence number 0. The second packet will have bytes 2 and

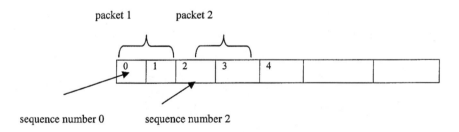

Figure 6.3 Sequencing of TCP Packets

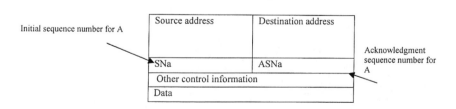

Figure 6.4 TCP Packet Structures with Initial and Acknowledgment Sequence Numbers

3 and will be assigned sequence number 2. Note that the sequence number is not the byte number but the first byte number in each packet. Upon receipt of the packets from A, B will send acknowledgments to A with an acknowledgment number. Recall TCP is a full-duplex communication protocol, meaning that during any communication session, there is a simultaneous two-way communication session during which A and B can talk to each other without one waiting for the other to finish before it can start. B acknowledges A's packets by informing A of the receipt of all the packets except the missing ones. So in this case B sends an ACK packet with an acknowledgment number and its own sequence number, which is the next number to the last sequence number it has received. For example, suppose A has sent packets with sequence numbers 0, 1, 2, ..., 15, B will send an acknowledgment of these packets through sequence number 15 with acknowledgment number 16.

Figure 6.4 shows a TCP Packet structures with initial and acknowledgment sequence numbers.

Figure 6.5 shows a TCP connection session using sequence numbers (SNs) and acknowledgment numbers(ACNs).

The initial sequence number (ISN) is supposed to be random and subsequent numbers are incremented by a constant based on time (usually seconds) and connection (RFC 793).

The initial sequence number attack is a technique that allows an attacker to create a one-way TCP connection with a target element while spoofing another element by guessing the TCP sequence numbers used. This is done by the attacker intercepting the communication session between two or more communicating elements and then guessing the next sequence number in a communication session. The intruder then slips the spoofed IP addresses into

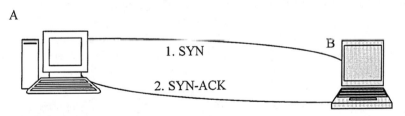

1.   A SYN (INSa – initial sequence number a) – A sends a first packet to B with initial sequence number a.
2.   B replies to A with ACK(SNb, SNa), two sequence numbers, its own sequence number (SNb) and acknowledging the sent number (SNa).

Figure 6.5 A TCP Connection Session

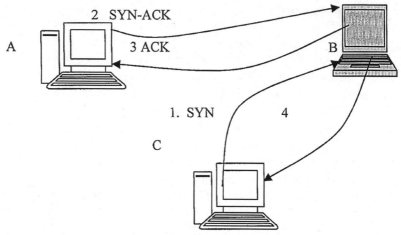

1. C, the attacker, opens a connection with B by sending (SYN, ISNa) masquerading as A, where ISNa is the initial sequence number for A.
2. B responds by sending an SYN-ACK to A (ACK, ISNb, ISNa).
3. A acknowledges B by sending ACK(ISNa, ISNb). Although A does NOT know anything about the SYN to B, it responds anyway by using the guessed ISNb.
4. B now believes it has a legitimate session with A.
   However C, the intruder, is actually communicating with B.

Figure 6.6 Initial Sequence Number Attack

---

packets transmitted to the server. The server sends an acknowledgment to the spoofed clients. Let us illustrate such an attack in Figure 6.6.

However, it is possible for client A to realize that server B is actually acknowledging a packet that A did not send in the first place. In this case, A may send a request (RST) to B to bring down the connection. However, this is possible only if A is not kept busy, and this is how the exploit occurs. The trick is to send a smurf attack on A to keep A as busy as possible so that it does not have time to respond to B with an RST. In this case then, the intruder successfully becomes a legitimate session member with server B.

Scanning and Probing Attacks

In a scanning and probing attack, the intruder or intruders send large quantities of packets from a single location. The activity involves mostly a Trojan horse remote controlled program with a distributed scanning engine that is configured to scan carefully selected ports. Currently, the most popular ports are port 80, used by World Wide Web applications, port 8080, used by World Wide Web proxy services, and port 3128, used by most common squid proxy services.

Low Bandwidth Attacks

A low bandwidth attack starts when a hacker sends a low volume, intermittent series of scanning or probing packets from various locations. The attack may involve several hackers from different locations, all concurrently scanning and probing the network for vulnerabilities. Low bandwidth attacks can involve as few as five to ten packets per hour, from as many different sources.

Session Attacks

Many other types of attacks target sessions already in progress and break into such sessions. Let us look at several of these, namely packet sniffing, buffer overflow, and session hijacking.

A packet sniffer is a program on a network element connected to a network to passively receive all Data Link Layer frames passing through the device's network interface. This makes all hosts connected to the network possible packet sniffers. If host A is transmitting to host B and there is a packet sniffer in the communication path between them, then all data frames sent from A to B and vice versa are "sniffed." A sniffed frame can have its content, message, and header altered, modified, even deleted and replaced. For example, in a network element in a local area network (LAN) with Ethernet protocols, if the network card is set to promiscuous mode, the interface can receive all passing frames. The intercepted frames are then passed over to the Application Layer program to extract any type of data the intruder may have an interest in. Figure 6.7 shows how packet sniffing works.

A buffer overflow is an attack that allows an intruder to overrun one or more program variables making it easy to execute arbitrary codes with the privilege of the current user. Intruders usually target the root (the highest privileged user on the system). The problem is always a result of bad program coding. Such coding may include a program that lacks good string or buffer data types in C, misuse of standard C library string functions, and if buffers are used, not being able to check the size of the buffer whenever data is inserted in the buffer. In a network environment, especially a UNIX environment,

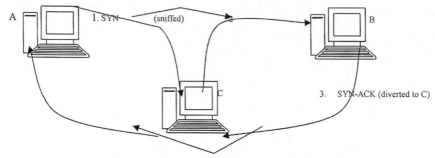

1.   A sends a SYN packet to B for login containing source and destination address and password.
2.   C, the intruder, sniffs the packet A is sending to B and gets A's and B's address and A's password to B.
3.   B, with no knowledge of C in the midiaum, sends a SYN-ACK and permission to enter to A.
4.   C is now in full access to both A and B after sniffing the SYN-ACK.

Figure 6.7 Packet Sniffing

---

buffer overflow can create serious security problems because an attacker can, from anywhere, execute an attack on a system of choice.

Session hijacking may occur in several situations. For example, quite often clients may desire services, like software stored at a server. In order to access such services, the server may require the client to send authenticating information that may include a password and username. In some cases, especially where requests from a client are frequent, the server may store the user ID with the access URL so that the server can quickly recognize the returning user without going through an authentication exercise every time a request comes from this client. Thus, a trust relationship is established. By doing this, however, the server automatically opens up loopholes through which an intruder, after sniffing the legitimate source IP address, can hijack a server TCP session without the knowledge of either the server or the client. A more common type of session hijacking is for the intruder to become a legal participant by monitoring a session between two communicating hosts and then injecting traffic that appears to be coming from those hosts. Eventually one of the legitimate hosts is dropped, thus making the intruder legitimate. Another type of session hijacking is known as *blind hijacking*, when an intruder guesses the responses of the two communicating elements and becomes a fully trusted participant without ever seeing the responses.

Session hijacking can take place even if the targeted communication element rejects the source IP address packets. This is possible if the initial connection sequence numbers can be predicted. Figure 6.8 illustrates a typical session hijacking using initial connection sequence numbers (ISN).

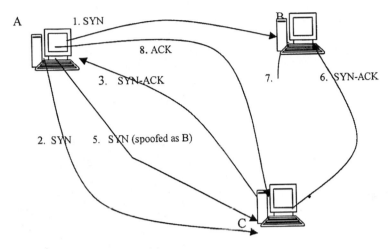

1. A sends a SYN flood to B – to keep it busy.
2. A also SYN to C.
3. C returns a SYN-ACK to A with initial sequence numbers (ISN).
4. C increments the ISN for this connection.
5. A then SYN to C spoofed as B. (recall B is busy).
6. C sends a SYN-ACK to B and an ISN (which A captures).
7. But there is no response from B to C (it is SYN-flooded).
8. A sends an ACK to C masquerading as B containing the guessed ISN+1.
    If the guess is correct, then C believes A to be B and A has successfully hijacked C's session.

Figure 6.8 Session Hijacking Using Sequence Numbers

Distributed Denial of Service Attacks

Distributed denial of service (DDoS) attacks are generally classified as nuisance attacks in the sense that they simply interrupt the services of the system. System interruption can be as serious as destroying a computer's hard disk or as simple as using up all the system's available memory. DDoS attacks come in many forms but the most common are the Ping of Death, smurfing, the teardrop, and the land.c.

Ping of Death

The Ping of Death is one of several possible Internet Control Message Protocol (ICMP) attacks. The ICMP is an IP protocol used in the exchange of messages. The IP-datagram encapsulates the ICMP message as shown in Figure 6.9.

According to RFC-791, an IP packet including those containing ICMP messages can be as long as 65,353 (2^{16-1}) octets. An octet is a group of eight

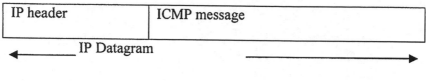

Figure 6.9 IP-ICMP Packet

items. When packets are bigger than the maximum allowable IP packet structure, such packets are fragmented into smaller products. ICMP ECHO_ REQUESTs are called pings. Normal network pings, as we have seen before, are done by the server broadcasting ICMP ECHO_REQUEST packets every second and waiting for a SIGALRM (short for signal alarm) packet signal from the clients. A ping flood occurs when the client sends lots of SIGALRM signals to the ping generator, in this case the server. The problem in this category is partly the size of these SIGALRM packets. If the SIGALRM packets sent by the client to the server are large and not fragmented into smaller packets, they can cause havoc. Large IP packets are known as the Ping of Death. You see, when packets get larger, the underlying protocols that handle them become less efficient. However, in normal data transmission, IP packets bigger than the maximum size are broken up into smaller packets which are then reassembled by the receiver.

Smurfing

A smurfing attack also utilizes the broken trust relationship created by IP-spoofing. An offending element sends a large amount of spoofed ping packets containing the victim's IP address as the source address. Ping traffic, also called Protocol Overview Internet Control Message Protocol (ICMP) in the Internet community, is used to report out-of-band messages related to network operation or mis-operation such as a host or entire portion of the network being unreachable, due to some type of failure. The pings are then directed to a large number of network subnets, a subnet being a small independent network like a LAN. If all subnets reply to the victim address, the victim element receives a high rate of requests from the spoofed addresses as a result and the element begins buffering these packets. When the requests come at a rate exceeding the capacity of the queue, the element generates ICMP Source Quench messages meant to slow down the sending rate. These messages are then sent, supposedly, to the legitimate sender of the requests. If the sender is legitimate, it will heed to the requests and slow down the rate of packet transmission. However, in cases of spoofed addresses, no action is taken because all sender addresses are bogus. The situation in the network can easily deteriorate further if each routing device takes part in smurfing.

Teardrop Attack

The teardrop attack exploits the fragmentation vulnerability mechanism of ICMP ECHO_REQUEST packets just like the Ping of Death attacks. However, the teardrop attack works by attacking the reassembling mechanism of the fragmented IP packets resulting in overlapping fragments that often lead targeted hosts to hang or crush altogether.[2]

Land.c Attack

The land.c attack is initiated by an intruder sending a TCP SYN packet giving the target host's addresses as both the source and destination addresses. It also uses the host's port number as both the source and destination ports.[3]

The techniques we have seen above are collectively known as distributed denial of service (DDoS) attacks. Any system connected to the Internet and using TCP and UDP protocol services like WWW, e-mail, FTP, and telnet is potentially subject to this attack. The attack may be selectively targeted to specific communicating elements or it might be directed to randomly selected victims.

Although we seem to understand how the DDoS problems arise, we have yet to come up with meaningful and effective solutions. What makes the search for solutions even more elusive is the fact that we do not even know when a server is under attack since the IP-spoofing connection requests, for example, may not lead to a system overload. While the attack is going on, the system may still be able to function satisfactorily establishing outgoing connections. It makes one wonder how many such attacks are going on without ever being detected, and what fraction of those attacks are ever detected.

Network Operating Systems and Software Vulnerabilities

Network infrastructure exploits are not limited to protocols. There are weaknesses and loopholes in network software that include network operating systems, Web browsers, and network applications. Such loopholes are quite often targets of aggressive hacker attacks like planting Trojan viruses, deliberately inserting backdoors, stealing sensitive information, and wiping out files from systems. Such exploits have become common. Let us look at some operating system vulnerabilities.

Windows NT and NT Registry Attacks

The Windows NT Registry is a central repository for all sensitive system and configuration information. It contains five permanent parts, called *hives*, that control local machine information such as booting and running the system, information on hardware configuration data, resource usage, per-machine software data, account and group databases, performance counters, and system-wide security policies that include hashed passwords, program locations, program default settings, lists of trusted systems, and audit settings. Almost all applications added to the NT machine and nearly all security settings affect the registry. The registry is a trove of information for attackers and it is a prime target of many computer attacks. Common NT Registry attacks include the L0pht Crack, the Chargen Attack, the SSPING/JOLT, and the RedButton.

The L0pht Crack works by guessing passwords on either the local or remote machine. Once a hacker succeeds in guessing a password and gains entry, the hacker then makes bogus passwords and establishes new accounts. Now the attacker can even try to gain access to privileged access accounts.

The Chargen Attack is a malicious attack that may be mounted against computers running Windows NT and 2000. The attack consists of a flood of UDP datagrams sent to the subnet broadcast address with the destination port set to 19 (chargen) and a spoofed source IP address. The Windows NT and 2000 computers running Simple TCP/IP services respond to each broadcast, creating a flood of UDP datagrams that eventually cripple the selected server.

The SSPING/JOLT is a version of the old SysV and Posix implementations. It effectively freezes almost any Windows 95 or Windows NT connection by sending a series of spoofed and fragmented ICMP packets to the target. A server running Windows 95/98/NT/2000 may crumble altogether. This is a version of the Ping of Death attack we saw earlier targeted on computers running Windows 95/98/NT/2000.

The RedButton allows an attacker of the NT Registry to bypass the traditional logon procedure that requires a valid username and password combination, or the use of a guest account. The bug grants that user access to intimate system information on an NT server without these requirements. It does this by exploiting an alternate means of access to an NT system using an anonymous account, which is normally used for machine-to-machine communication on a network. This anonymous account gives a successful attacker full access to all system resources available to an NT group named "everyone," that includes all system users.

UNIX

UNIX's source code, unlike Windows NT, has been publicly released for a long time. Its many flaws have been widely discussed and, of course, exploited. This leads to the perception that Windows NT is actually more secure—a false assumption. In fact, Windows NT has many of UNIX's flaws.

Knowledge of Users and System Administrators

The limited knowledge computer users and system administrators have about computer network infrastructure and the working of its protocols does not help advance network security. In fact, it increases the dangers. In a mechanical world where users understand the systems, things work differently. For example, in a mechanical system like a car, if a car has fundamental mechanical weaknesses, the driver usually understands and finds those weak points and repairs them. This, however, is not the case with computer networks. As we have seen, the network infrastructure has weaknesses, and this situation is complicated when both system administrators and users have limited knowledge of how the system works, its weaknesses and when such weaknesses are in the network. This lack of knowledge leads to other problems that further complicate network security. Among such factors are the following:

- Network administrators do not use effective encryption schemes and do not use or enforce a sound security policy.
- Less knowledgeable administrators and users quite often use blank or useless passwords, and they rarely care to change even the good ones.
- Users carelessly give away information to criminals without being aware of the security implications. For example, Kevin Mitnick, a notorious hacker, claims to have accessed the Motorola company computer network by persuading company employees to give up passwords on the pretext that he was one of them.[4] This very example illustrates the enormous task of educating users to be more proactive as far as computer security is concerned.
- Network administrators fail to use system security filters. According to security experts, network servers without filters "are the rule rather than the exception."

Society's Dependence on Computers

All the problems we have discussed so far are happening at a time when computer and Internet use are on the rise. Computer dependency is increasing as computers increasingly become part of our everyday lives. From Wall Street to private homes, dependency on computers and computer technology shows no signs of abating. As we get more and more entangled in a computer driven economy, very few in society have a sound working knowledge and understanding of the basics of how computers communicate and how e-mail and Internet surfing work. Indeed, few show any interest in learning. This has always been the case with the technology we use every day. From the business point of view, technology works better and is embraced faster if all its complexities are transparent to the user, and therefore, user-friendly. Few of us bother to learn much about cars, televisions, washers and dryers, or even faucets and drains, because when they break down and need fixing, we always call in a mechanic, a technician, or a plumber! What is so different about computers and computer networks?

What is different is the enormous amount of potential for abuse of computers and computer networks—and the possibility of damage over vast amounts of cyberspace.

Lack of Planning

Despite the potential for computer and computer network abuses to wreak havoc on our computer dependent society, as demonstrated by the "Love Bug" and the "Killer Resume" viruses, there are few signs that we are getting the message and making plans to educate the populace on computer use and security. Besides calling on the FBI to hunt abusers down and apprehend them, uring the courts to prosecute and convict them to the stiffest jail sentences possible to send a signal to other would-be abusers, and demanding tougher laws, there is nothing on the horizon. There is no clear plan or direction, no blueprint to guide the national efforts in finding a solution; very little has been done on the education front.

Complacent Society

When the general public holds some specialty in high regard, usually it is because the public has little knowledge of that specialty. The less knowledge we possess in some field, the more status we accord to those whose knowledge is great. I have little knowledge of how satellites are guided in the emptiness of space or how to land one on an outer space object in a specific preselected spot millions of miles away, so I really respect space scientists. However, when my bathroom faucet leaks, I can fix it in a few hours; therefore, I do not have as much respect for plumbers as I do for space scientists.

The same reasoning applies to computer users concerning computers and how they work. The public still accords "whiz kid" status to computer vandals. Do we accord them that status because they are young and computer literate and few of us used computers at their age, or because we think that they are smarter than we are? Not only do we admire the little vandals, but we also seem mesmerized with them and their actions do not seem to register on the radar, at least not yet. This is frightening, to say the least.

Inadequate Security Mechanisms and Solutions

Although computer network software developers and hardware manufacturers have tried to find solutions to the network infrastructure and related problems, sound and effective solutions are yet to be found. In fact, all solutions that have been provided so far by both hardware and software manufacturers have not really been solutions but patches. For example, when the distributed denial of service (DDoS) attack occurred, Cisco, one of the leading network router manufacturers, immediately, through its vendors, issued patches as solutions to DDoS attacks. This was followed by IBM, another leading router manufacturer; a few others followed the examples of the industry leaders. More recently, when both the "Love Bug" and the "Killer Resume" viruses struck e-mail applications on global networks, Microsoft, the developer of Outlook, which was the main conduit of both viruses, immediately issued a patch. These are not isolated incidents but a pattern of the computer industry's two major component manufacturers.

A computer communication network is only as good as its weakest hardware link and its poorest network protocol. In fact, infrastructure attacks like those outlined above have no known fixes. For example, there is no known effective defense against denial of service attacks. Several hardware manufacturers of network infrastructure items like routers and other switches have, in addition to offering patches, recommend to their customers that they boost the use of filters. Few of these remedies have worked effectively so far.

These best known security mechanisms and solutions, actually half solutions to the network infrastructure problems, are inadequate at best. More effective solutions to the network protocol weaknesses are not in sight. This, together with the FBI and other law enforcement agencies not being able to apprehend all perpetrators, highlights an urgent need for a solution that is still elusive. Yet, the rate of such crimes is on the rise. With such a rise, law enforcement agencies are trying to cope with the epidemic, limited as they are, with lack of modern technology. Michael Vatis, director of the FBI's National Infrastructure Protection Center, testifies to this when he says that due to limited capacity, attacks like spoofing make it very difficult for law enforcement to determine where an attack originates.[5] This explains why the FBI took so long to apprehend the recent cyber vandals of the DDoS attacks. Vatis, like many, sees no immediate solution coming from either the technology or the FBI and he proposes two possible solutions:

(i)   enabling civilians not bound by the Fourth Amendment to conduct investigations and

(ii) somehow defeating spoofing with better technology. None of his solutions is feasible yet.

Poor Reporting of a Growing Epidemic of Computer Crimes

Franz-Stefan Gady (2011) reports that data from the Norton Cyber Crime Report for 2011 show that 431 million adults worldwide were victims of cybercrime in 2010. The total cost of those crimes was north of $114 billion. However, data like this, routinely reported across the globe, is misleading. Because, that is not the true maginitude of the problem. We are falling short of the actual comprehensive picture of cybercrime data in assessing the true scale and scope of cybercrime. The main reason is that businesses, which are the main target of most cybercrimes, are reluctant to voluntarily report incidences of attacks and intrusions because of internal fear of sometimes critical business data exposure and a show of internal business weakness. According to reports, two-thirds of computer firms do not report hacker attacks.[6] According to a U.S. Senate report on security in cyberspace, many government departments, including Defense, have no mandatory reporting.[7] It is even worse when it comes to detection and intrusion. According to the same report, the Defense Information Systems Agency (DISA), an agency that performs proactive vulnerability assessments of the Defense Department computer networks, penetrated 18,200 systems and only five percent of those intrusions were detected by system administrators. And of the 910 systems users that detected the intrusions, only 27 percent reported the intrusions to their superiors.[8] In addition, even if businesses were to report, it is difficult for us to verify their statements.

We cannot fight this tide of cybercrime without having a clean picture and understanding of its true impact on the world economy.

Meanwhile headline-making vandals keep on striking, making more and more daring acts with impunity. Although the Internet Fraud Complaint Center—a partnership between the FBI and NW3C (funded by BJA), established in 2000 and later changing its name to the Internet Crime Complaint Center (IC3)—fights to address the ever-increasing incidence of online fraud and encourages victims of Internet crime to report all incidents, thousands of attacks are still not reported, making the number of reported cybercrimes tracked by IC3 and local enforcement authorities way below the actual numbers of cybercrimes committed.

Similar numbers are probably found in the private sector. In a study by the Computer Security Institute (CSI), 4,971 questionnaires were sent to information security practitioners, seeking information on system intrusions and only 8.6 percent responded. Of those responding, only 42 percent admitted that intrusions ever occurred in their systems.[9] This low reporting rate can be attributed to a number of reasons including the following:

- Many of those who would like to report such crimes do not do so because of the economic and psychological impact such news would have on shareholder confidence and on their company's reputation. Customer confidence is a competitive advantage and losing it could spell financial ruin for a company. Some companies are reluctant to report any form of computer attacks on their systems for fear that company management will be perceived as weak and having poor security policies.
- There is little to no interest in reporting.
- Most law enforcement agencies, especially the FBI, do not have the highly specialized personnel needed to effectively track down intruders. Those few highly trained professionals that do exist, however, are overworked and underpaid according to an ABC report.[10]
- Companies and businesses hit by cyber vandalism have little faith in law enforcement agencies, especially the FBI, because they think the FBI, in its present state and capacity, can do little. The burden to catch and apprehend cyber criminals is still on the FBI. This explains why there has been slow progress in apprehending the perpetrators of the recent denial of service and "Love Bug" attacks.

The FBI's problems are perpetuated by the fact that the law has not kept up with technology. According to an ABC News report, the FBI cannot quickly and readily share evidence of viruses and attack programs with private companies that have the capacity and technical know-how. By the time private industry gets hold of such evidence, the tracks left by the intruders are cold. The law enforcement situation is even more murky on a global scale. The global mosaic of laws, political systems, and law enforcement capacity make badly needed global efforts even more unattainable.

Also, current wiretap laws were designed for lengthy surveillance in one place in order to build a case. And, if there is cause to track down a perpetrator, a court order must be sought in every judicial district, which takes time and may lead to evidence getting altered or destroyed altogether. However, cyber attacks that are quick and can instantaneously have a global reach cannot be monitored from one place, and evidence cannot wait for court orders. This problem was highlighted in the attempted arrest of the authors of the "Love Bug." It took two days to even attempt to arrest a suspect because there were no computer crime laws on the books in the Philippines. So a judge could not issue an arrest warrant quickly. National laws have to be amended to make it easier to pursue attackers. To be effective, such laws must, among other things, allow investigators to completely trace an online communication to its source without seeking permission from each jurisdiction. More money must be allocated to hire prosecutors and analysts and to improve the research capability of all law enforcement agencies. In addition, there must be continuous training of the latest developments in digital forensics for those already in law enforcement agencies. If all these are put in place, then we will be on the way to making cyberspace safer for all.

Although the network infrastructure weaknesses we have discussed in this chapter seem simple, finding solutions will not be easy and it is an ongoing exercise of interest to lawmakers, law enforcement agencies, and the network community. The Holy Grail is to find a final solution to the dreaded computer network security problems. If we succeed, the solution will not last long, for the following reasons:

- The cyberspace infrastructure technology is constantly changing, adding new technologies along the way, and as new technologies are added, new loopholes and, therefore, new opportunities are created for cyber vandals.
- Solutions to social and ethical problems require a corresponding change in the legal structures, enforcement mechanisms, and human moral and ethical systems. None of these can change at the speed technology is changing. Pretty soon, any solution will be useless and we will be back to square one.
- As yet, there is no national or multinational plan or policy that can withstand the rapid changes in technology and remain enforceable.

- Most importantly, solutions that do not take into account and are not part of a general public education plan, do not stand a chance of lasting for any extended period of time. For any solution to the computer network security problem to last, public education and awareness are critical.

A workable and durable solution, if found, must include the following:

- Public awareness and understanding of the computer network infrastructure threats, its potential consequences and its vulnerabilities. We cannot rely on education acquired from science-fiction novels. Otherwise, when such attacks really occur, the public may take them to be science-fiction events.
- A well-developed plan based on a good policy for deterrence.
- A clear plan, again based on good and sound policy, for rapid and timely response to cyber attacks.

Chapter 7

Enterprise Security

Cybercrimes and other information-security breaches are widespread and diverse. — Patrice Rapalus, director of the Computer Security Institute

---

LEARNING OBJECTIVES:

After reading this chapter, the reader should be able to:
- Describe trends in computer crimes and information infrastructure protection.
- Describe and discuss the types and techniques of computer attacks.
- Understand computer attack motives.
- Discuss the most common information security flaws.

While Gibson's vision of cyberspace, as discussed in Chapter 5, captures the essence of cyberspace as a three-dimensional network of computers with pure information moving between these computers, the definition itself is not inclusive enough because it does not specifically tell us the small details that make up cyberspace. Let us examine that now here by giving an expanded definition of cyberspace to include all components that make the resources of cyberspace. They include:

- hardware, like computers, printers, scanners, servers and communication media;
- software, including application and special programs, system backups and diagnostic programs, and system programs like operating systems and protocols;
- data in storage, transition, or undergoing modification;
- people, including users, system administrators, and hardware and software manufacturers;

- documentation, including user information for hardware and software, administrative procedures, and policy documents; and
- supplies, including paper and printer cartridges.

These six components comprise the major divisions of cyberspace resources and together they form the cyberspace infrastructure and environment. Throughout this book, an attack on any one of these resources, therefore, will be considered an attack on cyberspace resources.

Although all of these resources make up cyberspace, and any one of them is a potential target for a cyberspace attack, they do not have the same degree of vulnerability. Some are more vulnerable than others and, therefore, are targeted more frequently by attackers. Cyberspace has brought about an increasing reliance on these resources through computers running national infrastructures like telecommunications, electrical power systems, gas and oil storage and transportation, banking and finance, transportation, water supply systems, emergency services that include medical, police, fire, and rescue, and, of course, government services. These are central to national security, economic survival, and the social well-being of people. Such infrastructures are deemed critical because their incapacitation could lead to chaos in any country.

A cyberspace threat is an intended or unintended illegal activity, an unavoidable or inadvertent event that has the potential to lead to unpredictable, unintended, and adverse consequences on a cyberspace resource. A cyberspace attack or *e-attack* is a cyberspace threat that physically affects the integrity of any one of these cyberspace resources. Most cyberspace attacks can be put in one of three categories: natural or inadvertent attacks, human errors, or intentional threats.[1]

Natural or inadvertent attacks include accidents originating from natural disasters like fire, floods, windstorms, lightning, and earthquakes. They usually occur very quickly and without warning, and they are beyond human capacity, often causing serious damage to affected cyberspace resources. Not much can be done to prevent natural disaster attacks on computer systems. However, precautions can be taken to lessen the impact of such disasters and to quicken the recovery from the damage they cause.

Human errors are caused by unintentional human actions. Unintended human actions are usually due to design problems. Such attacks are called *malfunctions*. Malfunctions, though occurring more frequently than natural disasters, are as unpredictable as natural disasters. They can affect any cyber resource, but they attack computer hardware and software resources more. In hardware, malfunctions can be a result of power failure or simply a power surge, electromagnetic influence, mechanical wear and tear, or human error. Software malfunctions result mainly from logical errors and occasionally from human errors during data entry. Malfunctions resulting from logical errors often cause a system to halt. However, there are times when such errors may not cause a halt to the running program, but may be passed on to later stages of the computation. If that happens and the errors are not caught in time, they can result in bad decision making. A bad decision may cost an organization millions of dollars.

Most cyberspace attacks are intentional, originating from humans, caused by illegal or criminal acts from either insiders or outsiders. For the remainder of this chapter we will focus on intentional attacks.

Types of Attacks

Because of the many cyberspace resources, the varying degrees of vulnerabilities of these resources, the motives of the attackers, and the many topographies involved, e-attacks fall into a number of types. We will put these types into two categories: penetration and denial of service attacks.

Penetration Attacks

Penetration attacks involve breaking into systems using known security vulnerabilities to gain access to any cyberspace resource. With full penetration, an intruder has full access to all of a system's cyberspace resources or *e-resources*. Full penetration, therefore, allows an intruder to alter data files, change data, plant viruses, or install damaging Trojan horse programs into the system. It is also possible for intruders, especially if the victim computer is on a network, to use a penetration attack as a launching pad to attack other network resources. According to William Stallings,[2] there are three classes of intruders:

(i)   Masquerader: This is a person who gains access to a computer system using other peoples' accounts without authorization.
(ii) Misfeasor: This is a legitimate user who gains access to system resources for which there is no authorization.
(iii) Clandestine user: This is a person with supervisory control who uses these privileges to evade or suppress auditing or access controls.

Penetration attacks can be local, where the intruder gains access to a computer on a LAN on which the program is run, or global on a WAN like the Internet, where an e-attack can originate thousands of miles from the victim computer. This was the case in the "Love Bug" e-mail attack.

For a long time, penetration attacks were limited to in-house employee generated attacks to systems and theft of company property. A limited form of system break-in from outsiders started appearing in the early 1970s when limited computer network communication became available. But as long as the technology was still in the hands of the privileged few, incidents of outsider system penetration were few. The first notable system penetration attack actually started in the mid–1980s with the San Francisco–based 414-Club. The 414-Club was the first national news-making hacker group. The group named themselves 414 after the area code. They started a series of computer intrusion attacks using a Stanford University computer to spread the attack across the country.[3]

From that small, but history-making attack, other headline-making attacks from Australia, Germany, Argentina and the United States followed. Ever since, we have been on a wild ride. There are three types of penetration attacks: viruses, non-virus malicious attacks from insiders, and non-virus malicious attacks from outsiders.

Viruses

Because viruses comprise a very big percentage of all cyberspace attacks, we will devote some time to them here. The term *virus* is derived from the Latin word *virus*, which means poison. For generations, even before the birth of modern medicine, the term remained mostly in medical circles and was used to refer to a foreign agent that injected itself into a living body, where it would feed, grow and multiply. As a virus reproduces itself in a host's body, it spreads throughout the body slowly disabling the body's natural resistance to foreign objects and weakening the body's ability to perform needed life functions, eventually causing serious, sometimes fatal, effects to the body.

A computer virus, defined as a self-propagating computer program designed to alter or destroy a computer system resource, follows almost the same pattern but instead of using a living body, it uses software to attach itself, grow, reproduce, and spread. As it spreads in the new environment, it attacks major system resources that include the surrogate software itself, data, and sometimes hardware, weakening the capacity of these resources to perform the needed functions and eventually bringing the system down.

The word *virus* was first assigned a nonbiological meaning in the 1972 science fiction stories about the G.O.D. machine that were compiled in the book *When Harly Was One* by David Gerrod (Ballantine Books, 1972). In the book, according to Karen Forcht, the term was first used to describe a piece of unwanted computer code.[4] Later, association of the term with a real world computer program was made by Fred Cohen, then a graduate student at the

University of Southern California. Cohen wrote five programs, actually viruses, to run on a VAX 11/750 running UNIX, not to alter or destroy any computer resources, but for class demonstration. During the demonstration, each virus obtained full control of the system within an hour.[5]

Since this simple and rather harmless beginning, computer viruses have been on the rise. In fact, the growth of the Internet together with massive news coverage of virus incidents have caused an explosion of all types of computer viruses from sources scattered around the globe, with newer attacks occurring at faster speeds than ever before. For more about the history and development of the computer virus the reader is referred to an extended discussion in Karen Forcht's book, *Computer Security Management* (Boyd and Fraser, 1994).

Where do computer viruses come from? Just like human viruses, they are contracted when there is an encounter with a species that already has the virus. There are four main sources of viruses: movable computer disks like floppies, zips, and tapes; Internet downloadable software like beta software, shareware, and freeware; e-mail and e-mail attachments; and platform-free executable applets, like those Java language applets.

Although movable computer disks used to be the most common way of sourcing and transmitting viruses, new Internet technology has caused this to decline. Viruses sourced from movable computer disks are either boot viruses or disk viruses.

Boot viruses attack boot sectors on both hard and floppy disks. Disk sectors are small areas on a disk that the hardware reads in single chunks. For DOS formatted disks, sectors are commonly 512 bytes in length. Disk sectors, although invisible to normal programs, are vital for the correct operation of computer systems because they form chunks of data the computer uses. A boot sector is the first disk sector or first sector on a disk or diskette that an operating system is aware of. It is called a boot sector because it contains an executable program the computer executes every time the computer is powered up. Because of its central role in the operations of computer systems, the boot sector is very vulnerable to virus attacks and viruses use it as a launching pad to attack other parts of the computer system. Viruses like this sector because from it they can spread very fast from computer to computer, booting from that same disk. Boot viruses can also infect other disks left in the disk drive of an infected computer.

Whenever viruses do not use the boot sector, they embed themselves, as macros, in disk data or software. A macro is a small program embedded in another program and executes when that program, the surrogate program, executes. Macro viruses mostly infect data and document files like Microsoft Word, templates, spreadsheets, and database files. All the following applications, for example, contain language which allow the introduction of macro viruses: Microsoft Word, Excel, Lotus 1–2-3, and Quattro Pro. Macro viruses spread only within these specific environments, and the speed with which they spread depends on the frequency of use of the infected documents in those applications. Examples of macro viruses are many including several varieties of the "Concept" virus and the "Nuclear" virus.

The advent of the Internet has made downloadable software the second most common source of viruses. Downloadable software include all downloadable types of software like freeware, shareware, and beta software. These types of software may have self-extracting viruses deliberately or accidentally implanted in them. Besides e-mail attachments, this is now the second fastest way to spread viruses. There are thousands of sites offering thousands of freeware, shareware, and beta software everyday. So, if a virus is embedded into any one of these, it is likely to spread very far, wide, and fast.

Currently, the most common sources of computer viruses are e-mail and e-mail attachments. This was demonstrated recently by "Melissa," "Love Bug," and "Killer Resume." All three viruses were embedded in e-mail attachments. One reason e-mail and e-mail attachments are popular is because more than 50 percent of all Internet traffic is e-mail, so virus developers see it as the best vehicle for transmitting their deadly payloads.

The newest and perhaps fastest-growing virus carrier is the Java applet. The Java Programming Language uses a Java applet to compile the source code on its Java machine and then migrate execution to a local browser. As Web pages become more animated, applets are becoming the medium of choice for virus transmission. There are some disadvantages to using Java applets as virus conduits that still keep this method of spreading viruses low-key. Applets are more complicated and one needs more expertise to create a virus and embed it in an applet other than one's own. And probably the most interesting disadvantage is that Java applets do not, as yet, have the capability to write to your machine's disk or memory; they simply execute in your browser. Until they acquire such capabilities, their ability to carry viruses remains limited.

Let us now consider how viruses are transmitted. In order for a computer virus to infect a computer it must have a chance to be transmitted and deposited in a good location where it can execute its code. The transmission of these viruses has improved as computer technology improved. In those days when computers were stand-alone and computer networks were a preserve of the lucky few, computer viruses used to be transmitted by passing infected floppy disks from one computer to another. The fully blown use of computer network communication, and the easy and almost universal access to the Internet have transformed and transcribed new methods of virus transmission. The proliferation of networking technologies, new developments in home personal

Ethernet networks, and the miniaturization of personal computers have resulted in new and faster virus transmission and exchange techniques. This is no better example than the successful transmission of the "Love Bug" e-mail virus that circumvented the globe in a mere 12 hours.

When a fertile environment is found by a downloaded virus, it attaches itself to a surrogate software or a safe location where it executes its code, modifying legitimate system resources so that its code is executed whenever these legitimate system resources are either opened or executed. Such resources may include the disk boot sector, which contains the code that is executed whenever the disk is used to boot the system, and other parts of the disk that contain software or data or other computer resources like memory. In non-boot sectors, the virus hides in software or data as macros, which are executed whenever documents on the disk are opened with the relevant application.

The downloaded virus, depending on the type and motive, can either be immediately active or can lie dormant for a specified amount of time waiting for an event to activate it. An active virus hidden in a computer resource can copy itself straight away to other files or disks, thus increasing its chances of infection. The speed at which the virus spreads depends not only on the speed of the network and transmission media but also on how fast and long it can replicate unnoticed. Most viruses go undetected for long periods of time. In fact, a lot of viruses manage to go undetected by either injecting themselves deep into legitimate code or disabling many of the code's options that would cause it to be detected. When they succeed in injecting themselves into a good hiding place, they may lie dormant for extended periods waiting for a trigger event to occur. The effects of a virus payload can range from harmless messages, data corruption and attrition to total destruction.

There are three ways viruses infect computer systems. The first of these is boot sector penetration. As we have seen in the previous section, a boot sector is usually the first sector on every disk. In a boot disk, the sector contains a chunk of code that powers up a computer, as we have already discussed. In a non-bootable disk, the sector contains a File Allocation Table (FAT), which is automatically loaded first into computer memory to create a roadmap of the type and contents of the disk for the computer to use when accessing the disk. Viruses imbedded in this sector are assured of automatic loading into the computer memory. This is a very insidious way of system memory penetration by viruses.

The second method of infection is macros penetration. Since macros are small language programs that can only execute after imbedding themselves into surrogate programs, their penetration is quite effective. They are becoming popular because modern system application programs are developed in such a way that they can accept added user macros. The virus uses the added loophole to penetrate and utilize the built-in macro language specific to some popular products such as Microsoft Office.

Parasites are the third method of infection. These are viruses that do not necessarily hide in the boot sector, or use an incubator like the macros, but attach themselves to a healthy executable program and wait for any event where such a program is executed. These days, due to the spread of the Internet, this method of penetration is the most widely used and the most effective. Examples of parasite viruses include "Friday the 13th" and "Michelangelo" viruses.

Once a computer attack, most often a virus attack, is launched the attacking agent scans the victim system looking for a healthy body for a surrogate. If one is found, the attacking agent tests to see if it has already been infected. Viruses do not like to infect themselves, hence, wasting their energy. If an uninfected body is found, then the virus attaches itself to it to grow, multiply, and wait for a trigger event to start its mission. The mission itself has three components:

(i)   to look further for more healthy environments for faster growth, thus spreading more;
(ii) to attach itself to any newly found body; and
(iii) once embedded, either to stay in the active mode ready to go at any trigger event or to lie dormant until a specific event occurs.

Not only do virus sources and methods of infection differ, but the viruses themselves are also of several different types. In fact, one type called a *worm* is actually not a virus at all, though the differences between a worm and a virus are few. They are both automated attacks, both self-generate or replicate new copies as they spread, and both can damage any resource they attack. The main difference between them, however, is that while viruses always hide in software as surrogates, worms are stand alone programs. The origin of a worm is not very clear, but according to Peter J. Denning,[6] the idea of a worm program that would invade computers and perform acts directed by the originator really started in 1975 in the science-fiction novel *The Shockwave Rider* by John Brunner (mass market paperback, 1990). However, the first real worm program was not written until early 1980 when John Shock and Jon Hupp, working at Xerox Palo Alto Research Center, wrote a program intended to replicate and locate idle workstations on the network for temporary use as servers.[7] Since then, worms have been on the rise. The most outstanding worm programs include the "Morris" worm. Robert T. Morris, a computer science graduate student at Cornell University, created and released perhaps the first headline-making worm program from an MIT computer. Instead of the program living on one infected computer, it created thousands of copies of itself on machines it infected. It is assumed to have infected approximately 6,000 computers, a great number in January 1990.[8]

A memory resident virus is more insidious, difficult to detect, fast spreading, and extremely difficult to eradicate. Once in memory, most viruses in this category simply disable a small part of or all of memory, making it unavailable for the system to use. Because they attack the central storage part of a computer system, memory resident viruses are considered to do the most damage to computer systems. Once in memory, they attack any other program or data in the system. There are two types of memory resident viruses: transient, the category that includes viruses that are only active when the inflicted program is executing, and resident, a brand that attaches itself via a surrogate software to a portion of memory and remains active long after the surrogate program has finished executing. Examples of memory resident viruses include all boot sector viruses like the "Israel" virus.[9]

Error generating viruses launch themselves most often in executable software. Once embedded, they attack the software, causing the software to generate errors. The errors can be either "hard" logical errors, resulting in a range of faults from simple momentary misses to complete termination of the software, or they can be "soft" logical errors which may not be part of the software but just falsely generate errors causing the user to believe that the software has developed errors.

Data and program destroyers are viruses that attach themselves to a software and then use it as a conduit or surrogate for growth, replication, and as a launch pad for later attacks to this and other programs and data. Once attached to a software, they attack any data or program that the software may come in contact with, sometimes altering, deleting, or completely destroying the contents. Some simply alter data and program files; others implant foreign codes in data and program files, yet others completely destroy all data and program files that they come in contact with. If code is introduced in data files that are used by thousands of users or data is altered or if removed from data files used by many, the effects can be severe. Familiar data and program destroying viruses are "Friday the 13th" and "Michelangelo."

Most deadly of all are the viruses known as *system crushers*. Once introduced in a computer system, they completely disable the system. This can be done in a number of ways. One way is to destroy the system programs like the operating system, compilers, loaders, linkers, and others. Another approach of the virus is to leave system software intact and to replicate itself filling up system memory, rendering the system useless.

In contrast, a computer time theft virus is not harmful in any way to system software and data. The goal of such a virus is to steal system time. The intruder has two approaches to this goal. One approach is for the intruder to first stealthily become a legitimate user of the system and then later use all the system resources without any detection. The other approach is to prevent other legitimate users from using the system by first creating a number of system interruptions. This effectively puts other programs scheduled to run into indefinite wait queues. The intruder then gains the highest priority, like a super user with full access to all system resources. With this approach, system intrusion is very difficult to detect.

While most viruses are known to alter or destroy data and programs, there are a few that literally attack and destroy system hardware. These are hardware destroyers, commonly known as *killer viruses*. Many of these viruses work by attaching themselves to micro-instructions, or *mic*, like bios and device drivers. Once embedded into the mic, they may alter it causing the devices to move into positions that normally result in physical damage. For example, there are viruses that are known to lock up keyboards, disable mice, and cause disk read/write heads to move to nonexisting sectors on the disk, thus causing the disk to crash.

Trojans are named after the famous Greek story about a wooden horse that concealed Greek soldiers as they tried to take over the city of Troy. According to the story, a huge, hollow wooden horse full of Greek soldiers was left at the gates of Troy as a gift from the Greeks to the people of Troy. Apparently, the Greeks had tried to take the city several times before and failed each time. The people of Troy took the horse inside the city walls and when night fell, the Greek soldiers emerged from the horse's belly, opened the city gates for the remainder of the Greek soldiers, and destroyed the city. Because of this legend, anything that abuses trust from within is referred to as a Trojan horse. Trojan horse viruses use the same tricks the legendary Greeks used. They hide inside trusted common programs like compilers and editors.

Logic or time bombs are viruses that penetrate a system and embed themselves in the system's software, using it as a conduit to attack once a trigger goes off. Trigger events can vary in type depending on the motive of the virus. Most triggers are timed events. There are various types of these viruses including "Columbus Day," "Valentine's Day," "Jerusalem-D," and the "Michelangelo," which was meant to activate on the anniversary of Michelangelo's 517th birthday. The most recent time bomb was the "Y2K" bug, which had millions of people scared as the year 2000 rolled in. The bug was an unintentional design flaw of a date where the year field did not use four digits. The scare was just a scare; very few effects were noted.

Trapdoor viruses find their way into a system through parts of the system and application software weak points. A trapdoor is a special set of instructions that allow a user to bypass normal security precautions to enter a system. Quite often software manufacturers, during software development and testing, intentionally leave trapdoors in their products, usually undocumented, as secret entry points into the programs so that modifications can be made on the programs at a later date. Trapdoors are also used by programmers as testing points. Trapdoors can also be exploited by malicious people, including programmers themselves. In a trapdoor attack, an intruder may deposit a virus-infected data file in a system instead of actually removing, copying, or destroying the existing data files. There is an interesting trapdoor scenario in the 1983 film *WarGames*, where a trapdoor was successfully used by a hacker to gain access to a military computer in the Cheyenne Mountains in Utah. The computer was programmed to react to nuclear attack threat and when the computer detected the intrusion, it mistook it to be a nuclear threat. According to the movie script, the computer automatically initiated pre-launch activities for launching a nuclear missile. The only way it could be stopped was through a trapdoor. However, without a password, neither the original programmer or the hacker could stop the launch program. At the end of the movie, as expected, the hacker manages to crack the military password file and save humanity.

Some viruses are jokes or hoaxes that do not destroy or interfere with the workings of a computer system. They are simply meant to be a nuisance to the user. Many of these types of viruses are sent to one or more users for no other reason than the sender wants to have fun. Joke and hoax viruses are for that purpose alone. Hoaxes usually are meant to create a scare while jokes are meant to create fun for the recipients. Fun, however, may not always be the result. Sometimes what is meant to be a joke or a hoax virus ends up creating mayhem.

We can follow Stephenson's[10] virus classification and put all these viruses into the following categories:

- Parasites: These are viruses that attach themselves to executable files and replicate in order to attack other files whenever the victim's programs are executed.
- Boot sector: These were seen earlier. They are viruses that affect the boot sector of a disk.
- Stealth: These are viruses that are designed to hide themselves from any antivirus software.
- Memory-resident: As seen earlier, these are viruses that use system memory as a beachhead to attack other programs.
- Polymorphic: These are viruses that mutate at every infection, making their detection difficult.

Theft of Proprietary Information

Theft of proprietary information involves acquiring, copying or distributing information belonging to a third party. This may also involve certain types of knowledge obtained through legitimate employment. It also includes all information as defined in the intellectual property statutes such as copyrights, patents, trade secrets, and trademarks. These types of attacks originate mainly from insiders within the employee ranks, who may steal the information for a number of motives. As we stated in Chapter 6, companies are reluctant to report these types of attacks for fear of bad publicity and public disclosure of their trade secrets.

Fraud

The growth of online services and access to the Internet have provided fertile ground for cyberspace fraud or *cyberfraud*. New novel online consumer services that include cybershopping, online banking, and other online conveniences have enabled consumers to do business online. However, crooks and intruders have also recognized the potential of cyberspace with its associated new technologies. These technologies are creating new and better ways to commit crimes against unsuspecting consumers.

Most online computer attacks motivated by fraud are in a form that gives the intruder consumer information like social security numbers, credit information, medical records, and a whole host of vital personal information usually stored on computer system databases.

Sabotage

Sabotage is a process of withdrawing efficiency. It interferes with the quantity or quality of one's skills, which may eventually lead to low quality and quantity of service. Sabotage as a system attack is an internal process that can be initiated by either an insider or an outsider. Sabotage motives vary depending on the attacker, but most are meant to strike a target, usually an employer, that benefits the attacker. The widespread use of the Internet has greatly increased the potential for and the number of incidents of these types of attacks.

Espionage

By the end of the cold war, the United States, as a leading military, economic, and information superpower, found itself a constant target of military espionage. As the cold war faded, military espionage shifted and gave way to economic espionage. In its pure form, economic espionage targets economic trade secrets which, according to the 1996 U.S. Economic Espionage Act, are defined as all forms and types of financial, business, scientific, technical, economic, and engineering information and all types of intellectual property including patterns, plans, compilations, program devices, formulas, designs, prototypes, methods, techniques, processes, procedures, programs, and codes, whether they are tangible or not, stored or not, or compiled or not.[11] To enforce this act and prevent computer attacks targeting American commercial interests, U.S. federal law authorizes law enforcement agencies to use wiretaps and other surveillance means to curb computer supported information espionage.

Network and Vulnerability Scanning

Scanners are programs that keep a constant electronic surveillance of a computer or a network, looking for computers and network devices with vulnerabilities. Computer vulnerabilities may be in the system hardware or software. Scanning the network computers for vulnerabilities allows the attacker to determine all possible weaknesses and loopholes in the system. This opens up possible attack avenues.

Password Crackers

Password crackers are actually worm algorithms. According to Don Seely, these algorithms have four parts: the first part, which is the most important, gathers password data used by the remaining three parts from hosts and user accounts.[12] Using this information, it then tries to either generate individual passwords or crack passwords it comes across. During the cracking phase, the worm saves the name, the encrypted password, the directory, and the user information field for each account.

The second and third parts trivially break passwords that can be easily broken using information already contained in the passwords. Around 30 percent of all passwords can be guessed using only literal variations or comparison with favorite passwords.[13] This list of favorite passwords consists of roughly 432 words, most of them proper nouns and common English words.[14] And the last part takes words in the user dictionaries and tries to decrypt them one by one. This may prove to be very time consuming and also a little harder. But with time, it may yield good guesses.

Employee Network Abuse

Although concerns of computer attacks on companies and corporations have traditionally been focused on outside penetration of systems, inside attacks have chronically been presenting serious problems in the workplace. An insider is someone who has been explicitly or implicitly granted access privileges that allow him or her the use of a particular system's facilities. Incidents of insider abuse are abound in the press highlighting the fundamental problems associated with insider system misuse. Insider net abuse attacks are fundamentally driven by financial fraud, vendettas, and other forms of intentional misuse. Nearly all insider net abuses are covered up.

A number of things have kept this rather serious problem off the radar including[15]:

- system security technology that does not yet distinguish inside system attacks from those originating from outside,
- a lack of system authentication that would prevent insiders from masquerading as someone else,
- top management's all-powerful and unchecked root privileges,
- employee assumption that once given access privileges they can roam the entire system,
- local system audit trails that are inadequate or compromised, and
- a lack of definitive policy on what constitutes insider net abuse in any given application.

Embezzlement

Embezzlement is an inside job by employees. It happens when a trusted employee fraudulently appropriates company property for personal gain. Embezzlement is widespread and happens every day in both large and small businesses, although small businesses are less likely to take the precautions necessary to prevent it. Online embezzlement is challenging because it may never be found. And, if found, sometimes it takes a long time to correct it, causing more damage.

Computer Hardware Parts Theft

In table 1.2 we notice that although theft of computing devices seem to be going down, the vice is still high after all these years. There are several reasons for this, including the miniaturization of computing devices, which makes them easier to conceal and be taken away. Also, because storage technology has approved in tandem with miniaturization, the devices are storing more valuable data, hence attracting more attention of device thieves. Thirdly, while the storage capacity and the computation power have been increasing as the sizes become smaller, the prices of these devices have been dramatically dropping, making them more available in many places and increasing their probability of being stolen. There are additional reasons that the theft of computing devices has remained in the top tier of the computing security problem.[16]

Denial of Service Attacks

Denial of service attacks, commonly known as distributed denial of service (DDoS) attacks, are not penetration attacks. They do not change, alter, destroy, or modify system resources. They do, however, affect a system by diminishing the system's ability to function; hence, they are capable of bringing a system down without destroying its resources. These types of attacks made headlines when a Canadian teen attacked Internet heavyweights Amazon, eBay, E*Trade, and CNN. DDoS attacks have been on the rise. Like penetration e-attacks, DDoS attacks can also be either local, shutting down LAN computers, or global, originating thousands of miles away on the Internet, as was the case in the Canadian generated DDoS attacks.

Most of the attacks in this category have already been discussed in Chapter 6. They include among others IP-spoofing, SYN flooding, smurfing, buffer overflow, and sequence number sniffing.

Motives of E-Attacks

Although hacking still has a long way to go before it can be considered a respectable pastime, it can be a full-time job or hobby, taking countless hours per week to learn the tricks of the trade, developing, experimenting, and executing the art of penetrating multiuser computer systems. Why do hackers spend such a good portion of their time hacking? Is it scientific curiosity, mental stimulation, greed, or personal attention? It is difficult to exclusively answer this question because the true roots of hacker motives run much deeper than that. Let us look at a few.

Some attacks are likely the result of personal vendettas. There are many causes that lead to vendettas. The demonstrations at the last World Trade Organization (WTO) meeting in Seattle, Washington, and the demonstrations at the World Bank and the International Monetary Fund meetings in Washington, D.C., and at the G8 meeting in Genoa, Italy, are indicative of the growing discontent of the masses; masses unhappy with big business, globalization, and a million other things. This discontent is driving a new breed of wild, rebellious young people to hit back at organizations that are not solving world problems or benefiting all of mankind. These mass computer attacks are increasingly being used to avenge what the attacker or attackers consider to be injustices. However, most vendetta attacks are for mundane reasons such as a promotion denied, a boyfriend or girlfriend taken, an ex-spouse given child custody, and other situations that may involve family and intimacy issues.

Some attacks at least begin as jokes, hoaxes, or pranks. Hoaxes are warnings that are actually scare alerts started by one or more malicious people and are passed on by innocent users who think that they are helping the community by spreading the warning. Most hoaxes are viruses although there are hoaxes that are computer-related folklore, urban legends or true stories. Virus hoaxes are usually false reports about nonexistent viruses that cause panic, especially to the majority of users who do not know how viruses work. Some hoaxes can get extremely widespread as they are mistakenly distributed by individuals and companies with the best of intentions. Although many virus hoaxes are false scares, some may have some truth about them, but they often become greatly exaggerated such as "Good Times" and "Great Salmon." Virus hoaxes infect mailing lists, bulletin boards, and Usenet newsgroups. Worried system administrators sometimes contribute to this scare by posting dire warnings to their employees, which become hoaxes themselves.

Some attacks are motivated by "hacker's ethics"—a collection of motives that make up the hacker character. Steven Levy lists these as follows[17]:

- Access to computers—and anything which might teach you something about the way the world works—should be unlimited and total.
- Always yield to the hands-on imperative!
- All information should be free.
- Mistrust authority—promote decentralization.
- Hackers should be judged by their hacking, not by bogus criteria such as degrees, age, race, or position.
- You can create art and beauty on a computer.
- Computers can change your life for the better.

If any of these beliefs are violated, a hacker will have a motive.

Our increasing dependence on computers and computer communication has opened up a can of worms we now know as electronic terrorism. Electronic terrorism—that is, hitting individuals by hitting the banking and the military systems—is perpetrated by a new breed of hacker, one who no longer holds the view that cracking systems is an intellectual exercise but that it is a way of gaining from the action. The new hacker is a cracker who knows and is aware of the value of the information that he or she is trying to obtain or compromise. But cyber terrorism is not only about obtaining information, it is also about instilling fear and doubt and compromising the integrity of the data.

Political and military espionage is another motive. For generations countries have been competing for supremacy of one form or another. During the cold war, countries competed for military spheres. At the end of the cold war, the espionage turf changed to gaining access to highly classified commercial information about what other countries were doing and to obtaining either a military or commercial advantage without spending a lot of money on the effort. It is not surprising, therefore, that the spread of the Internet has given a boost and a new lease on life to a dying cold-war profession. Our high dependency on computers in the national military and commercial establishments has given espionage new fertile ground. Electronic espionage has a lot of advantages over its old-fashioned, trench-coated, Hitchcock-style cousin. For example, it is far cheaper to implement. It can gain access into places which would be inaccessible to human spies, and it saves embarrassment in case of failed or botched attempts. And, it can be carried out at a place and time of choice. One of the first electronic espionage incidents that involved massive computer networks was by Marcus H., a West German hacker, who in 1986 along with accomplices attacked the military, universities, and research organization centers in the United States. Over a period of 10 months, he attacked over 450 computers and successfully penetrated over 40, starting with the Lawrence Berkeley Laboratory, through which he attacked U.S. Army bases in Japan, Germany, Washington, D.C., and Alabama; the U.S. naval base in Panama City, Florida, and the Naval Shipyard and Data Center in Norfolk, Virginia; U.S. Air Force bases in Germany and El Segundo, California; defense contractors in Richardson, Texas, and Redondo Beach, California; and universities including the University of Boston, a university in Atlanta, Georgia, the University of Pittsburgh, the University of Rochester, the University of Pasadena, and the University of Ontario. His list also included national research laboratories such as the Lawrence Livermore National Laboratory, the National Computing Center at Livermore, and research laboratories in Pasadena, California. As the list demonstrates, his main motive, according to Clifford Stoll, was computers operated by the military and by defense contractors, research organizations, and research universities.[18] Marcus and his accomplices passed the information they got to the KGB in the then–U.S.S.R. Marcus was arrested and convicted, together with his accomplices, Dirk B. and Peter C.[19]

Another type of espionage that may motivate a cyber attack is business (competition) espionage. As businesses become global and world markets become one global bazaar, business competition for ideas and market strategies is becoming very intense. According to Jonathan Calof, professor of management at the University of Ottawa, information for business competitiveness comes from primary sources, most of all the employees.[20] Because of this, business espionage mainly targets people, more specifically, employees. Company employees, and especially those working in company computer systems, are targeted the most.

Cyber sleuthing and corporate computer attacks are the most used business espionage techniques that involve physical system penetration for trophies like company policies and management and marketing data. It may also involve sniffing, electronic surveillance of the electronic communications of the company's executives and of the employee chat rooms for information.

Some cyber attacks spring from a very old motivation: hatred. Hate as a motive of attack originates from an individual or individuals with a serious dislike of another person or group of persons based on a string of human attributes that may include national origin, gender, race, or the manner of speech one uses. The attackers, then incensed by one or all of these attributes, contemplate and carry out attacks of vengeance often rooted in ignorance.

Some attacks may be motivated by a desire for personal gain. Such motives spring from the selfishness of individuals who are never satisfied with what they have and are always wanting more, usually more money. It is this need to get more that drives the attacker to plan and execute an attack.

Finally, cyber attacks sometimes occur as a result of ignorance. Unintended acts may lead to destruction of information and other systems resources. Such acts usually occur as a result of individuals (who may be authorized or not, but in either case are ignorant of the workings of the system) stumbling upon weaknesses or performing a forbidden act that results in system resource modification or destruction.

Topography of Attacks

E-attackers must always use specific patterns in order to reach their victims. When targeting one individual, they use a pattern of attack different from one they would use if their target was a group of green people. In this case, they would use a different pattern that would only reach and affect green people. However, if the e-attackers wanted to affect every one regardless, they would use still a different pattern. The pattern chosen, therefore, is primarily based on the type of victim(s), motive, location, method of delivery, and a few other things. There are four of these patterns and we will call them *topographies*. They are illustrated in Figures 7.1, 7.2, 7.3 and 7.4.

One-to-One

One-to-one e-attacks originate from one attacker and target a known victim. They are personalized attacks in which the attacker knows the victim and sometimes the victim may know the attacker. One-to-one attacks are usually motivated by hate, a personal vendetta, a desire for personal gain, or an attempt to make a joke, although business espionage may also be involved.

Figure 7.1 One-to-One Topology

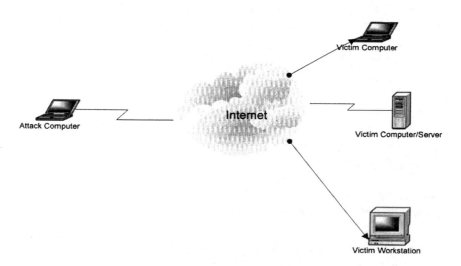

Figure 7.2 One-to-Many Topology

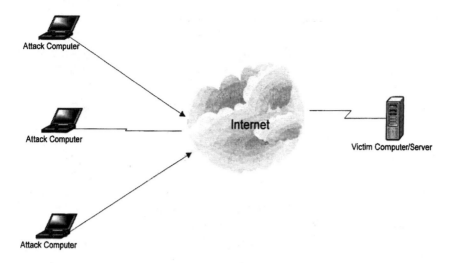

Figure 7.3 Many-to-One Topology

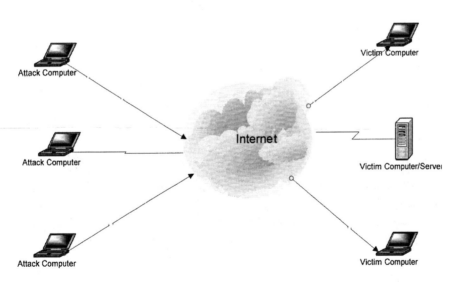

Figure 7.4 Many-to-Many Topology

One-to-Many

One-to-many attacks are fueled by anonymity. In most cases, the attacker does not know any of the victims. And in all cases, the attacker is anonymous to the victims. This topography has been the technique of choice in the last two to three years because it is one of the easiest to carry out. The motives that drive attackers to use this technique are hate, a desire for personal satisfaction, an attempt to play a joke or to intimidate people with a hoax.

Many-to-One

Many-to-one attacks so far have been rare, but they have recently picked up momentum as distributed denial of services attacks have once again gained favor in the hacker community. In a many-to-one attack technique, the attacker starts the attack by using one host to spoof other hosts, the secondary victims, which are then used as new sources of attacks on the selected victim. These types of attacks need a high degree of coordination and, therefore, may require advanced planning and a good understanding of the infrastructure of the network. They also require a very well-executed selection process in choosing the secondary victims and then eventually the final victim. Attacks in this category are driven by personal vendetta, hate, terrorism, or a desire for attention and fame.

Many-to-Many

As in the many-to-one topography, many-to-many attacks are rare; however, there has been an increase recently in reported attacks using this technique. For example, in some recent DDoS cases, there has been a select group of sites chosen by the attackers as secondary victims. These were then used to bombard another select group of victims. The numbers involved in each group may vary from a few to several thousands. Like the many-to-one topography, attackers using the many-to-many technique also need a good understanding of the network infrastructure and a good selection process to pick the secondary victims and to eventually select the final pool of victims. Attacks utilizing this topology are mostly driven by a number of motives including terrorism, a desire for attention and fame, or a desire to pull off a joke or hoax.

How Hackers Plan E-Attacks

Few computer attacks are developed and delivered in a few hours. The processes are always well drawn. There is always a motive followed by a plan. It is the carefully planned and fully developed e-attack that is successful. If only law enforcement agencies and society as a whole used these planning periods as windows of opportunity to snoop into these activities before they hatched, then computer crimes would be significantly reduced. But unfortunately, this may never happen because of the elaborate and varying sequences of steps leading to attacks. Studies of hacker activities from interviews and court papers have shown that an actual attack has the following sequence of steps:

- There is always a motive that must precede all other activities before the attack.
- Targets are always identified based on the motive(s).
- Programs are developed. Several programs may be needed, some to scan for network and system vulnerabilities and others to deliver the attacker payload.
- Once the targets are identified and the programs written, then, depending on the topography of attack, scanners are downloaded to search for network weak points and devices and to develop a full picture of the victim and LAN configuration. Operating systems and applications running on the victim site are also identified and platform and network vulnerabilities are noted.
- Using information from the scan, the first attempts are made from a list of selected target victims. The techniques used in the initial attack depend on whether the planned attack is a distributed denial of service or a penetration attack. In most penetration attacks, the initial attempt may include simple attacks using FTP, telnet, remote login, and password guessing. Once the initial penetration is successful, then penetration of the known system security loopholes (as revealed by the scanners) is attempted. These attempts may lead to the intruder gaining even higher security and access privileges that puts the intruder in full control before the full-blown attack commences.
- Once the initial attempts are successful, they are then used as a beachhead to launch a full-scale attack on the selected targets.

Most Common System and Software Vulnerabilities

Since the first edition of this book in 2002, vulnerabilities in major operating system keep changing. The top most common operating system vulnerabilities we have been giving in subsequent editions have, therefore, been changing. And so is the case in this fourth edition.

According to the National Vulnerability Database (NVD), a U.S. government repository of standards-based vulnerability management data represented using the Security Content Automation Protocol (SCAP), there were 3532 vulnerabilities reported in operating systems and applications like web browsers in 2011. This adds up to about ten new security vulnerabilities each day. While the rate of newly discovered vulnerabilities is impressive, both new and newer version of old operating systems and applications are getting better fortified because, as NVD reports, the trend is on a descending path. For example 4258 vulnerabilities were reported in 2010.[21]

Top Vulnerabilities to Windows Systems

According to Altius IT,[22] a network security audit and security consulting firm, the most recent top vulnerability in the Windows operating system at the writing of this edition are as follows:

- *Web Servers*—misconfigurations, product bugs, default installations, and third-party products such as php can introduce vulnerabilities.
- *Microsoft SQL Server*—vulnerabilities allow remote attackers to obtain sensitive information, alter database content, and compromise SQL servers and server hosts.
- *Passwords*—user accounts may have weak, nonexistent, or unprotected passwords. The operating system or third-party applications may create accounts with weak or nonexistent passwords.
- *Workstations*—requests to access resources such as files and printers without any bounds checking can lead to vulnerabilities. Overflows can be exploited by an unauthenticated remote attacker executing code on the vulnerable device.
- *Remote Access*—users can unknowingly open their systems to hackers when they allow *remote access* to their systems.
- *Browsers*—accessing cloud computing services puts an organization at risk when users have unpatched browsers. Browser features such as Active X and Active Scripting can bypass security controls.
- *File Sharing*—peer to peer vulnerabilities include technical vulnerabilities, social media, and altering or masquerading content.
- *E-mail*—by opening a message a recipient can activate security threats such as viruses, spyware, Trojan horse programs, and worms.
- *Instant Messaging*—vulnerabilities typically arise from outdated ActiveX controls in MSN Messenger, Yahoo! Voice Chat, buffer overflows, and others.
- *USB Devices*—plug and play devices can create risks when they are automatically recognized and immediately accessible by Windows operating systems.

Notice the persistence of some vulnerabilities in the Windows operating system to remain in the top tier by looking at the top vulnerabilities in the Windows operating system at the writing of the third edition below:

- Web Services & Services: These include Windows platforms default installations of various HTTP servers and additional components for serving HTTP requests as well as streaming media to the Internet. According to the report, attacks may result in denial of service, exposure or compromise of sensitive files or data, execution of arbitrary commands on the server, or complete compromise of the server.
- Workstation Service: This is a Windows Workstation service responsible for processing user requests to access resources such as files and printers. It determines if the resource is residing on the local system or on a network share and routes the user requests appropriately. An attack can result in a stack-based buffer overflow caused by a malicious DCE/RPC call.
- Windows Remote Access Services: These are various Windows operating systems services supporting different networking methods and technologies. An attack on these services may include Network Shares, Anonymous Logon, remote registry access, and remote procedure calls.
- Microsoft SQL Server (MSSQL): MSSQL is plagued by several serious vulnerabilities that allow remote attackers to obtain sensitive information, alter database content, compromise SQL servers, and, in some configurations, compromise server hosts. In fact, two recent MSSQL worms in May 2002 and January 2003 exploited several known MSSQL flaws. According to the report, hosts compromised by these worms generated a damaging level of network traffic when they scanned for other vulnerable hosts.
- Windows Authentication: Microsoft Windows does not store or transmit passwords in clear text. Instead it uses a hash, a mathematical function used like a password to obtain transformed data, instead of a password for authentication. Windows uses three authentication algorithms: LM (least secure, most compatible), NTLM and NTLMv2 (most secure and least compatible). Most current Windows environments have no need for LM (LAN Manager) support, however, Microsoft Windows locally stores legacy LM password hashes by default on Windows NT, 2000 and XP systems (but not in Windows server 2003). LM is a weak authentication algorithm because it uses a much weaker encryption scheme than more current Microsoft approaches (NTLM and NTLMv2). Therefore, LM passwords

can be broken in a relatively short period of time by a determined attacker.

- Web Browsers: Microsoft Internet Explorer (IE) is the default Web browser on Microsoft Windows platforms. The latest version, IE 8, like its predecessors has many vulnerabilities. Many of the vulnerabilities have been patched by Microsoft like the zero-day vulnerability that was first demonstrated on the first day of the Pwn2Own contest at the 2009 CanSecWest Conference in Vancouver. There are, of course, other vulnerabilities including filters designed by Microsoft to prevent some cross-site scripting (XSS) attacks which can be used to exploit IE 8.

- File-Sharing Applications: Peer-to-Peer File Sharing Programs (P2P) are popular applications used to download and distribute many types of user data including music, video, graphics, text, source code, and proprietary information. They are also used to distribute Open-Source/GPL binaries, ISO images of bootable Linux distributions, independent artists' creations, and even commercial media such as film trailers and game previews. Use of P2P applications introduces three types of vulnerabilities: technical vulnerabilities that can be exploited remotely, social vulnerabilities that are exploited by altering or masquerading binary content that others request, and legal vulnerabilities that can result from copyright infringement or objectionable material.

- LSAS Exposures: These are critical buffer overflows found and exploitable on Windows Local Security Authority Subsystem Service on Windows 2000, Server 2003 and Server 2003 64-bit, XP and XP 64-bit editions. These exposures can lead to a remote and anonymous attack over RPC on unpatched Windows 2000 and XP systems.

- Mail Client: Outlook Express (OE), a basic e-mail and contact management client bundled with Internet Explorer, has embedded automation features that are at odds with the built-in security controls leading to e-mail viruses, worms, malicious code to compromise the local system, and many other forms of attack. An attack exploiting these vulnerabilities can lead to infection of the computer with a virus or worm, spam e-mail, or Web beaconing, e-mail address validation triggered by the opening of an e-mail by recipient.

- Instant Messaging: Instant Messaging (IM) technology is very popular. Yahoo! Messenger (YM), AOL Instant Messenger (AIM), MSN Messenger (MSN) and Windows Messenger (WM), which is now fully integrated into Windows XP Professional and Home Editions, are all used on Windows systems. Remotely exploitable vulnerabilities in these programs or associated dependencies are a growing threat to the integrity and security of networks, directly proportional to their rapid integration and deployment on Windows systems. Attacks can result in remotely executed buffer overflows, URI/maliciouslink based attacks, file transferring vulnerabilities, and Active X exploits.

Top Vulnerabilities to UNIX/Linux Systems

Since Unix is a dated operating system, its vulnerabilities tend to remain stable. Also, since Linux is based on Unix, vulnerabilities in Unix are also the same vulnerabilities in Linux.

- BIND Domain Name System: The Berkeley Internet Name Domain (BIND) is one of the most widely used implementations of the Domain Name Service (DNS). It enables the binding conversion of host names into the corresponding registered IP addresses making it easy to locate systems on the Internet by name without having to know specific IP addresses. This binding has security weaknesses that can be exploited by an intruder. Many DNS servers are still vulnerable to attacks that range from denial of service to buffer overflows and cache poisoning. Since the Berkeley Internet Name Domain package is the most widely used implementation of Domain Name Service, it is a favorite target for attack.
- Web Server: UNIX and Linux Web servers such as Apache and the Sun Java System Web Server (formerly iPlanet) serve a majority of Internet traffic and are therefore the most targeted for attack. At the same time, they also suffer from various vulnerabilities that include vulnerabilities within the server itself, add-on modules, default/example/test cgi scripts, PHP bugs, and various other attack vectors.
- Authentication: UNIX and Linux, just like Windows, suffer from password authentication weaknesses. The most common password vulnerabilities are:
  - ° User accounts with weak or nonexistent passwords.
  - ° Weak or well-known password hashing algorithms and/or user password hashes that are stored with weak security and that are denial of service to the Concurrent Versions System (CUS) server, or execute arbitrary code on the CUS server.
- Version Control Systems: Version control systems are applications that provide tools to manage different versions of documents or source code, and facilitate multiple users to concurrently work on the same set of files. Concurrent Versions System (CVS), the most popular source code control system used in UNIX and Linux environments, can be remotely configured for remote access via the pserver protocol that runs on port 2401/tcp by

default. A server configured in such a fashion contains the following vulnerabilities:

° A heap-based buffer overflow resulting from malicious access to Entry-Lines.
° A denial of service to the CVS server, or execute arbitrary code on the CVS server.

- Sendmail: This is a general purpose internetwork email routing facility that supports many kinds of mail-transfer and -delivery methods, including the Simple Mail Transfer Protocol (SMTP) used for email transport over the Internet. Simple Mail Transport Protocol (SMTP) is one of the oldest of the mail protocols. Mail Transport Agent (MTA) servers transport mail from senders to recipients using SMTP protocol, usually encrypted with SSL on insecure ports with TLS if both ends support it. Sendmail is the most widely used UNIX-based MTA. Most of the vulnerabilities are therefore targeting it. Attacks on MTA servers are looking for:
° Unpatched systems and systems that can easily suffer from buffer overruns and heap overflows.
° Systems with open relays for spamming.
° Systems with nonrelay misconfiguration, like a user-account database, for spam or social engineering purposes.

- Simple Network Management Protocol (SNMP) is a network management protocol developed in 1988 to solve communication problems between different types of networks. Since then, it has become a de facto standard. It works by exchanging network information through five protocol data units (PDUs). This protocol suite manages information obtained from network entities such as hosts, routers, switches, hubs, and so on. The information collected from these various network entities via SNMP variable queries is sent to a management station. Information events, called *traps*, such as critical changes to interface status and packet collisions can also be sent from entities to these management stations. These domains of SNMP management stations and entities are grouped together in communities. These communities, commonly known as *community strings*, are used as an authentication method in information retrieval/traps. Two types of community strings are in common use: read, which is default public, and write, which is default private. A read community has privileges to retrieve variables from SNMP entities and a write community has privileges to read as well as write to entity variables. SNMP employs these units to monitor and administer all types of network-connected devices, data transmissions, and network events such as terminal start-ups or shutdowns. However, these SNMP entities are unencrypted. It is possible for any intruder to have full administrator access to these SNMP facilities which has the potential for abuse of privileges including the ability to modify host name, network interface state, IP forwarding and routing, state of network sockets (including the ability to terminate active TCP sessions and listening sockets) and the ARP cache. An attacker also has full read access to all SNMP facilities.[23]

- Open Secure Sockets Layer: Open Secure Sockets Layer (OpenSSL) is a cryptographic library to support applications communicating over the network. Its SSL/TLS protocol is used widely in commercial communication. Popular UNIX and Linux applications like Apache Web Server, POP3, IMAP, SMTP and LDAP servers use OpenSSL. Because of its wide integration, many applications may suffer if the library has vulnerabilities. For example, multiple exploits are publicly available that can compromise Apache servers compiled with certain versions of the library.

- U5 File Transfer Protocol (FTP): Network File System (NFS) is designed to share ("export") file systems/directories and files among UNIX systems over a network, while Network Information Service (NIS) is a set of services that work as a loosely distributed database service to provide location information, called *maps*, to other network services such as NFS. Both NSF and NIS are commonly used in UNIX servers/networks that have had security problems over the years like buffer overflows, DDoS and weak authentication, thus, becoming attractive to hackers.

- Databases: Databases, as collections of a variety of things like business, financial, banking, and Enterprise Resource Planning (ERP) systems, are widely used systems. However, unlike operating systems, they have not been subjected to the same level of security. Partly because of that, they have a wide array of features and capabilities that can be misused or exploited to compromise the confidentiality, availability, and integrity of data.

- Kernel: This is the core of an operating system. It does all of the privileged operations that can cause the security of the system to be compromised. Any weaknesses in the kernel can lead to serious security problems. Risks from kernel vulnerabilities include denial of service, execution of arbitrary code with system privileges, unrestricted access to the file system, and root level access.

- General Unix Authentication—Accounts with no passwords or weak passwords.

Top Vulnerabilities to Apple OS Systems

According to eSecurity Planet,[24] in the past, and even up to now as we have seen already, most malware writers have targeted systems running Microsoft's Windows operating system. This has led many Mac users to believe falsely that OS X is a highly secure operating system that can't be compromised. As a result, most computers running the operating system have little or no anti-malware protection. However, machines running Apple's OS X operating system are increasingly being targeted. For Mac OSs, apart from vulnerabilities in the operating system, which Apple is often slow to patch, malware writers are also exploiting vulnerabilities in software such Java, which run on these systems.[25] According to Paul Rubens (2010), Apple Macs are secure because they don't get computer viruses, and because OS X, the operating system they run, is based on the rock-solid and highly secure BSD UNIX.

Rubens also blames Apple, the company, for its inaccurate perception that Macs are "secure" based on the company's current security line that "Mac OS X doesn't get PC viruses." Since most OS X systems have little or no protection and the user base is inexperienced with security, it will increasingly be targeted by attackers in the future.

The most current Apple OS-specific threats include:

- rootkits such as WeaponX
- fake codec Trojans
- malicious code with Mac-specific DNS changing functionality
- fake or rogue anti-malware
- keyloggers
- disruptive adware
- multi-platform threats that include phishing attacks (and social engineering)
- non-Mach-O binaries, that include bash, Perl, and other scripts, and Java bytecode.
- And JavaScript in particular can wreak havoc in many browsers, regardless of the operating system they are running on. "JavaScript is a now infamous tool for exploiting vulnerabilities in browsers, and there is no reason to suspect that Safari suffers any less vulnerability in this respect than any of the other popular browsers," Harley concludes in his EICAR presentation.

Before this edition, the list of vulnerabilities was even longer, as shown below.

Apple Mac OS Classic*

- The TCP/IP stack responds to packets from a multicast address (known as a spank attack) which allows Denial of Service through network saturation or stealth scans.[26]

- The Web server tested positive for an Oracle9i crash through an incorrectly crafted, long URL.
- The system can be crashed through a "land" attack, where a packet's return port and address are identical to the destination port and address.
- The Web server is vulnerable to an infinite HTTP request loop resulting in a server crash.
- The Web server can be crashed through an HTTP 1.0 format string value in the header request.

Apple OS X 10.4 Server

- The OS X version was identified as older than the current 10.4.8 meaning the system has vulnerabilities in the binaries: AFP Server, Bluetooth, CFNetwork, Dashboard, Flash Player, ImageIO, Kernel, launchd, LoginWindow, OpenLDAP, Preferences, QuickDraw Manager, SASL, Security Agent, TCP/IP, WebCore, Workgroup Manager.
- The Directory Services could be remotely shut down by making excessive connections to the server.
- The DNS server is vulnerable to Cache Snooping attacks.
- The Web server reveals the existence of user accounts by querying against UserDir.
- The Web server is vulnerable to an infinite HTTP request allowing an attacker to exhaust all available resources.
- The Web server crashes when issued a long argument to the Host: field on an HTTP request.
- The JBoss server allows information disclosure about the system configuration.
- The Streaming server allows remote code execution because OpenLink is vulnerable to buffer overflows on two crafted URLs: GET AAA[...] AAA and GET /cgi-bin/testcono?AAAAA[...]AAA HTTP/1.0.
- The DNS server still allows Cache Snooping.
- The Web server allowed downloading the source code of scripts on the server (specifically files served by weblog feature).
- The Web server (port 80, 8080, 8443) allows for username enumeration because the "UserDir" option is enabled.
- The Web server (port 8080) has HTTP TRACE enabled allowing for a potential cross-site scripting attack.
- The SSL Coyote service on port 8443 is vulnerable to a format string

attack on the method name allowing remote execution of code or Denial of Service.

- The Web server (port 80, 1085) accepts unlimited requests making the system vulnerable to Denial of Service attacks that consume all available memory.
- The Web server (port 80) crashes when issued a long argument to the Host: field on an HTTP request.
- The OS X Directory service could be remotely shut down.
- The DNS server permits external cache snooping and allows for recursive queries.
- The Web server (port 80, 8080, 8443) allows for username enumeration because the "UserDir" option is enabled.
- The Web server (port 8080) has HTTP TRACE enabled allowing for a potential cross-site scripting attack.
- The Web server (port 80, 1085) accepts unlimited requests allowing attackers to consume all available resources.
- The Web server (port 80) crashes when a long argument is passed to the Host: field of an HTTP request.

Apple OS X 10.4 Tiger*

- The SSH service is subject to a PAM timing attack allowing for user enumeration.
- The web server allows user enumeration through an HTTP response timing issue.

The vulnerabilities discussed above, most of them appearing in the dated SANS Institute annual Top 20 Vulnerability Reports, tended to focus only on operating systems. However, the threat landscape is very dynamic and has changed over the years. This has necessitated us to broaden our focus beyond operating systems to cover vulnerabilities found in other systems like antivirus, backup or other application software, client-side vulnerabilities, including vulnerabilities in browsers, in office software, in media players and in other desktop applications. These vulnerabilities are continuously being discovered on a variety of operating systems and are also massively exploited in the wild. So newer SANS vulnerability reports are covering areas such as*:

- Client-side vulnerabilities:
  ° Web browsers
  ° Office software

- ° Email clients
- ° Media players
- Server-side Vulnerabilities:
  - ° Web applications
  - ° Windows services
  - ° Unix and Mac OS services
  - ° Backup software
  - ° Anti-virus software
  - ° Management servers
  - ° Database software security policy and personnel
- Application abuse:
  - ° Instant messaging
  - ° Peer-to-peer programs
- Network devices:
  - ° VoIP servers and phones
- Zero-day attacks

For more details on these vulnerabilities, the reader is referred to SANS's Top–20 2007 Security Risks (2007 Annual Update), http://www.sans-ssi.org/top20/.

Forces Behind Cyberspace Attacks

Just a few years ago it almost looked like there was a big one every few days—a big computer network attack, that is. E-attacks were, and still are, very frequent, but they are now more designer-tailored, more bold, gang-like and more state sponsored and are taking on more systems than ever before. In fact, if we look at the chronology of computer attacks, there is a progressive pattern in the number of targeted systems and in the severity of these attacks. Early attacks were far less dangerous and they were targeted on a few selected systems. Through the years, this pattern has been morphing and attacks are becoming more daring, broader, and more indiscriminate.

One of these reasons is rapid technology growth. The unprecedented growth in both the computer and telecommunication industries has enabled access to the Internet to balloon into millions. Portable laptops and palms have made Internet access easier because people can now logon the Internet anytime, anywhere. Laptops, palms, and cellular and satellite phones can be used in many places on earth like in the backyard of any urban house, in the Sahara Desert, in the Amazon or in the Congo, and the access is as good as in a major city like London, New York, or Tokyo. The arena of possible cyber attacks is growing.

Another reason for cybercrime growth is the easy availability of hacker tools. There are an estimated 30,000 hacker-oriented sites on the Internet, advertising and giving away free hacker tools and hacking tips.[27] As the Philippine-generated "Love Bug" demonstrated, hacking prowess is no longer a question of affluence and intelligence but of time and patience. With time, one can go through a good number of hacker sites, picking up tips and tools and coming out with a ready payload to create mayhem in cyberspace.

Anonymity is a third reason for cybercrime growth. Those times when computer access was only available in busy well-lit public and private areas are gone. Now, as computers become smaller and people with those small Internet-accessible gizmos become more mobile, hacker tracing, tracking, and apprehending have become more difficult than ever before. Now hackers can hide in smaller places and spend a lot of time producing deadlier viruses drawing very little attention.

Cybercrime has also grown as a result of cut-and-paste in programming technology. This removed the most important impediment for would-be hackers. Historically, before anybody could develop a virus, one had to write a code for it. The code had to be written in a computer programming language, compiled, and made ready to go. This means, of course, that the hacker had to know or learn a programming language! Learning a programming language is not a one-day job. It takes long hours of study and practice. Well, today this is no longer the case. We're in an age of cut-and-paste programming. The pieces and technical know-how are readily available from hacker sites. One only needs to have a motive and the time.

Communications speed is another factor to consider. With the latest developments in bandwidth, high volumes of data can be moved in a short time. This means that intruders can download a payload, usually developed by cut-and-paste offline, very quickly log off and possibly leave before detection is possible.

The high degree of internetworking also supports cybercrime. There is a computer network in almost every country on earth. Nearly all these networks are connected on the Internet. In many countries, Internet access is readily available to a high percentage of the population. In the United States, for example, almost 50 percent of the population has access to the Internet.[28] On a global scale, studies show that currently up to 40 percent of developed countries and 4 percent of all developing countries on average have access to the Internet and the numbers are growing daily.[29] As time passes, more and more will join the Internet bandwagon, creating the largest electronic human community in the history of humanity. The size of this cybercommunity alone is likely to create many temptations.

Finally, we must realize that crime is encouraged by our increasing dependency on computers. The ever increasing access to cyberspace, together with the increasing capacity to store huge quantities of data, the increasing bandwidth in communication networks to move huge quantities of data, the increased computing power of computers, and plummeting computer prices have all created an environment of human dependency on computers. This, in turn, creates numerous problems and fertile ground for hackers.

Challenges in Tracking Cyber Vandals

All the reasons for cybercrime growth that we gave in the previous section make it extremely difficult for law enforcement agencies and other interested parties, like computer equipment manufacturers and software producers, to track down and apprehend cyber criminals. In addition to the structural and technological bonanzas outlined above that provide a fertile ground for cyber-crime, there are also serious logistical challenges that prevent tracking down and apprehending a successful cyber criminal. Let us consider some of those challenges.

As computer networks grow around the globe, improvements in computer network technology and communication protocols are made, and as millions jump on the Internet bandwagon, the volume of traffic on the Internet will keep on growing, always ahead of the technology. This makes it extremely difficult for law enforcement agencies to do their work. The higher the volume of traffic, the harder it gets to filter and find cyber criminals. It is like looking for a needle in a haystack or looking for a penny on the bottom of the ocean.

The recent distributed denial of service (DDoS) attacks have demonstrated how difficult it is to trace and track down a well-planned cyber attack. When the attackers are clever enough to mask their legitimate sources in layers of multiple hoops that use innocent computers in networks, the task of tracking them becomes even more complicated. Because we explained in detail how this can be achieved in Chapter 6, we will not do so again here. However, with several layers of hoops, DDoS and other penetration attacks can go undetected.

Law enforcement and other interested parties lack a good hacker profile to use to track down would-be hackers before they create mayhem. The true profile of a computer hacker has been changing along with the technology. In fact the Philippine-generated "Love Bug" demonstrated beyond a doubt how this profile is constantly changing. This incident and others like it discredited the widely held computer hacker profile of a well-to-do, soccer playing, suburban, privately schooled, teen. The incident showed that a teenager in an underdeveloped nation, given a computer and access to the Internet, can create as much mayhem in cyberspace as his or her counter-parts in industrialized, highly computerized societies. This lack of a good computer hacker profile has made it extremely difficult to track down cyber criminals.

The mosaic of global jurisdictions also makes it difficult for security agencies to track cyber criminals across borders. The Internet, as a geographically boundaryless infrastructure, demonstrates for the first time how difficult it is to enforce national laws on a boundaryless community. Traditionally, there were mechanisms to deal with cross-border criminals. There is Interpol, a loose arrangement between national police forces to share information and sometimes apprehend criminals outside a country's borders. Besides Interpol, there are bilateral and multinational agreements and conventions that establish frameworks through which "international" criminals are apprehended. In cyberspace, this is not the case. However, there are now new voices advocating for a form of *cyberpol*. But even with cyberpol, there will still be a need to change judicial and law enforcement mechanisms to speed up the process of cross-border tracking and apprehension.

There is a lack of history and of will to report cybercrimes. This is a problem in all countries. We have already discussed the reasons that still hinder cybercrime reporting.

Because of the persistent lag between technology and the legal processes involving most of the current wiretaps and cross-state and cross-border laws, effective tracing, tracking and apprehension of cyber criminals is a long way off. And as time passes and technology improves, as it is bound to, the situation will become more complicated and we may even lose the fight.

The Cost of Cyberspace Crime

According to the InfoSecurity Report of 2012,[30] although the frequency of successful cyber attacks has more than doubled over the last three years, the annual cost to organizations has slowed dramatically in the last two years. The report noted that for the period of the study the "most costly cyber crimes are those caused by malicious insiders, denial of services, and malicious code." The U.S. companies were more likely to suffer insider attacks than the other countries. A study like this and other in the security domain looking at the cost of cybercrimes, continue to indicate that cybercrimes, where ever they are committed, are getting more frequent and more costly. However, as we have indicated and will continue to urge in the rest of the book, this cost especially in some major crimes can be contained with a proper ethical framework, strong security protocols and encryption regimes, and a carefully chosen basket of security best practices. Organizations with a stronger security posture are continuously experiencing less cybercrimes costs, sometimes than half the cost of less prepared ones. We will talk more about these in the coming chapters.

The universality of cyber attacks creates new dimensions to cyberspace security, making it very difficult to predict the source of the next big attack, to monitor, let alone identify, trouble spots, to track and apprehend hackers, or to put a price on the problem that has increasingly become a nightmare to computer systems administrators, the network community, and users in general.

As computer prices plummet, as computer and Internet devices become smaller, and as computer ownership and Internet access sky-rocket, estimating the cost of e-attacks becomes increasingly difficult to do. For one thing, each type of e-attack (seen earlier) has its own effects on the resources of cyberspace, and the damage each causes depends on the time, place, and topography used.

Then, too, it is very difficult to quantify the actual true number of attacks. Only a tiny fraction, of what everyone believes is a huge number of incidents, is detected and an even smaller number is reported. In fact, as we reported in the previous section, only one in 20 of all system intrusions is detected and of those detected only one in 20 is reported.[31]

Because of the small number of reports, there has been no conclusive study to establish a valid figure that would at least give us an idea of the scope of the problem. The only known studies have been regional and sector based. For example, there have been studies in education, on defense, and in a select number of industries and public government departments.

According to Terry Guiditis of Global Integrity, 90 percent of all reported and unreported computer attacks is done by insiders.[32] Insider attacks are rarely reported. As we reported in Chapter 6, companies are reluctant to report any type of cyber attack, especially insider ones, for fear of diluting integrity and eroding investor confidence in the company.

Another problem in estimating the numbers stems from a lack of cooperation between emergency and computer crime reporting centers worldwide. There are over 100 such centers worldwide, but they do not cooperate because most commercially compete with each other.[33]

It is difficult, too, to estimate costs when faced with so many unpredictable types of attacks and viruses. Attackers can pick and choose when and where to attack. And, attack type and topography cannot be predicted. Hence, it is extremely difficult for system security chiefs to prepare for attacks and thus reduce the costs of each attack that might occur.

Virus mutations are another issue in the rising costs of cyber attacks. The "Code Red" virus is an example of a mutating virus. The original virus started mutating after about 12 hours of release. It put enormous strain on system administrators to search and destroy all the various strains of the virus and the exercise was like looking for a needle in a haystack.

Another problem is the lack of system administrators and security chiefs trained in the latest network forensics technology who can quickly scan, spot, and remove or prevent any pending or reported attack and quickly detect system intrusions. Without such personnel, it takes longer to respond to and clear systems from attacks, so the effectiveness of the response is reduced. Also, failure to detect intrusion always results in huge losses to the organization.

A final problem is primitive monitoring technology. The computer industry as a whole, and the network community in particular, have not achieved the degree of sophistication necessary to monitor a computer system continuously for full proof detection and prevention of system penetration. The industry is always on the defensive, always responding after an attack has occurred and with inadequate measures. In fact, at least for the time being, it looks like the attackers are setting the agenda for the rest of us. This kind of situation makes every attack very expensive.

Input Parameters for a Cost Estimate Model

Whenever an e-attack occurs and one is interested in how to estimate the costs of such an attack, what must be considered in order to generate a plausible estimate? There is not an agreed-on list of quantifiable costs from any user, hardware or software manufacturer, network administrator, or network community as a whole. However, there are some obvious and basic parameters we can start with in building a model such as:

- Actual software costs.
- Actual hardware costs.
- Loss in host computer time. This is computed using a known computer usage schedule and costs per item on the schedule. To compute the estimate, one takes the total system downtime multiplied by cost per scheduled item.
- Estimated cost of employee work time. Again, this is computed using known hourly employee payments multiplied by the number of idle time units.
- Loss in productivity. This may be computed using known organizational performance and output measures.

If one has full knowledge of any or several of the items on this list and knows the type of e-attack being estimated, one can use the model to arrive at a plausible estimate.

Lack of coordinated efforts to estimate the costs of e-crimes has led to a confusing situation with varying and sometimes conflicting estimates of one e-attack flying around after each attack.

Social and Ethical Consequences

Although it is difficult to estimate the costs of e-attacks on physical system resources, it can be done, as we have seen above. However, estimating the cost of such attacks on society is almost impossible.

For example, we are not able to put a price tag on the psychological effects, which vary depending on the attack motive. Attack motives that result in long-term psychological effects include hate and joke, especially on an individual. Psychological effects may lead to reclusion and such a trend may lead to dangerous and costly repercussions on the individual, corporations, and society as a whole.

What about the cost of moral decay? There is a moral imperative in all our actions. When human actions, whether bad or good, become so frequent, they create a level of familiarity that leads to acceptance as "normal." This type of acceptance of actions formerly viewed as immoral and bad society is moral decay. There are numerous e-attacks that can cause moral decay. In fact, because of the recent spree of DDoS and e-mail attacks, one wonders whether the people doing these acts seriously consider them immoral and illegal anymore!

We must also take into account the overall social implications. Consider the following scenario: Suppose in society X, cheating becomes so rampant that it is a daily occurrence. Children born in this cheating society grow up accepting cheating as normal since it always happens. To these children and generations after them, cheating may never ever be considered a vice. Suppose there is a neighboring society Y which considers cheating bad and immoral, and the two societies have, for generations, been engaged in commerce with each other. But as cheating becomes normal in society X, the level of trust of the people of X by the people of Y declines. Unfortunately, this results in a corresponding decline in business activities between the two societies. While society Y has a choice to do business with other societies that are not like X, society X loses business with Y. This scenario illustrates a situation that is so common in today's international commerce, where cheating can be like any other human vice. It also illustrates huge hidden costs that are difficult to quantify and may cause society to suffer if it continuously condones certain vices as normal.

Then there is the cost of loss of privacy. After the headline-making e-attacks on CNN, eBay, E*Trade, and Amazon, and the e-mail attacks that wreaked havoc on global computers, there is a resurgence in the need for quick solutions to the problem that seems to have hit home. Many businesses are responding with patches, filters, ID tools, and a whole list of solutions as we will discuss in Chapter 8. Among these solutions are profile scanners and straight e-mail scanners like Echlon. Echlon is a high-tech U.S. government spying software housed in England. It is capable of scanning millions of e-mails given specific keywords. The e-mails trapped by it are further processed and subsequent actions are taken as warranted. Profile scanners are a direct attack on individual privacy. This type of privacy invasion in the name of network security is a threat to all of us. We will never estimate its price, and we are not ready to pay! The blanket branding of every Internet user as a potential computer attacker or a criminal until proven otherwise, by a software of course, is perhaps the greatest challenge to personal freedoms and very costly to society.

Finally, who can put a price tag on the loss of trust? Individuals, once attacked, lose trust in a person, group, company, or anything else believed to be the source of the attack or believed to be unable to stop the attack. E-attacks, together with draconian solutions, cause us to lose trust in individuals and businesses, especially businesses hit by e-attacks. Customer loss of trust in a business is disastrous for that business. Most importantly, it is the loss of innocence that society had about computers.

As the growth of the Internet increases around the globe and computer prices plummet, Internet access becomes easier and widespread, and as computer technology produces smaller computers and other communication gadgets, the number of e-attacks are likely to increase. The current, almost weekly, reports of e-attacks on global computers is an indication of this trend. The attacks are getting bolder, more frequent, indiscriminate, widespread, and destructive. They are also becoming more difficult to detect as new programming technologies and delivery systems are developed, thus making estimating costs more complicated, difficult, specialized, and of course, expensive.

Currently very few people, including system administrators and security chiefs, are able to estimate the costs of the many types of e-attacks. This is not likely to get better soon because of the ever-increasing numbers of better-trained hackers, the pulling together of hacker resources, the creation and sharing of hacking tools, and the constantly changing attack tactics. Administrators and security personnel, already overburdened with the rapidly changing security environments, are not able to keep up with these fast changing security challenges. So whenever attacks occur, very few in the network community can make a plausible estimate for any of those attacks. In fact, we are not even likely to see a good estimate model soon because:

- There is not one agreed-on list of parameters to be used in estimates.
- The costs, even if they are from the same type of attack, depend on

incidents. The same attack may produce different losses if applied at different times on the same system.

- There is a serious lack of trained estimators. Very few system managers and security chiefs have the know-how to come up with good input parameters.
- Many of the intrusions still go undetected; even the few detected are not properly reported.
- There is no standard format for system inventory to help administrators and security experts put a price on many of the system resources.
- Poor readings from ID tools can result in poor estimates. Many of the current ID tools are still giving false negatives and positives which lead to sometimes overestimating or underestimating the outcomes.
- Although systems intrusion reporting is on the rise, there is still a code of silence in many organizations that are not willing to report these intrusions for both financial and managerial reasons. Some organizations even undervalue the costs and underreport the extent of system intrusions for similar reasons.
- Depending on the sensitivity of the resources effected in an attack, especially if strategic information is involved, management may decide to underreport or undervalue the true extent of the intrusions.

Because of all these, a real cost model of e-attacks on society will be difficult to determine. We will continue to work with "magic figures pulled out of hats" for some time to come. Without mandatory reporting of e-crimes, there will never be a true picture of the costs involved. However, even mandatory reporting will never be a silver bullet until every sector, every business, and every individual gets involved in voluntary reporting of e-crimes.

Conclusion

The computer revolution that gave birth to the Internet, and hence to cyberspace, has in most ways changed human life for the better. The benefits of the revolution far outweigh the problems we have so far discussed in this and preceding chapters. People have benefited far more from the revolution in every aspect of life than they have been affected negatively. And it is expected, from almost all signs, that new developments in computer technology and new research will yield even better benefits for humanity.

However, we should not ignore the inconveniences or the social and ethical upheavals that are perpetuated by the technology. We need to find ways to prevent future computer attacks. Our focus, as we work on the root causes of these attacks, is to understand what they are, who generates them, and why. Dealing with these questions and finding answers to them are not easy tasks for a number of reasons. Among those reasons are the following:

- The nature, topography, and motives of e-attacks change as computer technology changes.
- Since 80 to 90 percent of all e-attacks are virus based, the development of computer viruses is getting better and faster because of new developments in computer programming. If current trends continue, the cut-and-paste programming we use today will get even better, resulting in better viruses, virus macros, and applets.
- Current development in genetic programming, artificial intelligence, and Web-based script development all point to new and faster developments of viruses and other programming-based types of e-attacks.
- The development in network programming, network infrastructure, and programming languages with large API libraries will continue to contribute to a kind of "team" effort in virus development, where virus wares and scripts are easily shared and passed around.
- Free downloadable header tools are widely available. There are thousands of hacker tools and wares on hundreds of hacker Web sites that will eventually make designing viruses a thrilling experience.
- The public is still impressed by the "intelligence" of hackers.

For these and other reasons we have not touched on, e-attacks are likely to continue, and the public, through legislation, law enforcement, self-regulation, and education, must do whatever possible to keep cyberspace civilized.

Chapter 8

Information Security Protocols and Best Practices

LEARNING OBJECTIVES:

After reading this chapter, the reader should be able to:
- Describe the evolution of and types of computer networks.
- Understand the fundamentals of a security protocol.
- Know what makes a good protocol.
- Know some of the best practices in a given type/area of information security.
- Understand how the network infrastructure helps to perpetuate online crimes.
- Recognize the difficulties faced in fighting online crime.

Throughout this book, we discussed the vulnerability of computer networks, and the dangers, known and unknown, that computer networks face from an unpredictable user clientele. Although it is difficult to know all possible types of attacks to computer networks, we have, based on what is currently known, tried to discuss and categorize these attacks and how they affect the victim computer network systems. In this chapter we will continue with this discussion. However, we will focus on the known security protocols and best practices that can be used to protect an enterprise network.

In securing networks, or cyberspace in general, the following protocols and best practices are worth investing in: a good security policy, thorough and consistent security assessments, an effective firewall regime, strong cryptographic systems, authentication and authorization, intrusion detection, vigilant virus detection, legislation, regulation, self-regulation, moral and ethics education, and a number of others.

A Good Security Policy

According to RFC 2196, a security policy is a formal statement of the rules by which people who are given access to an organization's technology and information assets must abide.[1] The strength of an organization's systems security is determined by the details in its security policy. The security policy is the tool that says *no* when no needs to be said. The no must be said because the system administrator wants to limit the number of network computers, resources, and capabilities people use to ensure the security of the system. One way of doing this fairly is by implementing a set of policies, procedures, and guidelines that tell all employees and business partners what constitutes acceptable and unacceptable use of the organization's computer system. These policies, procedures, and guidelines constitute the organization's security policy. The security policy also spells out what resources need to be protected and how the organization can protect such resources. A security policy is a living set of policies and procedures that impact and potentially limit the freedoms and, of course, levels of individual security responsibility of all users. Such a structure is essential to an organization's security. There are, however, those in the security community who do not think much of a security policy. We believe security policies are very important in the overall security plan of a system for several reasons including:

- Firewall installations: If a functioning firewall is to be configured, its rule base must be based on a sound security policy.
- User discipline: All users in the organization who connect to a network like the Internet through a firewall, must conform to the security policy.

Without a strong security policy to which every employee must conform, the organization may suffer a loss of data and employee productivity all because employees spend time fixing holes, repairing vulnerabilities, and recovering lost or compromised data, among other things.

The security policy should be flexible enough to allow as much access as necessary for individual employees to do their assigned tasks; full access should only be granted to those whose work calls for such access. Also, the access policy, as a rule of thumb, should be communicated as fully as possible to all employees and employers. There should be no misunderstanding whatsoever. According to Mani Subramanian, a good security policy should[2]:

- Identify what needs to be protected;
- Determine which items need to be protected from authorized access,

unauthorized or unintended disclosure of information and denial of service;
- Determine the likelihood of attack;
- Implement the most effective protection; and
- Review the policy continuously and update it if weaknesses are found.

Merike Kaeo[3] suggests that a security policy must:

- Be capable of being implemented technically;
- Be capable of being implemented organizationally;
- Be enforceable with security tools where appropriate and with sanctions where prevention is not technically feasible;
- Clearly define the areas of responsibility for users, administrators, and management; and
- Be flexible and adaptable to changing environments.

A security policy covers a wide variety of topics and serves several important purposes in the system security cycle. Constructing a security policy is like building a house, it needs a lot of different components that must fit together. The security policy is built in stages and each stage add value to the overall product making it unique to the organization. To be successful, a security policy must:

- Have the backing of the organization's top management.
- Involve everyone in the organization by explicitly stating everyone's role and the responsibilities in the security of the organization.
- Precisely describe a clear vision of a secure environment, stating what needs to be protected and the reasons for it.
- Set priorities and costs of the items to be protected.
- Be a good teaching tool for everyone in the organization about security, the items to be protected and why and how they are protected.
- Set boundaries on what constitutes appropriate and inappropriate behavior as far as security and privacy of the organization resources are concerned.
- Create a security clearinghouse and authority.
- Be flexible enough to adapt to new changes.
- Be consistently implemented throughout the organization.

To achieve all those, Jasma suggests the following core steps[4]:

- Determine the resources that must be protected and for each resource draw a profile of its characteristics. Such resources should include physical, logical, network, and system assets. A table of these items, in order of importance should be developed.

- For each identified resource, determine from whom you must protect it.
- For each identified resource, determine the types of potential threats and the likelihood of such threats. Threats can be denial of service, disclosure or modification of information, or unauthorized access. For each threat, identify the security risk and construct a table for these in order of importance.
- Develop a policy team consisting of at least one member each from senior administration, legal, the employees on the frontline, and the IT department. Also include an editor or writer to help with drafting the policy.
- Determine what needs to be audited. Use programs like Tripwire to perform audits on systems including security events on servers, firewalls and on selected network hosts. Auditable logs include logfiles and object accesses on servers, firewalls and selected network hosts.
- Define acceptable use of system resources like e-mail, news, and the Web.
- Consider how to deal with encryption, passwords, key creation and distributions, and wireless devices that connect on the organization's network.
- Provide for remote access to accommodate workers on the road, those working from home, and business partners who may need to connect through a VPN.

From all this information develop two structures, one describing user access rights to the resources identified and the other describing user responsibilities in ensuring security for a given resource.

And finally, a good security policy must have the following components:

- A security policy access rights matrix.
- Logical access restriction to the system resources.
- Physical security of resources and site environment.
- Cryptographic restrictions.
- Policies and procedures.
- Common attacks and possible deterrents.
- A well-trained workforce.
- Equipment certification.
- Audit trails and legal evidence.
- Privacy concerns.

- Security awareness training.
- Incident handling.

Vulnerability Assessment

Vulnerability assessment is a periodic process that works on a system to identify, track, and manage the repair of vulnerabilities on the system. Vulnerability assessment does a health check of the system. It is an essential security process and best practice for the well-being of the system. The assortment of items that are checked in this process vary depending on the organization. It may include all desktops, servers, routers and firewalls. Most vulnerability assessment services will provide system administrators with:

- Network mapping and system fingerprinting of all known vulnerabilities.
- A complete vulnerability analysis and ranking of all exploitable weaknesses based on potential impact and likelihood of occurrence for all services on each host.
- A prioritized list of mis-configurations.

At the end of the process, a final report is always produced detailing the findings and the best way to go about overcoming such vulnerabilities. This report consists of prioritized recommendations for mitigating or eliminating weaknesses and, based on the organization's operational schedule, it also contains recommendations for further reassessments of the system on given time intervals or on a regular basis.

Because of the necessity of the practice, vulnerability assessment has become a very popular security practice and as a result, there has been a flurry of software products created to meet the need. The popularity of the practice has also led to a high level of expertise in the process as many security assessment businesses have sprung up. However, because of the number of such companies, trust is an issue. It is, however, advisable that a system administrator periodically employ the services of an outsider to get a more objective view.

Security assessment services, usually target the perimeter and internal systems of a private computer network, including scanning, assessment and penetration testing, and application assessment.

Vulnerability Scanning

System and network scanning for vulnerabilities is an automated process where a scanning program sends network traffic to all or selected computers in the network and expects to receive return traffic that will indicate whether those computers have known vulnerabilities. These vulnerabilities may include weaknesses in operating systems, application software, and protocols.

Since vulnerability scanning is meant to provide a system administrator with a comprehensive security review of the system, including both the perimeter and system internals, the vulnerability scanning services are aimed at spotting critical security vulnerabilities and gaps in the current system's security practices. Because of the accuracy needed and aimed at by these services, comprehensive system scanning usually results in a number of both false positives and negatives. It is the job of the system administrator to find ways of dealing with these false positives and negatives. The final report produced after each scan consists of strategic advice and prioritized recommendations to ensure critical holes are addressed first. System scanning can be scheduled, depending on the level of the requested scan, by the system user or the service provider, to run automatically and report by automated, periodic e-mails to a designated user. The scans can also be stored on a secure server for future review.

Vulnerability scanning has so far gone through three generations. The first generation required either code or script, usually downloaded from the Internet or fully distributed, to be compiled and executed for specific hardware or platforms. Because they were code and scripts that were platform and hardware specific, they always needed updates to meet specifications for newer technologies.

These limitations led to the second generation, which had more power and sophistication and provided more extensive and comprehensive reports. Tools were able to scan multiple platforms and hardware and to isolate checks for specific vulnerabilities. This was a great improvement. However, they were not extensive or thorough enough, and quite often they gave false positives and negatives.

The third generation was meant to reduce false reports by incorporating a double, and sometimes triple, scan of the same network resources. It used data from the first scan to scan for additional and subsequent vulnerabilities. This was a great improvement because those additional scans usually revealed more datagram vulnerabilities, the so-called second-level vulnerabilities. Those second-level vulnerabilities, if not found in time and plugged, are used effectively by hackers when data from less secure servers is used to attack more system servers, thus creating cascade defects in the network.

System scanning for vulnerabilities in a network is a double-edged sword. It can be used effectively by both system intruders and system security chiefs to compile an electronic inventory of the network. As the scanner continuously scans the network, it quickly identifies security holes and generates reports identifying what the holes are and where they are in the network. The information contained in the electronic inventory can be used by inside and outside intruders to penetrate the network and by the system security team to plug the identified loopholes. So to the network security team, vulnerability scanning has a number of benefits including the following:

- It identifies weaknesses in the network, the types of weaknesses, and where they are. It is up to the security team to fix the identified loopholes.
- Once network security administrators have the electronic network security inventory, they can quickly and thoroughly test the operating system privileges and permissions, the chief source of network loopholes, test the compliance to company policies, the most likely of network security intrusions, and finally set up a continuous monitoring system. Once these measures are taken, it may lead to fewer security breaches, thus increasing customer confidence.
- When there are fewer and less serious security breaches, maintenance costs are lower and the worry of data loss is diminished.

Types of Scanning Tools

There are hundreds of network security scanning tools and scripts on the market today. Each one of these tools, when used properly, will find different vulnerabilities. As network technology changes, accompanied by the changing landscape of attacks and the advances in virus generation and other attack tools, it is difficult for any one vulnerability tool or script to be useful for a large collection of system vulnerabilities. So most security experts, to be most effective, use a combination of these tools and scripts. The most commonly used tools usually have around 140 settings which are carefully used to change the sensitivity of the tool or to target the tool to focus the scan.

For commercial vulnerability scanners and scripts, we will review the most current tools and scripts. They are divided into two categories: network based and host based. Network-based tools are meant to guard the entire network and they scan the entire network for a variety of vulnerabilities. They scan all Internet resources including servers, routers, firewalls, and local-based facilities. Since a large percentage of network security risk comes from within the organization, from inside employees, host-based scanning, focuses on a single host that is assumed to be vulnerable. It requires an installation on the host to scan the operating system and hardware of the machine. At the operating system level, the scanner checks on missing security checks, vulnerable service configurations, poor password policies, and bad or poor passwords.

One of the most commonly used scanners today is Nmap, a network port scanning utility for single hosts and small and large networks. Nmap supports many scanning techniques including Vanilla TCP connect, TCP SYN (half open), TCP FIN, Xmas or NULL, TCP FTP proxy (bounce attack), SYN/FIN, IP fragments, TCP ACK and Windows, UDP raw ICMP port unreachable, ICMP (ping-sweep), TCP ping, direct (non-portmapper) RPC, remote OS identification by TCP/IP fingerprinting, and reverse-identity scanning.

When fully configured, Nmap can perform decoy scans using any selection of TCP addresses desired by its operator. Nmap can also simulate a coordinated scan to target different networks in one country or a number of countries all at the same time. It can also hide its activities in a barrage of what appears to the user or system administrator to be multinational attacks. It can spread out its attacks to hide below a monitoring threshold set by the system administrator or the system security team. Nmap is extremely effective at identifying the types of computers running in a targeted network and the potentially vulnerable services available on every one of them.

Vulnerability Assessment and Penetration Testing

Vulnerability assessment and penetration testing is another important phase of system security vulnerability assessment. It should be intensive, comprehensive and thorough in the way it is carried out. It is aimed at testing the system's identified and unidentified vulnerabilities. All known hacking techniques and tools are tested during this phase to reproduce real-world attack scenarios. From this phase of intensive real-life system testing, sometimes obscure vulnerabilities are found, processes and procedures of attack are identified, and sources and severity of vulnerabilities are categorized and prioritized based on the user provided risks.

Application Assessment

Demands on system application software increase as the number of services provided by computer network systems skyrocket, and there are corresponding demands for application automation and new dynamism of these applications. Such dynamism introduced in application software has opened a new security paradigm in system administration. Many organizations have gotten a sense of these dangers and are making substantial progress in protecting their systems from attacks via Web-based applications. Assessing the security of system applications is, therefore, becoming a special skills requirement needed to secure critical systems.

Firewalls

A firewall is a combination of hardware and software used to police network traffic that enters and leaves a network, thus isolating an organization's internal network from a large network like the Internet. In fact, a firewall is a computer with two network cards as interfaces—that is, an ordinary router, as we discussed in Chapter 5.

According to both Smith[5] and Stallings,[6] firewalls commonly use the following forms of control techniques to police network traffic inflow and outflow:

- Direction control: This is to determine the source and direction of service requests as they pass through the firewall.
- User control: This controls local user access to a service within the firewall perimeter walls. By using authentication services like IPSec, this control can be extended to external traffic entering the firewall perimeter.
- Service control: This control helps the firewall decide whether the type of Internet service is inbound or outbound. Based on this, the firewall decides if the service is necessary. Such services may range from filtering traffic using IP addresses or TCP/UDP port numbers to provide an appropriate proxy software for the service.
- Behavior control: This control determines how particular services at the firewall are used. The firewall chooses from an array of services available to it.

Firewalls are commonly used in organizational networks to exclude unwanted and undesirable network traffic entering the organization's systems. Depending on the organization's firewall policy, the firewall may completely disallow some traffic or all of the traffic, or it perform a verification on some or all of the traffic. There are two commonly used organization firewall policies:

(i) Deny everything: A deny-everything-not-specifically-allowed policy sets the firewall to deny all services and then add back those services allowed.

(ii) Allow everything: An allow-everything-not-specifically-denied policy sets the firewall to allow everything and then deny the services considered unacceptable.

Each one of these policies enables well-configured firewalls to stop a large number of attacks. For example, by restricting and/or limiting access to host systems and services, firewalls can stop many TCP-based, denial of service attacks by analyzing each individual TCP packet going into the network and they can stop many penetration attacks by disallowing many protocols used by an attacker. In particular firewalls are needed to prevent intruders from[7]:

- Entering and interfacing with the operations of an organization's network system,
- Deleting or modifying information that is either stored or in motion within the organization's network system, and
- Acquiring proprietary information.

There are two types of firewalls: packet filtering and application proxy. In addition, there are variations in these two types, commonly called *gateway* or *bastion*.

Packet Filter Firewalls

A packet filter firewall is a multilevel firewall, in fact a router, that compares and filters all incoming and sometimes outgoing network traffic passing through it. It matches all packets against a stored set of rules. If a packet matches a rule, then the packet is accepted. If a packet does not match a rule, it is rejected or logged for further investigation. Further investigations may include further screening of the datagram, in which case the firewall directs the datagram to the screening device. After further screening, the datagram may be let through or dropped. Many filter firewalls use protocol specific filtering criteria at the data link, network, and transport layers. At each layer, the firewall compares information in each datagram, like source and destination addresses, type of service requested, and the type of data delivered. A decision to deny, accept, or defer a datagram is based on one or a combination of the following conditions[8]:

- Source address.
- Destination address.
- TCP or UTP source and destination port.
- ICMP message type.
- Payload data type.
- Connection initialization and datagrams using TCP ACK bit.

A packet filter firewall is itself divided into two configurations. One is a straight packet filter firewall, which allows full-duplex communication. This two-way communication is made possible by following specific rules for communicating traffic in each direction. Each datagram is examined for the specific criteria given above and if conformity to direction-specific rules is established, the firewall lets the datagram through.

The second configuration is the stateful inspection packet filter firewall, also a full-duplex filter firewall; however, it filters using a more complex set of criteria that involves restrictions that are more than those used by a straight packet filter firewall. These complex restrictions form a set of one-way rules for the stateful inspection filter firewall.

Figure 8.1 shows a packet filter firewall in which all network traffic from source address xxx.xx.1.4 using destination port y, where y is some of the well-known port numbers and X is an integer, is dropped or put in a trash.

Application Proxy Firewalls

Application proxy firewalls provide higher levels of filtering than packet filter firewalls by examining individual packet data streams. An application proxy can be a small application or a part of a big application that runs on the firewall. Because there is no direct connection between the two elements communicating across the filter, unlike in the case of the packet filter firewalls, the

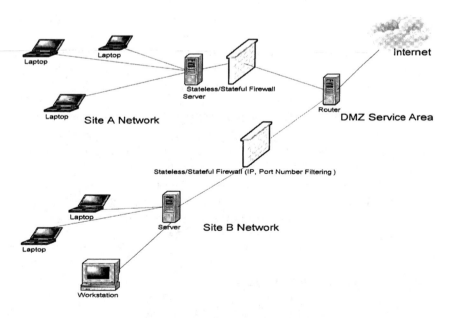

Figure 8.1 A Packet Filter Firewall

firewall generates a proxy for each application generated by a communicating element. The proxy inspects and forwards each application-generated traffic. Because each application proxy filters traffic based on application, it is able to log and control all incoming and outgoing traffic and to offer a higher degree of security and flexibility in accepting additional security functions, like user level authentication, end-to-end encryption, intelligent logging, information hiding, and access restrictions based on service types. A proxy filter firewall is shown in Figure 8.2.

Internal networks like LANs usually have multiple application proxy firewalls that may include telnet, WWW, FTP, and SMTP (e-mail). Although application proxy firewalls are great as high-level filtering devices, they are more expensive to install because they may require installing a proxy firewall for each application an organization has and that can be expensive to acquire, install, and maintain.

According to Lincoln Stein,[9] proxy firewalls are themselves divided into two types:

(i) Application-level proxy firewall with specific application protocols: For example, there is an application-level proxy for HTTP, one for FTP, one for e-mail, and so on. The filtering rules applied are specific to the application network packet.

(ii) Circuit-level proxy firewall with low-level general propose protocols: This type of proxy firewall treats all network packets like many black boxes to be forwarded across the filter or a bastion or not. It only filters on the basis of packet header information. Because of this, it is faster than its cousin the application-level proxy.

A combination of the filter and proxy firewalls is a gateway commonly called a *bastion* gateway which gives it a medieval castle flavor. In a firewall, packets originating from the local network and those from outside the network can only reach their destinations by going through the filter router and then through the proxy by station. The gateway or bastion firewall is shown in Figure 8.3.

Each application gateway combines a general purpose router to act as a traffic filter and an application-specific server through which all applications data must pass.

Use of Strong Cryptography

When there is no trust in the media of two communicating elements, there is always a need to "hide" the message before transmitting it through the untrusted medium. The concept of hiding messages is as old as humanity itself.

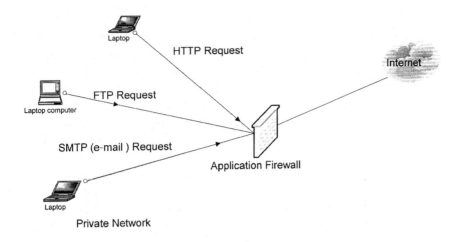

Figure 8.2 A Proxy Filter Firewall

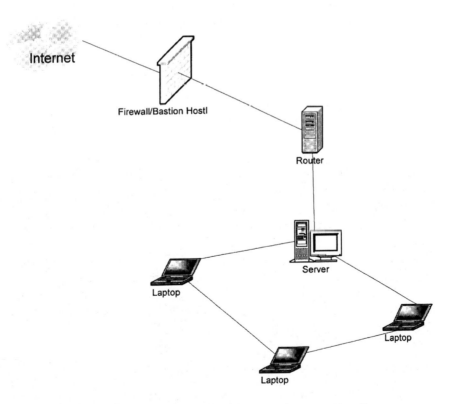

Figure 8.3 An Application Gateway/Bastion Firewall

Julius Caesar used to hide his messages whenever he sent them to acquaintances or to his generals in battle. A method of hiding or disguising messages is called a *cryptosystem*. A cryptosystem is a collection of algorithms. Messages are disguised using these algorithms. Each algorithm has a key used to decrypt the message encrypted using that algorithm. Cryptography is the art of creating and using cryptosystems. The word *cryptography* comes from Greek meaning "secret writing." But cryptography is one side of the coin of dealing with disguised messages; the other side is analyzing and making sense of a disguised message. Cryptanalysis is the art of breaking cryptosystems. Cryptology, therefore, is the study of both cryptography and cryptanalysis. Cryptographic systems have four basic parts:

(i)   Plaintext: This is the original message before anything is done to it. It is still in either the human readable form or in the format the sender of the message created it in.
(ii) Ciphertext: This is the form the plaintext takes after it has been encrypted using a cryptographic algorithm. It is an intelligible form.
(iii) Cryptographic algorithm: This is the mathematical operation that converts plaintext into ciphertext.
(iv) Key: This is the tool used to turn ciphertext into plaintext.

There are two types of cryptosystems: symmetric and asymmetric.

Symmetric Encryption

In symmetric cryptosystems, usually called conventional encryption, only one key, the secret key, is used to both encrypt and decrypt a message. Figure 8.4 shows the essential elements of a symmetric encryption.

For symmetric encryption to work, the two parties must find a sharable and trusted scheme to share their secret key. The strength of algorithms rests with the key distribution technique, a way to deliver the key to both parties. Several techniques are used including Key Distribution Centers (KDC). In the KDC, each participant shares a master key with the KDC. Each participant requests a session key from the KDC and uses the master key to decrypt the session key from the KDC.

Asymmetric Encryption

In asymmetric cryptosystems two keys are used. To encrypt a message, a public key is used and to decrypt the message a private key is used. Figure 8.5 shows the basic elements in asymmetric encryption.

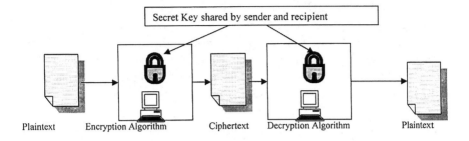

Figure 8.4 Symmetric Encryption

Figure 8.5 Asymmetric Encryption

The public key is made available to the public and the private key is kept private. The sender encrypts the message using the recipient's public key. The recipient decrypts the ciphertext using his or her private key.

While there are many algorithms for the conventional or symmetric encryption, there are only a few asymmetric algorithms.

Authentication and Authorization

Authentication is the process of verifying the identity of a person or a source of information. The process uses information provided to the authenticator to determine whether someone or something is, in fact, who or what it is declared to be. In computing, the process of authentication commonly involves someone, usually the user, presenting a password provided by the system administrator to logon. The user's possession of a password is meant to guarantee that the user is authentic. It means that at some previous time, the user requested a self-selected password from the system administrator, and the administrator assigned or registered one to the user.

Generally, authentication requires the presentation of credentials or items of value to the authenticating agent to prove the claim of who one is. The items of value or the credentials are based on several unique factors that show something you know, something you have or something you are[10]:

- Something you know means something you mentally possess. This could be a password, a secret word known by the user and the authenticator. While this method is cheap to administrate, people often forget their passwords, and system administrators must ensure that password files are stored securely. The user may use the same password on all system logons or may change it periodically, which is recommended. Examples of this factor include passwords, pass-phrases, and PINs (Personal Identification Numbers).
- Something you have is any form of issued or acquired self-identification like a SecurID, CryptoCard, Activcard, or SafeWord. This form is slightly safer than something you know because it is hard to abuse individual physical identifications. For example, it is easier to forget the number on the card than losing the card itself.
- Something you are is a physical attribute or characteristic like voice, fingerprint, iris pattern or other biometric. While one can lose something they have and forget something they know, it is not possible to lose something you are. So this seems to be the safest way to guarantee the authenticity of an individual. This is why biometrics are now a very popular way of identification. Although biometrics are very easy to use, biometric readers are still very expensive.

To the top three factors above, let us also add another factor, though it is seldom used—somewhere you are:

- Somewhere you are is usually based on either physical or logical location of the user. Consider for example a terminal that can be used to access certain resources.

In everyday use, authentication is implemented in three ways[11]:

(i)   Basic authentication involves a server which maintains a user file of either passwords and usernames or some other useful piece of authenticating information. This information is always examined before authorization is granted. Although this is the most common way computer network systems authenticate users, it has several weaknesses, including forgetting and misplacing authenticating information like passwords.

(ii) In challenge-response authentication, the server or any other authenticating system generates a challenge to the host requesting authentication and expecting a response.

(iii) Centralized authentication is when a central server authenticates, authorizes, and audits all network users. If the authentication process is successful, the client seeking authentication is then authorized to use the requested system resources, otherwise the authentication process fails and authorization is denied.

Types of Authentication

There are two types of authentication in use today: non-repudiable and repudiable authentication.

Non-Repudiable Authentication

Something you are involves physical characteristics that cannot be denied, therefore, authentication based on it cannot be denied. This is a non-repudiable authentication. Biometrics can positively verify the identity of an individual because biometric characteristics cannot be forgotten, lost, stolen, guessed or modified by an intruder. They, therefore, present a very reliable form of access control and authorization. It is also important to note that contemporary applications of biometric authorization are automated, which further eliminates human error in verification. As technology improves and our understanding of human anatomy increases, newer, more sensitive and accurate biometrics are being developed.

Next to biometrics as non-repudiable authentication items are undeniable and confirmer digital signatures. These signatures, developed by Chaum and van Antwerpen, cannot be verified without the help of a signer and cannot, with nonnegligible probability, be denied by the signer. Signer legitimacy is established through a confirmation or denial protocol.[12] Many undeniable digital signatures are based on RSA structure and technology, which gives them provable security making the forging of undeniable signatures as hard as forging standard RSA signatures.

Confirmer signatures[13] are a type of undeniable signatures where signatures may also be further verified by an entity called the confirmer, designated by the signer.

Lastly, there are chameleon signatures, a type of undeniable signatures where the validity of the content is based on the trust of the signer's commitment to the contents of the signed document. In addition, the recipient of the signature is not allowed to disclose the contents of the signed information to any third party without the signer's consent.[14]

Repudiable Authentication

Any information derivable from "what you know" and "what you have" can present problems if presented to the authenticator because the information can be unreliable. It can be unreliable because such information suffers from several well-known problems, including possessions that are lost, forged or easily duplicated, knowledge that is forgotten, and taken together, knowledge and possessions that are shared or stolen. Authentication based on this information is, therefore, easy to repudiate.

Authentication Methods

Several authentication methods are in use today. The most common are password authentication, public-key authentication, remote authentication, and anonymous authentication.

Password Authentication

Password authentication is the oldest, most durable, and most widely used of all the methods we will discuss. It is set up by default in many systems. Sometimes, it can be interactive, using the newer keyboard-interactive authentication. Password authentication has several flavors including, reusable passwords, one-time passwords, challenge-response passwords, and combined-approach authentication.

- Reusable passwords have two types: user and client authentication. User authentication, the most common and most familiar to most users, is always initiated by the user, who sends a request to the server for authentication and authorization for use of a specified system resource. Upon receipt of the request, the server prompts the user for a username and password. Upon submission of these, the server checks for a match against copies in its database. Based on the match, authorization is granted. In client authentication, on the other hand, the user first requests authentication and then authorization from the server to use a system or a specified number of system resources. An authenticated user may not be able to use any system resource the user wants.

This authentication establishes user authorization to use the requested resources in the amount requested and no more.

- One-time passwords, also known as session authentication, are used one time and then are disposed of after each session. Passwords are randomly generated using powerful random number generators which reduce the chances of their being guessed. There are several schemes of one-time passwords. The most common are: S/Key and token. An S/Key password is a one-time password generation scheme defined in RFC 1760 and is based on MD4 and MD5 encryption algorithms. It was designed to fight against replay attacks where, in a login session for example, an intruder eavesdrops on the network login session and gets the password and user ID for the legitimate user. Its protocol is based on a client-server model, where the client initiates the S/Key exchange by sending the first packet, to which the server responds with an ACK and a sequence number. A token password is a password generation scheme that requires the use of a special card like a smart card. The scheme is based on two schemes: challenge response and time synchronous.

- Challenge-response passwords uses a handshake authentication process in which the authenticator issues a challenge to the user seeking authentication. The user must provide a correct response in order to be authenticated. The challenge may take many forms depending on the system. In some systems the challenge is in the form of a message indicating "unauthorized access" and requesting a password. In other systems, it may be a simple request for a password, a number, a digest, or a nonce (a server-specified data string which may be uniquely generated each time a server generates a 401 server error). The person seeking authentication must respond to the system challenge. Nowadays, responses are a one-way function using password tokens, commonly referred to as *asynchronous tokens*. When the server receives the user response, it checks to be sure the password is correct. If so, the user is authenticated. If not, or if for another reason the network does not want to accept the password, the request is denied.

- Combined-approach authentication uses several combined authentication schemes for enhanced security. One of the most secure authentication methods is to use a random challenge-response exchange using digital signatures. When the user attempts to make a connection, the authentication system, a server or a firewall, sends a random string back as a challenge. The random string is signed using the user's private key, and sent back as a response. The authenticating server or firewall can then use the user's public key to verify that the user is indeed the holder of the associated private key.[15]

Public Key Authentication

As we discussed earlier in this chapter, the process of public-key authentication requires each user of the scheme to first generate a pair of keys and store each in a file. Each key is usually between 1,024 and 2,048 bits in length. Public-private key pairs are typically created using a key generation utility. As we will discuss in the next chapter, the pair will consist of a user's public and private key pair. The server knows the user's public key because it is published widely. However, only the user has the private key.

Public key systems are routinely used by authentication systems to enhance system security. The centralized authentication server commonly known as the *access control server* (ACS), is in charge of authentication using public key systems. When a user tries to access an ACS, it looks up the user's public key and uses it to send a challenge to the user. The server expects a response to the challenge where the user must use his or her private key. If the user then signs the response using his or her private key, he or she is authenticated as legitimate. To enhance public key security, the private key never leaves the user's machine, and therefore, cannot be stolen or guessed like a password. In addition, the private key has a passphrase associated with it, so even if the private key is stolen, the attacker must still guess the passphrase in order to gain access.

Public-key authentication has several flavors including secure sockets layer, kerberos, and MD5 authentication:

- In Secure Sockets Layer (SSL) authentication, authentication, encryption, and data integrity are provided using public key infrastructure (PKI). SSL authentication, being cryptographic based, uses a public/private key pair that must be generated before the process can begin. Communicating elements acquire verification certificates from a certificate authority (CA), a trusted third party between any two communicating elements like network servers, that certify that the other two or more entities involved in the intercommunication, including individual users, databases, administrators, clients, and servers are who they say they are. These certificates are signed by calculating a checksum over the certificate, encrypting the checksum and other information using the private key of a signing certificate. User certificates can be created and signed by a signing certificate which can be used in the SSL protocol for authentication purposes.
- Kerberos authentication is a network authentication protocol that provides strong authentication for client/server applications by using PKI technology. Kerberos is typically used when a user on a network

is attempting to make use of a network service and the service wants assurance that the user is who he says he is. To that end, the kerberos user gets a ticket that is issued by the kerberos authentication server (AS). The service then examines the ticket to verify the identity of the user. If all checks out, then the user is issued an access ticket.[16]

- MD5 authentication is one of the standard encryption algorithms in use today for authentication. The authentication process using MD5 is very simple. Each user has a file containing a set of keys that are used as input into an MD5 hash. The information being supplied to the authenticating server, like passwords, has its MD5 checksum calculated using these keys, and is then transferred to the authenticating server, along with the MD5 hash result. The authenticating server then gets user identity information like a password, obtains the user's set of keys from a key file, and then calculates the MD5 hash value. If the two are in agreement, authentication is successful.[17]

Remote Authentication

Not all users are directly connected to the networks whose services they want to use. In fact, many workers use company resources remotely while they are on the road. So remote authentication is essential for many system administrators. Remote authentication is used to authenticate those users who dial in to the ACS from a remote host. This can be done several ways including using secure remote procedure call, dial-up, and remote authentication dial-in user services authentication:

- Secure Remote Procedure Call (RPC) authentication is used by clients who do not need to identify themselves to the server, and the server does not require any identification from the client. Services falling in this category, like the Network File System (NFS), require stronger security than the other services and RPC authentication provides that degree of security. Since the RPC authentication subsystem package is open ended, different forms and multiple types of authentication can be used by RPC including: NULL authentication, UNIX authentication, data encryption standard (DES) authentication, DES Authentication Protocol, and Diffie-Hellman Encryption.
- Dial-up authentication authenticates a remote user, who is usually on a serial line or ISDN. The most common dial-up connection is the Point-to-Point Protocol (PPP). Dial-up authentication services authenticate the peer device, not the user of the device. There are several dial-up authentication mechanisms. For example, PPP authenti-

cation has the following mechanisms: Password Authentication Protocol (PAP), the Challenge Handshake Protocol (CHAP), and the Extensible Authentication Protocol (EAP).[18]

- Remote Authentication Dial-in User Services (RADIUS) is a common user protocol that provides user dial-in to the ACS which does the user authentication. Because all information from the remote host travels in the clear, RADIUS is considered to be vulnerable to attacks and, therefore, not secure.

Anonymous Authentication

There are many times a system administrator may want outside users to access public areas of the network without accessing the entire system. Clients who need this type of access typically use anonymous authentication. In order to give them access to some system resources, for example to a company Web site, these users, usually customers, are given access to the resources via a special anonymous account. System services that are used by many users who are not indigenous, like the World Wide Web service or the FTP service, must include an anonymous account to process anonymous requests.

Digital Signature-Based Authentication

Digital signature-based authentication is an authentication technique that does not require passwords and usernames. A digital signature is a cryptographic scheme used by the message recipient and any third party to verify the sender's identity and/or message for authenticity. It consists of an electronic signature that uses public key infrastructure (PKI) to verify the identity of the sender of a message or the signer of a document. The scheme may include a number of algorithms and functions including the digital signature algorithm (DSA), Elliptic curve digital signature and algorithm (ECDSA), account authority digital signature, authentication function, and signing function.[19]

Wireless Authentication

Because of the growing use of wireless technology, mobile computing has skyrocketed in the last several years. However, wireless technology has had a persistent low security problem that this rapid growth makes worse. There is a growing need for wireless network authentication for mobile devices since they connect to fixed networks as well as mobile networks. The IEEE 802.1X, through its Extensible Authentication Protocol (EAP), has built-in authentication for mobile unit users. This authentication requires Wi-Fi mobile units to authenticate with the network servers that they seek to connect to.

Intrusion Detection

Intrusion detection (ID) is a new technology that detects the characteristic signatures of software used in cyber attacks. The detection software uses the signatures to determine the nature of the attacks. At each different level of network investigative work, there is a different technique of network traffic information gathering, analysis, and reporting.

Intrusion detection operates on network traffic entering or already within the network. Designers of ID tools believe that anomalies in the traffic will lead to distinguishing between intruders and legitimate users of the network. The anomalies resulting from the ID analyses are actually large and noticeable deviations from historical patterns of usage. ID systems are supposed to identify three categories of users: legitimate users, legitimate users performing unauthorized activities, and, of course, intruders who have illegally acquired the required identification and authentication.

ID sensors are commonly and conveniently placed on the perimeter of a private network, outside the organization's firewalls. This usually behaves as the last defense of the organization's network, the last fence to the outside network, usually the Internet. It is also becoming common to have sensors on the same machine as the firewall. This approach gives the sensors more protection, making them less vulnerable to coordinated attacks. Although there are some attacks that some sensors cannot see, this location is good as the first line of defense since all possible attacks coming into the organization network pass through this point. Other good locations for ID sensors are inside the network on network subnets and on network hosts to monitor inside activities.

As more research is done in ID and as linkages are established between ID and artificial intelligence, newer ID tools with embedded extended rule bases that enable them to learn are being developed and, over time, they will be able to make better analyses and, therefore, decisions. The debate is not what kind of rule base to put in the ID tools, but what type. Currently, the rule bases have been those that teach the ID tools the patterns to look for in the traffic signature and to learn those patterns. For example, if an application is not supported by the server, that application's port number should never be active. However, the new movement differs from the traditional embedded rule bases. The focus now is actually to embed into these ID tools what Marcus J. Tanum calls "artificial ignorance," a rule base that teaches them the things not to look for.[20] People following this line of thought believe the rule base will then be simpler and the product will be more effective.

The scope of ID systems is also changing in another direction. For a while now, it has been assumed—wrongly—by management and many in the network community that ID systems protect network systems from outside intruders. But studies have shown that the majority of system intrusions are actually from insiders. So newer ID tools focus on this issue. Also, the human mind is the most complicated and unpredictable machine ever, so as new ID tools are being built to counter system intrusions, new attack patterns are being developed to take unpredictable human behavior into account. To keep abreast of all these changes, ID systems must be constantly changing.

As all these changes are taking place, the primary focus of ID systems is on the network as a unit where network packet data is collected by watching network packet traffic and then it is analyzed based on network protocol pattern norms, normal network traffic signatures, and network traffic anomalies built in the rule base. The ID systems look for three things: signatures of known attacks, anonymous behavior, and misuse patterns.[21]

Signatures of known attacks usually involve one of three common types[22]:

(i)   String: These signatures are used to monitor text strings that may indicate a possible attack.
(ii) Port: These signatures are used to monitor for applications that make port connection attempts. The monitoring is usually done on well-known and frequently attacked ports. Most attacked ports include port 20 for TCP, port 21 for FTP, and port 23 for telnet. A full list of TCP ports that are attacked frequently was given in earlier chapters.
(iii) Header: These signatures monitor abnormal combinations in packet headers for a number of known signatures like the IP address and sequence number signatures.

Anonymous behaviors are detected when the ID tools take observed activities and compare them to the rule-based profiles for significant deviations. The profiles are commonly for individual users, groups of users, system resource usages, and a collection of others as discussed below:

- An individual profile is a collection of common activities a user is expected to do, with little deviation from the expected norm. This may cover specific user events like the time being longer than usual usage, recent changes in user work patterns, and significant or irregular user requests.
- A group profile covers a group of users with common work patterns,

resource requests and usage, and historic activities. It is expected that each individual user in the group follows the group activity patterns.
- A resource profile includes the monitoring of the use patterns of the system resources like applications, accounts, storage media, protocols, communications ports, and a list of many others the system manager may wish to include. It is expected, depending on the rule-based profile, that common uses will not deviate significantly from these rules.

Other profiles include executable profiles that monitor how executable programs use the system resources. This, for example, may be used to monitor strange deviations of an executable program if it has an embedded Trojan worm or a trapdoor virus. In addition to executable profiles, there are also the following profiles: work profile, which includes monitoring the ports; static profile, which monitors other profiles, periodically updating them so that those profiles cannot slowly expand to sneak in intruder behavior; and, a variation of the work profile called the *adaptive profile*, which monitors work profiles automatically updating them to reflect recent upsurges in usage. And finally, there is also the adoptive rule-based profile which monitors historic usage patterns of all other profiles and uses them to make updates to the rule base.[23]

Misuse patterns—that is, patterns of known misuse of system resources—are also an effective focus for ID tools. These patterns, once observed, are compared to those in the rule base that describe "bad" or "undesirable" usage of resources. To achieve this, a knowledge database and a rule engine must be developed to work together. Misuse pattern analysis is best done by expert systems, model-based reasoning, or neural networks. We will not go further in explaining how each one works. An interested reader is referred to the well-written paper "AINT Misbehaving: A Taxonomy of Anti-Intrusion Techniques" by R. Kenneth Bauer (http://www.sans.org/newlook/ resources/ID FAQ/aint.htm).

But since networks are getting larger and traffic heavier, it is becoming more and more difficult for the ID system to "see" all traffic on a switched network like an Ethernet. This has led to a new approach of looking closer at the host. So in general, ID systems fall into two categories: host based and network based.

Host-Based Intrusion Detection Systems

Host-based intrusion detection systems (HIDS) techniques focus on the network server to monitor specific user and application traffic handled by that server. It is actually tracking log files and auditing traffic in and out of this one machine. Besides tracking in and out traffic, HIDS also check on the integrity of system files and watch the activities of all processes on the machine for abnormal process behavior. Host-based ID systems are indeed either personal firewalls or sensor agents. Personal firewalls, sometimes called *wrappers*, are configured to look at all network packets, connection attempts, login attempts and nonnetwork communications.

Agents are configured to monitor accesses and changes to critical system files and changes in user privileges.[24] Whether personal firewalls or agents, host-based ID tools are good for monitoring a network system for intrusion from insiders.

Advantages of HIDS

The concept of HIDS is slightly new. They came into widespread use in the early and mid–1980s after studies showed that a large number of illegal and illegitimate activities in organization networks actually originated with the employees. Over the succeeding years as technology advanced, the HIDS technology also advanced in tandem. More and more organizations are discovering the benefits of HIDS on their overall security. Besides being faster than their cousins the network-based intrusion detection systems (NIDS) and because they are dealing with less traffic, HIDS offer additional advantages including the following[25]:

- The ability to verify success or failure of an attack quickly. Because they log continuing events that have actually occurred, HIDS have information that is more accurate and less prone to false positives than their cousins the NIDS. This information can accurately and quickly infer whether an attack was successful or not and a response can be started early. In this role, HIDS complement the NIDS, as a verification system.
- Low-level monitoring. Because HIDS monitor at a local host, they are able to "see" low-level local activities such as file accesses, changes to file permissions, attempts to install new executables, attempts to access privileged services, changes to key system files and executables, attempts to overwrite vital system files or attempts to install Trojan horses or backdoors. These low-level activities can be detected very quickly and the reporting is quick and timely, giving the administrator time for an appropriate response. Some of these low-level attacks are so small that no NIDS can detect them.
- Near real-time detection and response. HIDS have the ability to detect minute activities at the target hosts and to report them to the administrator very quickly—at a rate near real-time. This is possible because

the operating system can recognize the event before any IDS can, in which case, an intruder can be detected and stopped before substantial damage is done.

- The ability to deal with encrypted and switched environments. Large networks are routinely switch chopped into many smaller network segments. Each one of these smaller networks is then tagged with a NIDS. In a heavily switched network, it can be difficult to determine where to deploy a network-based IDS to achieve sufficient network coverage. This problem can be solved by using traffic mirroring and administrative ports on switches, but this is not as effective. HIDS provides the needed greater visibility into these switched environments by residing on as many critical hosts as needed. In addition, because the operating systems see incoming traffic after encryption has already been decrypted, HIDS that monitor the operating systems can deal with these encryptions better than NIDS, which may not even deal with them at all.

- Cost effectiveness. Because no additional hardware is needed to install HIDS, there may be great savings for the organization. This compares favorably with the big costs of installing NIDS, which requires dedicated and expensive servers. In fact, in large networks that are switch chopped require a large number of NIDS per segment, this cost can add up.

Disadvantages of HIDS

Although they offer many advantages, HIDS have limitations in what they can do. These limitations include the following[26]:

- HIDS have a myopic viewpoint. Since they are deployed at a host, they have a very limited view of the network.
- Since HIDS are close to users, they are more susceptible to illegal tampering.

Network-Based
Intrusion Detection Systems

NIDS are network sensors configured to monitor all network traffic including traffic on the communication media and on all network servers and firewalls. They monitor the traffic on the network to detect intrusions. They are responsible for detecting anomalous, inappropriate, or other data that may be considered unauthorized and harmful occurring on a network. NIDS may or may not run with firewalls because there are striking differences between NIDS and firewalls. Firewalls are configured to allow or deny access to a particular service or host based on a set of rules. Only when the traffic matches an acceptable pattern is it permitted to proceed, regardless of what the packet contains. While NIDS also captures and inspects every packet that is destined for the network regardless of whether it's permitted or not, it is a silent listener, acting only by generating an alert if the packet signature, based on the contents of the packet, is not among the acceptable signatures.

There are several ways an NIDS sensor may be placed and run. It can either be placed and run as an independent stand-alone machine where it watches over all traffic entering the network from the outside, watches traffic entering a subnet, or just monitors itself as the target machine to watch over its own traffic. For example, in this mode, it can watch itself to see if somebody is attempting a SYN flood or a TCP port scan.

While NIDS, if well placed, can be very effective in capturing all incoming network traffic, it is possible that an attacker can evade this detection by exploiting ambiguities in the traffic stream as seen by the NIDS. Mark Handley, Vern Paxson, and Christian Kreibich list the sources of these exploitable ambiguities as follows[27]:

- Many NIDS do not have the capabilities to analyze the full range of behavior that can be exposed by the user and allowed by a particular protocol. The attacker can also evade the NIDS even if the NIDS performs analysis for the protocol.
- Since NIDS are far removed from individual hosts, they do not have full knowledge of each host's protocol implementation. This knowledge is essential for the NIDS to be able to determine how the host may treat a given sequence of packets if different implementations interpret the same stream of packets in different ways.
- Again, since NIDS do not have a full picture of the network topology between the NIDS and the hosts, the NIDS may be unable to determine whether a given packet will even be seen by the hosts.

Advantages of NIDS

NIDS focus, placement, running, and requirements, all seem to give them wonderful advantages over their cousins the firewalls and host-based IDS (as we will see soon).[28] These advantages are:

- The ability to detect attacks that a host-based system would miss because NIDS monitor network traffic at a Transport Layer. At this level, NIDS are able to look at, not only the packet addresses, but also the packet port numbers from the packet headers. HIDS which monitor traffic at a lower Link Layer may fail to detect some types of attack.

- A difficulty removing evidence. Because NIDS are on dedicated machines that are routinely protected, it is more difficult for an attacker to remove evidence than it is with HIDS, which are near or at the attacker's desk. Also, since NIDS use live network traffic and it is this traffic that is captured by NIDS when there is an attack, this also makes it difficult for an attacker to remove evidence.
- Real-time detection and response. Because NIDS are at the most opportune and strategic entry points in the network, they are able to detect foreign intrusions into the network in real-time and report as quickly as possible to the administrator for a quick and appropriate response. Real-time notification, which many NIDS have now, allows for a quick and appropriate response and can even let the administrators allow the intruder more time as they do more and targeted surveillance.
- The ability to detect unsuccessful attacks and malicious intent. Because the HIDS are inside the protected internal network, they never come into contact with many types of attack, since such attacks are often stopped by the outside firewall. NIDS, especially those in the DMZ, come across these attacks (those that escape the first firewall) that are later rejected by the inner firewall and those targeting the DMZ services that have been let in by the outer firewall. Besides showing these attacks, NIDS can also record the frequency of these attacks.

Disadvantages of NIDS

Although NIDS are very well suited to monitor all the traffic coming into the network or subnet, they have limitations[29]:

- Blind spots: Deployed at the borders of an organization's network, NIDS are blind to the whole inside network. As sensors are placed in designated spots, especially in switched networks, NIDS have blind spots—sometimes whole network segments they cannot see.
- Encrypted data: One of the major weaknesses of NIDS is on encrypted data. They have no capabilities to decrypt encrypted data. They can only scan unencrypted parts of the packets such as headers.

Challenges to Intrusion Detection

While ID technology has come a long way, and there is an exciting future for it as the marriage between it and artificial intelligence takes hold, it faces many challenges. Several problems still limit ID technology.

One problem is false alarms. Although the tools have come a long way and are slowly gaining acceptance as they gain widespread use, they still produce a significant number of both false positives and negatives.

A second problem is that technology is not yet ready to handle a large scale attack. This is because of ID's very nature: It has to literally scan every packet, every contact point, and every traffic pattern in the network. For larger networks during a large scale attack, it is not possible to rely on the technology to keep working with acceptable quality and grace. Unless there is a breakthrough today, the technology in its current state cannot handle very fast and large quantities of traffic efficiently.

Probably the biggest challenge is ID's perceived, and sometimes exaggerated, capabilities. The technology, while good, is not a cure for all computer network ills as some have pumped it up to be. It is just like any other good security tool.

Virus Detection

A virus detection program, commonly called an *antivirus* program, is a software program that monitors or examines a system, including its data and program files, for the presence of viruses. Once a virus has infected a system, it is vitally important that the virus be removed, whether it is active or dormant. There are a number of techniques used by antivirus programs to detect a virus in whatever stage it is in. Such techniques include detecting virus signatures, file length, checksum, and symptoms.

A virus signature is a specific and unique series of bytes bearing unique virus characteristics that is used like a human fingerprint to detect a virus. The most common of these characteristics are part of the virus instructions. Every virus has its own specific characteristics. The known characteristics are used to build up defenses against future viruses. Although there are new viruses created and distributed almost everyday, the most common viruses in circulation, according to virus and e-attack reporting agencies and centers, are the same old ones. So, it makes sense to use the historical facts of viruses and their characteristics to create defenses against future e-attacks. Most of today's antivirus scanners use this technique to detect viruses in systems. One weakness with signature detection is that only known viruses can be detected. This calls for frequent updates to virus scanners to build up an archive of signatures.

File length is a useful detection item because viruses work by attaching themselves to software as their surrogates. Usually when this happens, the length of the surrogate software increases. Antivirus software works by comparing the length of the original file or software with the length of the file or software whenever it is used. If the two lengths differ, this signals the existence of a virus. Note that this method does not reveal the type of virus in the file or data, it only detects the presence of a virus.

A checksum is a value calculated in a file to determine if data has been altered by a virus without increasing file length. There are two ways a checksum is used by antivirus checkers. One way is to compute the total number of bytes in the file and store it somewhere. Every time the file is used, the antivirus software recalculates the checksum and compares it with the original checksum. If the new value differs from the stored original, then the antivirus program reports the existence of a virus. In the second approach, probably in small files, checksum is computed as a sum of all binary words in a file. This method is better used to detect those viruses that do not, in any way, increase the length of a file, but simply alter its content. In transmission data, the checksum is computed for data before it is transmitted and again after transmission. If a virus was introduced between the source and destination, the checksum will reveal it. Checksum should be used only when it is clear that the first time a checksum was computed the file was virus free; otherwise, it will never detect a virus that was already in the file the first time the file was used.

The symptoms of a virus, if found in a file or software, indicate the presence of a virus. Virus symptoms usually depend on the type of virus. Remember that symptoms are not unique to any one virus. Several viruses may have similar symptoms. Some of the most common symptoms are the following:

- Frequent or unexpected computer reboots.
- Sudden size increases in data and software.
- Disappearance of data files.
- Difficulty saving open files.
- Shortage of memory.
- Presence of strange sounds or text.

Legislation

As the Internet and its activities increase and as e-commerce booms, the citizenry of every nation who represent special interests such as environmental protection, media-carried violence, pornography, gambling, free speech, intellectual property rights, privacy, censorship, and security are putting enormous pressures on their national legislatures and other lawmaking bodies to enact laws to curb Internet activities in ways that those groups feel best serve their interests.

Already this is happening in countries like the United States, the United Kingdom, Germany, France, China, and Singapore. The list grows every passing day. In all these countries, laws, some good, many repressive, are being enacted to put limits on Internet activities. The recent upsurge of illegal Internet activities, like the much publicized distributed denial of service and headline-making e-mail attacks, have fueled calls from around the world for legislative action to stop such activities. Yet, it is not likely that such actions will stop or arrest the escalating rate of illegal activities in cyberspace. The patchwork of legislation will not, in any meaningful way, put a stop to these malicious activities in the near future. If anything, such activities are likely to continue unabated unless and until long-term plans are in place. Such efforts and plans should include, first and foremost, an education in ethics.

Regulation

As the debate between the freedom of speech advocates and the protection of children crusaders heats up, governments around the world are being forced to revisit, amend, and legislate new policies, charters, and acts. As we will see in detail in the next section, this has been one of the most popular and for politicians, the most visible means of Internet control. Legislative efforts are backed by judicial and law enforcement machinery. In the United States, a number of acts are in place and are enforceable. In the last few years, many outdated acts have been revisited and updated.

Besides purely legislative processes which are more public, there are also private initiatives working in conjunction with public judicial systems and law enforcement agencies or through workplace forces. Examples abound of large companies, especially high technology companies like software, telecommunications, and Internet providers, coming together to lobby their national legislatures to enact laws to protect their interests. Such companies are also forming consortiums or partnerships to create and implement private control techniques.

Self-Regulation

There are several reasons why self-regulation as a means of Internet control is appealing to a good cross section of people around the globe. One reason, supported mostly by the free-speech advocates, is to prevent the heavy hand of government from deciding what is or is not acceptable.

Although legislation and enforcement can go a long way in helping to curb cybercrime, they are not the magic bullets that will eventually eradicate cybercrime. They must be combined with other measures that must work together. Probably one of the most effective prevention techniques is to give users enough autonomy to regulate themselves, each taking on the responsibility to the degree and level of control and regulation that best suits his or her needs and environment. This self-regulated cyberspace control can be done through two approaches: hardware and software.

Hardware-Based Self-Regulation

Hardware security controls and cyberspace regulation set by individual users are varied and involve controlling access to hardware resources like memory, files, authentication routines for file access, password protection, and firewalls. Hardware controls are focused in six areas:

(i)   Prevention restricts access to information on system resources like disks on network hosts and network servers using technologies that permit only authorized people to the designated areas. Such technologies include, for example, firewalls.

(ii) Protection routinely identifies, evaluates, and updates system security requirements to make them suitable, comprehensive, and effective.

(iii) Detection deploys an early warning monitoring system for early discovery of security breaches both planned and in progress.

(iv) Limitation cuts the losses suffered in cases of failed security.

(v)   Reaction analyzes all possible security lapses and plans relevant remedial efforts for a better security system based on observed failures.

(vi) Recovery recovers what has been lost as quickly and efficiently as possible and updates contingent recovery plans.

Software-Based Self-Regulation

The software approach is less threatening and, therefore, more user-friendly and closer to the user. This means that it can either be installed by the user on the user's computer or by a network system administrator on a network server. If installed by the user, the user can set the parameters for the level of control needed. At a network level, whether using a firewall or specific software package, controls are set based on general user consensus. Software controls fall into two categories: ratings programs and filtering programs.[30]

Rating programs rate Internet content using the same principle the movie industry uses when rating movies for violence, language, and sexual content. Software rating labels enable Internet content providers to place voluntary labels on their products according to a set of criteria. However, these labels are not uniform throughout the industry, because they are provided by different rating companies, including CyberPatrol, CYBERsitter, Net Nanny, and SurfWatch. They all claim to provide a simple, yet effective rating system for Web sites to protect children and free speech for everyone who publishes on the World Wide Web. These labels are then used by the filtering program on the user's computer or server. The filtering programs always examine each Web document header looking for a label.

Filtering software blocks documents and Web sites that contain materials designated on a filter list, usually bad words and URLs. Filters are either client based, where a filter is installed on a user's computer or server based, where the filters are centrally located and maintained. Server-based filters offer better security because they are not easy to tamper with. Even though filtering software, both server based and client based, has recently become very popular, it still has serious problems and drawbacks like inaccuracies in labeling, restrictions on unrated material and just mere deliberate exclusion of certain Web sites by an individual or individuals. Inaccuracies have many sources. Some Web sites are blocked because they are near a file with some adult content. For example, if some materials are in the same directory as the file with adult content, the Web site with the file without adult content may be blocked. Sometimes Web sites are blocked because they contain words deemed to be distasteful. Such words are sometimes foreignwords with completely different meanings. Further, the decision of the user to either block or unblock unrated materials can limit the user's access to useful information. Blocking software works best only if all web materials are rated. But as we all know, with hundreds of thousands of Web sites submitted everyday, it is impossible to rate all material on the Internet, at least at the moment.

Mass Moral and Ethics Education

Perhaps one of the most viable tools to prevent and curb illegal cyberspace activities, we believe, is mass moral and ethics education. This strong belief we have about the value of teaching moral and ethics to all computer users explains and justifies our inclusion of Chapters 2 through 4. In these chapters we emphasized the importance of having a strong moral and ethics background and how this creates a strong person with character. We are very aware that character education is not easy and that schools across the United States have been struggling with this issue. However, we believe character education should not be left to the schools. Character education should start in the home. There must be a strong family role in character education. Without this vital component, there is limited value in character education and there will continue to be the controversy we have today about it.

Although we advocate a strong mass moral and ethics education both at home and in school, we are also aware of our diverse society and the difficulties that come with that. However, the sooner we face these problems head-on the better, because with modern technology and the forces of globalization, there is no turning back. Societies the world over are heading to diversity full steam.

There are many people not convinced that character education alone can do the job. To them we say, let us devise a strong framework that involves all of us—the parents, the teachers, and you and I—to educate our children about this new technology, the best use of it, and its perils. If action is to be taken, now is the time to do so.

Formal character education should target the whole length of the education spectrum from kindergarten through college. The focus and contact, however, will differ depending on the selected level. For example, in elementary education, it is appropriate to educate kids about the dangers of information misuse and computer ethics in general, and the content and the delivery of that content are measured for that level. In high school where the students are more mature and curious, the content and the delivery system is more focused and more forceful. The approach changes in college because here the students are more focused on their majors and the intended education should reflect this.

Occasional or continuous education is based on the idea that teaching responsible use of information in general, and computer ethics in particular, is a lifelong process. This responsibility should be and is usually passed on to professionals. There are a variety of ways professions enforce this education with their members. For many traditional professions, this is done through the introduction and enforcement of professional codes, guidelines, and canons. Other professions supplement their codes with a requirement of in-service training sessions and refresher courses. Quite a number of professions require licensing as a means of ensuring continuing education of its members.

Reporting Centers

The recent skyrocketing rise in e-attacks has prompted authorities looking after the welfare of the general public to open up e-attack reporting centers. The purpose of these centers is to collect all relevant information on cyber attacks and make that information available to the general public. The centers also function as the first point of contact whenever one suspects or has confirmed an electronic attack. Centers also act as advice-giving centers for those who want to learn more about measures to take to prevent, detect, and recover from attacks.

In the United States, there are several federally supported and privately funded reporting centers including the NIST Computer Security Resource Clearinghouse, the Federal Computer Incident Response Capacity, the Center for Education and Research in Information Assurance and Security, the Carnegie-Mellon Emergency Response Team, the FedCIRC, and the National Infrastructure Protection Center. These centers fall into two categories:

(i)   Non–law enforcement centers that collect, index, and advise the population of all aspects of cyber attacks including prevention, detection, and survivability.

(ii) Law enforcement centers that act as national clearinghouses for computer crime, linking up directly with other national and international computer emergency response teams to monitor and assess potential threats. In addition, law enforcement centers may provide training for local law enforcement officials in cooperation with private industry and international law enforcement agencies. These centers do not only focus on government break-ins but also on those in the private sector, and they cover any crimes perpetrated over the wires, including those involving telephones.[31]

Advisories

The rise in e-attacks has also prompted private industry and government agencies to work together to warn the public of the dangers of e-attacks and of the steps to take to remove the vulnerabilities thereby lessening the chances of being attacked. Both major software and hardware manufacturers have been very active and prompt in posting, sending, and widely distributing advisories, vulnerability patches, and antivirus software whenever their products are hit. Cisco, a major Internet infrastructure network device manufacturer, has been calling and e-mailing its customers, mainly Internet service providers (ISPs), worldwide notifying them of the possibilities of e-attacks that target Cisco's products. It also informs its customers of software patches that can be used to resist or repair those attacks. It has also assisted in the dissemination of vital information to the general public through its Web sites concerning those attacks and how to prevent and recover from them. On the software front

Microsoft, the most affected target in the software arena, has similarly been active, posting, calling, and e-mailing its customers with vital and necessary information on how to prevent and recover from attacks targeting its products. Besides the private sector, public sector reporting centers have also been active, sending advisories of impending attacks and techniques to recover from attacks.

Ad Hoc

There are many other efforts by groups, organizations, and individuals that we have not so far discussed. In this section let us look at some of these.

The Role of Application Service Providers

Businesses that choose to install computer networks soon find that they are in for a shocking surprise: The cost of the associated equipment is only the tip of the monetary iceberg. The major cost of owning a network is the preventive and reactionary maintenance and the people it takes to keep the network running efficiently. Application service providers (ASPs), is a new industry that has arisen over the past few years to alleviate the problems associated with trying to keep up with computer networks. They take most of the network functions, including security, outside the business to a centralized location where efficient and reliable computers to take over the job of providing data storage, application software, data backup, virus checks, and a host of other functions that would normally be performed by the equipment and people in the business. Small businesses especially do not have the capacity or resources to do this. Teams of network specialists in all areas of network functionalities are available around the clock.

Patching

Quite often companies release software to the public only to later find errors and loopholes through which attackers can gain access to the resources on which the software is running. Upon becoming aware of these errors and loopholes, companies issue patches in order to plug those errors. Security chiefs, system administrators, and individuals should look for the most up-to-date patches from software manufacturers and vendors.

Individual Responsibility

Newly installed operating systems on their first runs enable all available networking features of the computer system, giving hackers a chance to explore system vulnerabilities. It is advisable for all individuals to play their role by turning off all unneeded network services when installing a new operating system.

Chapter 9

Security and Privacy in Online Social Networks

LEARNING OBJECTIVES:

After reading this chapter, the reader should be able to:
- Understand the concepts of social networks.
- Learn about the growth of social networks.
- Understand security issues in social networks.
- Understand privacy issues in social networks.
- Learn the ethical framework of cyberspace.

Online Social Networks (OSNs)

A social network is a social mesh or structure consisting of individuals (or organizations) called "nodes." The nodes are then connected together by one or more specific types of interdependency, such as friendship, kinship, common attribute such as interest, like and dislike, common relationships, beliefs, knowledge or prestige.[1] The concept of social networking is not new. Sociologists and psychologists have been dealing with and analyzing social networks for generations. In fact social networks have been in existence since the beginning of man. Prehistoric man formed social networks for different reasons including security, access to food and the social wellbeing.

Online social networks (OSNs) are social networks with underlining communication infrastructure links enabling the connection of the interdependencies between the network nodes either digital or analog. The discussion in this chapter will focus on these OSNs. In particular we will focus on two types of online social networks:

- The traditional OSNs such as Facebook and MySpace. Many of these can be accessed via mobile devices without the capability of dealing with mobile content, and

161

- The Mobile OSNs (mOSNs) which are newer OSNs that can be accessed via mobile devices and can deal with the new mobile context.

The interdependency between nodes in the OSNs support social network services among people as nodes. These interdependencies as relations among people participating in the network services define the type of OSNs.

Types of Online Social Networks

The growth of the OSNs over the years since the beginning of digital communication, saw them evolving through several types. Let us look at the most popular types using a historical chronology.

The chat network was born out of the digital chatting anchored on a *chat room*. The chat room was and still is a virtual room where people "gather" just to chat. Most chat rooms have open access policies meaning that anyone interested in chatting or just reading others' chats may enter the chat room. People can "enter" and "exit" any time during the chats. At any one time several threads of the public chats may be going on. Each individual in the chat room is given a small window on his or her communication device to enter a few lines of text contributing to one or more of the discussion threads. This communication occurs in real time and whatever every one submits to the chat room can be seen by anyone in the chat room.

Chat rooms also have a feature where a participating individual can invite another individual currently in the public chat room into a private chat room where the two can continue with limited "privacy." To be a member of the chat room you must create a user name and members of the chat room will know you by that. Frequent chatters will normally become acquaintances based on user names. Some chat room software allows users to create and upload their profiles so that users can know you more via your profile.

Although chat rooms by their own nature are public and free for all, some are monitored for specific compliance based usually on attributes like topics under discussion.

With the coming of more graphical based online services, the use of chat room is becoming less popular especially to youth.

Another online social network is the blog network. "Blogs" are nothing more than people's online journals. Avid bloggers keep diaries of daily activities. These diaries sometimes are specific on one thread of interest to the blogger or a series of random logs of events during a specific activity. Some blogs are comment on specific topics. Some bloggers have a devoted following depending on the issues.

The Instant Messaging Network (IMN) supports real time communication between two or more individuals. Like chat rooms, each participant in the IMN must have a user name. To IM an individual, one must know that individual's username or screen name. The initiator of the IM is provided with a small window to type the message and the recipient is also provided with a similar window to reply to the message. The transcript of the interchange is kept scrolling up both users' screens. Unlike the chat room however, these exchanges of short messages are private. Like in Chat Networks, some IMN allow users to keep profiles of themselves.

Online Social Networks (OSNs) are a combination of all the network types we have discussed above and other highly advanced online features with advanced graphics. There are several of these social networks including Facebook, Twitter, Myspace, Friendster, YouTube, Flickr, and LinkedIn. Since these networks grew out of those we have seen before, many of the features of these networks are like those we have discussed in the above networks. For example, users in these networks can create profiles that include their graphics and other enclosures and upload them to their network accounts. They must have a username or screen name. Also communication, if desired, can occur in real time as if one is using chat or IM capabilities. In additional to real time, these networks also give the user the delayed and archiving features so that the users can store and search for information. Because of these additional archival and search capabilities, network administrators have fought with the issues of privacy and security of users as we will see later in this chapter. As a way to keep users data safe, profiles can be set to a private setting, thus limiting access to private information by unauthorized users.

Types of OSN Services

OSNs have been growing in popularity, along with the growth of the Internet, because of the growing popularity with the services these networks are offering to the users. Some of the more durable and most popular of these services are:

- Creating and accessing users profiles: A profile in general terms is an outlined view of an object. A personal profile in particular is an informal biography or a sketch of the life and character of a person. Since the beginning of the growth of social networks, profiles of users have been central to social networks. Social networks have provided differing capabilities of presenting and accessing users profiles.
- Search in social graph: The search feature in social networks makes it

possible to tag user profiles and other user provided data so that search engines can crawl through the social graph in the network to pick up metadata and links to other profiles.

- Updates: The update feature helps users to constantly update their profiles and add new information into the social graph. This helps users to keep track of the status of other users.

The type of services a social network offers helps in creating user interest groups called "tribes." Major tribes are created in the following areas of interests:

- Social
- Business
- Religious
- Ethnicity
- Profession

There is no limit on the number of tribes a social network may have as long as they are members to create it. And tribes are not restricted to special social networks although some networks are more known by specific tribes than others. Within each tribe, entities can share one or more relations. The more relations two entities have and how frequent these ties are maintained, the closer the pair becomes and the stronger the corroboration between them and the more intimate information and resources they share. Strong collaboration creates cohesive tribes. As interactions and collaborations between pairs of entities and within tribes grow, a strong sense of belonging start to develop among the pairs and within tribes. These feelings of belonging and of community among pairs and within tribes may lead to greater commitment of individual entities to the others or the tribe which in turn may lead to change in behavior as the individual gets closer to the others within the tribe.

The Growth of Online Social Networks

OSNs have blossomed as the Internet exploded. The history and the growth of OSNs have mirrored and kept in tandem with the growth of the Internet. At the infant age of the Internet, computer-mediated communication services like Usenet, ARPANET, LISTSERV, bulletin board services (BBS) helped to start the growth of the current OSNs as we know them today. Let us now see how these contributed to the growth of OSNs.

BITNET was an early world leader in network communications for the research and education communities, and helped lay the groundwork for the subsequent introduction of the Internet, especially outside the United States.[2] Both BITNET and Usenet, invented around the same time in 1981 by Ira Fuchs and Greydon Freeman at the City University of New York (CUNY), were both "store-and-forward" networks. BITNET was originally named for the phrase "Because It's There Net," later updated to "Because It's Time Net"[3] on the IBM Virtual Machine (VM) mainframe operating system. But it was later emulated on other popular operating systems like DEC VMS and Unix. What made BITNET so popular was its support of a variety of mailing lists supported by the LISTSERV software.

BITNET was updated in 1987 to BITNET II to provide a higher bandwidth network similar to the NSFNET. However, by 1996, it was clear that the Internet was providing a range of communication capabilities that fulfilled BITNET's roles, so CREN ended their support and the network slowly faded away.[4]

A Bulletin Board System (BBS) is a software running on a computer allowing users on computer terminals far away to login and access the system services like uploading and downloading files and reading news and contribution of other members through emails or public bulletin boards. In "Electronic Bulletin Boards, A Case Study: The Columbia University Center for Computing Activities," Janet F. Asteroff[5] reports that the components of computer conferencing that include private conferencing facilities, electronic mail, and electronic bulletin boards started earlier than the electronic bulletin board (BBS). Asteroff writes that the concept of an electronic bulletin board began around 1976 through ARPANET at schools such as the University of California at Berkeley, Carnegie Mellon University, and Stanford University. These electronic bulletin boards were first used in the same manner as physical bulletin boards, i.e., help wanted, items for sale, public announcements, and more. But electronic bulletin boards soon became a forum for user debates on many subjects because of the ability of the computer to store and disseminate information to many people in text form. In its early years, BBS connections were via telephone lines and modems. The cost of using them was high, hence they tended to be local. As the earlier form of the World Wide Web, BBS use receded as the Web grew.

LISTSERV started in 1986 as an automatic mailing list server software which broadcasts emails directed to it to all on the list. The first Listserv was conceived of by Ira Fuchs from BITNET and Dan Oberst from EDUCOM (later EDUCAUSE), and implemented by Ricky Hernandez also of EDUCOM, in order to support research mailing lists on the BITNET academic research network.[6]

By the year 2000, LISTSERV ran on computers around the world managing more than 50,000 lists, with more than 30 million subscribers, delivering more than 20 million messages a day over the Internet.[7]

As time went on and technology improved, other online services came along to supplement and always improve on the services of whatever was in use. Most of the new services were commercially driven. Most of them were moving towards and are currently on the web. These services including news, shopping, travel reservations and others were the beginning of the web-based services we are enjoying today. Since they were commercially driven, they were mostly offered by ISPs like AOL, Netscape, Microsoft and the like. As the Internet grew millions of people flocked onto it and the web and services started moving away from ISP to fully fledged online social network companies like Facebook, Flicker, Napster, LinkedIn, Twitter and others.

Security and Privacy

Privacy is a human value consisting of four rights. These rights are solitude, the right to be alone without disturbances; anonymity, the right to have no public personal identity; intimacy, the right not to be monitored; and reserve, the right to control one's personal information, including the dissemination methods of that information. As humans, we assign a lot of value to these four rights. In fact, these rights are part of our moral and ethical systems. With the advent of the Internet, privacy has gained even more value as information has gained value. The value of privacy comes from its guardianship of the individual's personal identity and autonomy.

Autonomy is important because humans need to feel that they are in control of their destiny. The less personal information people have about an individual, the more autonomous that individual can be, especially in decision making. However, other people will challenge one's autonomy depending on the quantity, quality, and value of information they have about that individual. People usually tend to establish relationships and associations with individuals and groups that will respect their personal autonomy, especially in decision making.

As information becomes more imperative and precious, it becomes more important for individuals to guard their personal identity. Personal identity is a valuable source. Unfortunately, with rapid advances in technology, especially computer technology, it has become increasingly difficult to protect personal identity.

Privacy Issues in OSNs

Privacy can be violated, anywhere including in online social network communities, through intrusion, misuse of information, interception of information, and information matching.[8] In online communities, intrusion, as an invasion of privacy, is a wrongful entry, a seizing, or acquiring of information or data belonging to other members of the online social network community. Misuse of information is all too easy. While online, we inevitably give off our information to whomever asks for it in order to get services. There is nothing wrong with collecting personal information when it is authorized and is going to be used for a legitimate reason. Routinely information collected from online community members, however, is not always used as intended. It is quite often used for unauthorized purposes, hence an invasion of privacy. As commercial activities increase online, there is likely to be stiff competition for personal information collected online for commercial purposes. Companies offering services on the Internet may seek new customers by either legally buying customer information or illegally obtaining it through eavesdropping, intrusion, and surveillance. To counter this, companies running these online communities must find ways to enhance the security of personal data online.

As the number and membership in online social networks skyrocketed, the issues of privacy and security of users while online and the security of users' data while off-line have taken center stage. The problems of online social networking have been exhibited by the already high and still growing numbers especially of young people who pay little to no attention to privacy issues for themselves or others. Every passing day, there is news about and growing concerns over breaches in privacy caused by social networking services. Many users are now worried that their personal data is being misused by the online service providers. All these privacy issues can be captured as follows:

- Sharing of personal information with all OSN users:
  - Users in the network give out too much personal information without being aware who might wrongly use that information. Sexual predators are known to use information from teens on these networks. Currently many of the OSNs are working with law enforcement to try to prevent such incidents.[9] Information such as street address, phone number, and instant messaging names are routinely disclosed to an unknown population in cyberspace.
  - Ease of access to OSNs. Currently it is very easy for anyone to set up an account on anyone of these networks with no requirements to specific identifications. This can lead to identity theft or impersonation.[10]
  - Privacy threat resulting from placing too much personal information in the hands of large corporations or governmental bodies, allowing a profile to be produced on an individual's behavior on which detrimental decisions may be taken.[11]
  - Updating profiles with current activities poses a great threat, for example,

updating your profile informing people of your whereabouts.

- Lack of precise rules by the OSNs on who should use which data.
- Leakage of private information to third-parties:
  - ° On many of these networks, information altered or removed by a user may in fact be retained and/or passed on to third parties.[12]
    - Inter-linkages in OSNs. In their paper "(Under)mining Privacy in Social Networks," Monica Chew, Dirk Balfanz and Ben Laurie of Google, Inc., point to three distinct areas where the highly-interlinked world of social networking sites can compromise user privacy. They are[13]:
  - ° Lack of control over activity streams: An *activity stream,* according to the authors, is a collection of events associated with a single user including changes a user makes to his or her profile page, the user adding or running a particular application on the social networking site, news items shared, or communication with friends. Activity streams may compromise a user's privacy in two ways:
    - A user may not be aware of all the events that are fed into their activity streams in which case the user lacks control over those streams.
    - A user may not be aware of the audience who can see their activity streams in which case the user lacks control over the audience who could see the activity stream.
      - ° Unwelcome linkage: *Unwelcome linkage* occurs when links on the Internet reveal information about an individual that they had not intended to reveal. Unwelcome linkage may occur wherever graphs of hyperlinks on the World Wide Web are automatically created to mirror connections between people in the real world. Maintaining separation of individual activities and different personae is important in OSNs.
  - ° Deanonymization of users through merging of social graphs: OSN sites tend to extract a lot of personally identifiable information from people such as birth date and address. With this information, it is possible to de-anonymize users by comparing such information across social networking sites, even if the information is partially obfuscated in each OSN.

As the growth in Online Social Networks continues unabated, there is a new comer in the mix that is making the already existing problems more complex. The newcomer is mobile devices with cell phones which are explodng in popularity. These new devices are not only small and very portable but they are also increasingly becoming smarter with additional services like voice communication, playing music and videos, accessing the Internet over WiFi and have their own additional communication networks.[14] Not surprising, an increasing number of accesses to OSNs are now via mobile devices. In addition to the privacy issues mentioned above in traditional OSNs,[15] new issues arising because of these new technologies include:

- The presence of a user. Unlike in the most traditional OSNs where users were not automatically made aware of the presence of their friends, most mobile OSN (mOSN) now allow users to indicate their presence via a "check-in" mechanism, where a user establishes their location at a particular time. According to Krishnamurthy and Wills,[16] the indication of presence allows their friends to expect quick response and this may lead to meeting new people who are members of the same mOSN. Although the feature of automatic locate by oneself is becoming popular, it allows leakage of personal private information along two tracks: the personal information that may be sent and the destination to which it could be sent.
  - Geographical location. This is a feature that is widespread in the mobile environment. However, users must be aware that allowing their location to be known by friends, their friends who are currently online on this mOSN, their friends in other mOSNs and others may lead to leakage of personal information to third-parties.
  - Interaction potential between mOSNs and traditional OSNs. According to Krishnamurthy and Wills,[17] such connections are useful to users who, while interacting with a mOSN can expect some of their actions to show up on traditional OSNs and be visible to their friends there. However, a lot of their personal information can leak to unintended users of both the traditional OSNs and the mOSNs.

Strengthening Privacy in OSNs

As more and more people join OSNs and now the rapidly growing mOSNs, there is a growing need for more protection to users. Chew et al. suggest the following steps needed to be taken[18]:

- Both OSN and mOSN applications should be explicit about which user activities automatically generate events for their activity streams.
- Users should have control over which events make it into their activity streams and be able to remove events from the streams after they have been added by an application.
- Users should know who the audience of their activity streams is and should also have control over selecting the audience of their activity streams.

- Both OSN and mOSN applications should create activity stream events which are in sync with user expectation.

Other suggestions that may help in this effort are:

- Use of secure passwords.
- User awareness of the privacy policies and terms of use for their OSNs and mOSNs.
- Both OSNs and mOSNs providers should devise policies and enforce existing laws to allow some privacy protection for users while on their networks.

Chapter 10

Security in Mobile Systems

LEARNING OBJECTIVES:

After reading this chapter, the reader should be able to:
- Understand the architecture of mobile networks.
- Learn about the operating systems upon which mobile systems run.
- Understand security issues in mobile systems.
- Understand privacy issues in mobile systems.
- Learn the ethical framework most suited for mobile systems.

Introduction

A mobile communication systems consists of two or more of the following devices, running specifically developed software to sustain, for a time, a wireless communication link between them: mobile telephone, broadly construed here to include devices based on Code Division Multiple Access (CDMA), Time Division Multiple Access (TDMA), Global System for Mobile Communications (GSM), and Wireless Personal Digital Assistants (WPDA) digital technologies and follow-ons, as well as satellite telephones and email appliances. Mobile communication systems are revolutionising the world, shrinking the world to between two or more small handheld mobile devices. The rapid changes in communication technologies, revolutionary changes in software and the growth of large powerful communication network technologies all have eased communication and brought it to large swaths of the globe. The high end competition between the mobile telecommunication operators is resulting in plummeting device prices and quickly developing smart phone technology, and a growing number of undersea cables and cheaper satellites technologies are bringing Internet access to almost every one of the global rural poor faster than many had anticipated.

Current Major Mobile Operating Systems

To fully understand the working of mobile systems, one has to start with understanding the role operating systems play in the infrastructure and the ecosystem of mobile systems. The mobile operating system, commonly called the mobile OS, or just mOS, is an operating system that is specifically designed to run on mobile devices such as mobile phones, smartphones, PDAs, tablet computers and other handheld devices. The mobile operating system is the software platform on top of which an ecosystem of other programs, called application programs, can run on mobile devices. The mOS performs the same functionalities as its bigger brother that runs laptops and PCs. The differences, however, are in the size of memory an ordinary and modern operating system will need to perform those functions. In the case of mOS, we are talking small sizes for everything. In additional to running in limited everything, modern mOSs must combine the required features of a personal computer with touch-screen, cellular, Bluetooth, WiFi, GPS navigation, camera, video camera, speech recognition, voice recorder, music player, near field communication, personal digital assistant (PDA), and many others still in development.

Mobile operating systems are as crucial and central to the running and security of the mobile device as they are in the bigger, less mobile devices like PCs and laptops. When it comes to security related issues, the mobile device is as secure as its operating system. So every mobile device integrates in its operating systems as much security as it can possibly carry without sacrificing speed, ease of use and functionalities expected by consumers. Most mobile operating systems are similar in a number of ways to their older brothers, the operating systems in the PCs and laptops, which have seen and continue to see growing security problems like backdoors, spyware, worms, Trojans, and others. The best way to protect these devices with mOS is not to wait and respond to attacks, as we did with laptops and PC, but rather to anticipate what kind of attacks can occur and plan for them. Quick preemptive measures like these probably could help safeguard the mobile device a lot faster.

At the writing of this chapter, the most popular mOSs are: Android, Symbian, iOS, BlackBerry OS, Bada and Windows Phone. Of course they are many others. Let us very briefly look at a few of these in a limited details.[1]

Android

Android is a Linux-derived OS backed by Google, originally developed by a small start-up company, along with major hardware and software developers (such as Intel, HTC, ARM, Samsung, Motorola and eBay, to name a few), that form the Open Handset Alliance. Android's major features, at the time of this writing, include:

—Multitasking
—"Zoom-to-fill" screen compatibility mode
—Support of connectivity technologies: GSM/EDGE, IDEN, CDMA, EV-DO, UMTS, Bluetooth, Wi-Fi, LTE, NFC and WiMAX
—Threaded SMS view
—Multi-Touch input support
—Notification bar
—Customizable home screen and keyboard.

iOS

iOS is Apple's mobile operating system, originally developed for the iPhone, it has since been extended to support other Apple devices such as the iPod touch, iPad and Apple TV. iOS is not licensed for installation on third-party hardware. Interaction with the OS includes gestures such as swipe, tap, pinch, and reverse pinch, all of which have specific definitions within the context of the iOS operating system and its multi-touch interface. iOS's major features, at the time of this writing, include:

—Multitasking
—A dock at the bottom of the screen where users can pin their most frequently used apps
—Notification Center (similar to notification bar)
—iMessage (allow iPod touch, iPhone, and iPad users to communicate, much like a chat service only used between these devices)
—Newsstand
—Location based reminders (get an alert as soon as you enter a particular location/area)
—WI-Fi Sync
—Improved multi-touch input gestures

Windows Phone 7.5 ("Mango")

Windows Phone 7.5 is a major software update for Windows Phone, the mobile operating system, by Microsoft. Windows Phone OS's major features, at the time of this writing, include:

—Multitasking
—Dynamic Live tile information

—Facebook Places check-in support
—Windows Live Messenger and Facebook Chat integration
—All in one thread view: SMS, MMS, IMs, Facebook Chat together in
  one conversation
—Threaded email conversations support
—Built-in voice-to-text/text-to-voice functionality
—Twitter and Facebook integration
—Geolocation support
—Multi-Touch input support
—Internet Explorer 9

Bada (Samsang)

"Bada" is a Korean word meaning "ocean" and "seashore." The Bada operating system was first introduced at Mobile World Congress 2010 in Barcelona in February 2010, running the Samsung S8500 Wave. Bada's major features, at the time of this writing, include:

—Multitasking
—Multi-Touch input support
—Notification bar
—Multiple homescreens with widgets support
—Improved user Interface

BlackBerry OS/RIM

BlackBerry OS is a proprietary mobile operating system, developed by Research in Motion for its BlackBerry line of smartphone handheld devices. The operating system provides multitasking and supports specialized input devices that have been adopted by RIM for use in its handhelds, particularly the trackwheel, trackball, trackpad and touchscreen. The BlackBerry platform is perhaps best known for its native support for corporate email, through MIDP 1.0 and, more recently, a subset of MIDP 2.0, which allows complete wireless activation and synchronization with Microsoft Exchange, Lotus Domino, or Novell GroupWise email, calendar, tasks, notes, and contacts, when used with BlackBerry Enterprise Server. The BlackBerry OS's major features, at the time of this writing, include:

—Multitasking
—NFC (near field communication)
—Ajax and HTML5 support

—Notifications preview on homescreen
—Multi-touch support (for touch screen)
—Geotagging
—Liquid Graphics technology, which in OS 7 delivers high resolution displays, slicker graphics and a more responsive touchscreen, as compared to OS 6
—Integrated BlackBerry Messenger 6 and Facebook Application
—40 percent faster web browsing experience in OS 7 as compared to OS 6, and 100 percent when compared to OS 5

Symbian

Symbian mOS is used on more phones and smartphones globally than any other mobile OS. Symbian's strengths include its longevity, widespread use, and maturity as an operating system. With its most recent release, Symbian 9, increased emphasis has been placed on improved e-mail functionality, enhanced capabilities to assist third-party developers, and additional security functions.

Security in the Mobile Ecosystems

As mobile devices become more and more ubiquitous, the risk for using them is increasing. They are increasingly holding and storing more private data, personal and business, and they are roaming in public spaces on public networks with limited security and cryptographic protocols to protect the data. In fact the kind of security threats towards these devices is similar and probably more than that experienced by PCs and laptops in their heydays. The security threats to these mobile devices are comparable if not more than those facing servers in that these devices can remain on without user attention and are always connected to a network. Also, because these devices have the ability to roam on several networks, there is a wider sphere of attack beset by geographical, legal and moral differences. Because of the high demand for global connectivity, especially in developing countries, service providers are responding with zeal to consolidate networks and standardize communication protocols, thus making it easier for these devices to roam in large spaces and networks, creating fertile ground for attackers. The penetration trend of these smart mobile devices is not limited to faraway rural places, but more scary is their rapid penetration on enterprise IT spaces where security is paramount for any device. This extension of smart devices into the enterprise IT spaces is a result of their popularity as they slowly eat away the enterprise laptop as the enterprise mobile device. This in turn is increasingly causing enterprise management to start focusing on their security issues. Although anti-virus client applications have been available and security best practices have been in place for most high level operating systems, this is not the case with small mobile devices. In his article, "New Security Flaws Detected in Mobile Devices," Byron Acohido reports of two recent examinations by Cryptography Research. In one study, Cryptography Research showed how it's possible to eavesdrop on any smartphone or tablet as it is being used to make a purchase, conduct online banking or access a company's virtual private network. Also, McAfee, an anti-virus software company and a division of Intel, showed ways to remotely hack into Apple iOS and steal secret keys and passwords and pilfer sensitive data, including call histories, e-mail and text messages. What is more worrying is the reported fact that the device under attack would not in any way show that an attack is under way. Almost every mobile system user, security experts and law enforcement officials are all anticipating that cyber-gangs will accelerate attacks as consumers and companies begin to rely more heavily on mobile devices for shopping, banking and working. So there is an urgent need for a broader array of security awareness of the community and actions by community to assist in providing all users the highest level of protection.

The smartphone security company Lookout Mobile Security, in its "2011 Mobile Threat Report," discusses security threats to mobile devices in four major areas: application, web-based access, network and physical environments. Major threats are encountered by mobile devices on a daily basis.

Application-Based Threats

For every mobile device, the biggest appealing feature is the ability to run thousands of applications (apps) to accomplish a variety of tasks. These applications are written by unknown people with limited to no allegiance to anybody and taking no command from anyone. Do downloadable applications present the greatest security issues for any mobile device that is capable of downloading software? Application-based threats, in downloadable applications, present a great security risk through malware, software designed with the intent to engage in malicious behavior on a device; spyware, a software designed with the intent to collect or use data without a user's knowledge or approval; functionality features, the device's normal functionality features that reveal or threaten an individual's privacy; and vulnerable applications, software that may have vulnerabilities that can be exploited for malicious purposes.

Web-based Threats

Mobile devices, once on, are continuously roaming in public spaces on public networks with limited security and cryptographic protocols to protect them. In many cases, they are often constantly connected to the Internet for normal web-based services. Under such circumstances, they are exposed to a variety of web-based threats including phishing scams, a way intruders, masquerading as a trustworthy friend in electronic communication like email and text, use web-based services to launch attacks on those devices connected to the web to acquire information such as usernames, passwords, and credit card details and other private data of the device owner; drive-by downloads, pop-ups written by scammers to automatically begin uploading treacherous application as soon as the device visits a web page; and web exploits.

Network Threats

As stated above, once mobile devices are on, they immediately start looking for networks to connect on either cellular networks or the internet. Once connected, they are prone to network exploits.

Physical Threats

Physical threats, unlike threats based on the nature and the functionality of the mobile device, are based on the size and the surroundings of the owner of the mobile device. Such threats include lost or stolen devices—due mainly to the miniaturization of mobile devices.

Operating System Based Threats

A mobile device is as secure as its operating system. We need to note that most operating system threats are specific to the brand. So let us focus on a few known operating system-based threats:

- KDataAtruct—This is a Windows Mobile (WM) operating system problem based on the vulnerability that in WM Microsoft placed all main system functions are in one coredll.dll file so that developers do not have to include the code for functions in their own programs. They just call the coredll addresses of all the APIs it uses into memory space it is allocated. In so doing an address to the list of modules is provided so that the address of the coredll can be determined. From here one can search through memory looking for the virtual address of the API wanted. This can open up the device for exploitation. This vulnerability is exploited by the virus WinCE.Duts.A.

- Pocket IE—another Windows vulnerability found in the small Internet Explorer—commonly known as Pocket IE (PIE), default Web Browser for the WM OSs. The PIE has all the vulnerabilities found in the standard IE for the big brothers PC and laptops. See all these vulnerabilities in the "General Mobile Devices Attack Types" below.
- Jailbreaking—is a process by which a user can alter the phone's operating system to gain full access (or root access) to the operating system and allow applications not officially vetted by Apple's review policies. For example JailbreakMe 3.0 for iOS devices is a non-malicious web page that exploits two vulnerabilities to jailbreak a device.[2]
- DroidDream—is an Android malware that utilizes two exploits, Exploid and RageAgainstTheCage to break out of the Android security sandbox, gain root control of the operating system, and install applications without user intervention.[3]
- Update Attacks—there a growing problem of using application updates as an attack method in the Android Market. A malware writer first releases a legitimate application containing no malware. Once they have a large enough user base, the malware writer updates the application with a malicious version.
- Malvertising—is malicious advertising where an attacker lures victims into downloading malware, especially on the Android Market. They rely on the fact that developers commonly use in-app advertisements to gain more users, so people are used to downloading apps via advertisements.
- Other threats include flowed shell model (iOS), root account (iOS), static addressing (iOS), static systems (iOS) and reuse of code (iOS).

General Mobile Devices Attack Types

Besides specific operating systems' attack discussed above, there also major general mobile system attacks launched against specific mobile devices or operating systems or applications. Some of these, mostly carry-overs from the laptop and PC era, include the following:

Denial-of-service (DDoS)

This technique is meant to cause system disruption so that the device, the service or the network on which the device operates cannot complete the operation under way involving the device.

Phone Hacking

This is a technique used to intercept phone calls or voicemail messages, either by accessing the voicemail or text messages of a mobile phone without the knowledge or consent of the phone's owner. You may recall the *News of The World* phone hacking events in the United Kingdom.

Mobile Malware/Virus

A mobile malware or virus is software that deliberately targets mobile phones or wireless-enabled PDAs.

Spyware

Spyware is a type of malware that automatically installs itself or in some cases is installed manually on computers so that it continuously or periodically collects information about a range or one event, user, or application without the owner's knowledge.

Exploit

An exploit is software code that takes advantage of a bug, glitch or vulnerability to cause unintended or unanticipated consequences to occur on computer software, hardware, or something electronic.

Everything Blue

The following are some of the malware and spyware that take advantage of Bluetooth technology. They include the following[4]:

- Bluejacking—this is similar to spamming but here, the criminal sends unsolicited messages to the victim's device, which opens up communication between the paired devices. This can lead to the attacker gaining access to the victim's device.
- Bluesnarfing—a form of Bluetooth hacking which can allow a hacker to gain access to the victim's device's contact list, text messages, emails and other vital information. The hacker can even use brute force attack, even if the device is invisible, to guess the victim's MAC address.
- Bluebugging—is the type of attack, like a Trojan Horse, where the hacker uses sophisticated attack techniques to gain control of the vic-

tim's mobile device. Once in control, the attacker can do anything with the mobile device.

- Bluetoothing—this is social engineering, where a hacker can use traditional social engineering tricks to masquerade as the legitimate user of the mobile device.
- BlueBumping—is an attack involving two mobile devices. The attacking device gets the victim to accept a connection for a trivial data exchange such as a picture, then uses that pairing to attack other services. While the connection is still open, the attacker requests for a link key regeneration which it uses later for access to the victim's device, thus getting full access to any of the services on the victim's device.
- BlueChopping—is an attack that targets Bluetooth piconet (an ad-hoc Bluetooth network linking other Bluetooth devices. It allows one *master* device to interconnect with many other active *slave* devices) for disruption by spoofing one of the participating piconet slaves, leading to confusion of the master's internal state and thus disrupting the piconet.
- BlueDumping—is the act of sniffing a Bluetooth device's key-exchange by forcing the Bluetooth victim's mobile device to dump its stored link key. Before the sniff, the attacker needs to know the BDADDR of a set of paired devices. To get this, the attacker spoofs the address of one of the devices and connects to the other. Since the attacker has no link key, when the target device requests authentication, the attacker's device will respond with an "HCI_Link_Key_Request_Negative_Reply," which will, in some cases, cause the target device to delete its own link key and go into pairing mode.[5]
- BlueSmucking—is a Bluetooth Denial of Service attack that knocks out some Bluetooth-enabled devices immediately. It is carried out using the old "Ping of Death" but transformed to work in Bluetooth. On the L2CAP (echo request) layer there is the possibility to request an echo from another Bluetooth peer, to check connectivity and to measure round-trip time on the established link. This is possible in Bluetooth because, the l2ping in BlueZ utils allows the user to specify a packet length that is sent to the respective peer. This is done by means of the -s <num> option.[6]
- BlueSniffing—is a Bluetooth version of war driving.

Phishing

Phishing in Bluetooth devices takes the same attempting techniques used in PCs and laptops in that it is intended to acquire information such as usernames, passwords, credit card details and other private data of the device owner by the intruder masquerading as a trustworthy friend in an electronic communication like email and text.

SMiShing

SMiShing is social engineering crime like phishing in that it uses the mobile devices and texts as baits to pull in the mobile device owner to divulge private and sometimes personal information.

Vishing

Vishing is another criminal practice in the social engineering class just like the last two. It mostly uses the mobile device phone features facilitated by Voice over IP (VoIP) to gain access to private personal and financial information from the public for the purpose of financial reward. The term is a combination of "voice" and phishing.

Mitigating Mobile Devices Attacks

With the growing use of mobile devices and the growing trend of employers allowing employees to bring their own devices (BYOD) to work, there is a growing threat and increasingly uneasiness of unmanaged, personal devices accessing sensitive enterprise resources and then connecting these devices to third-party services outside of the enterprise security controls. This potentially exposes the enterprise sensitive data to possible attackers. The security teams in these enterprises are beginning to feel exposed to mobile device security risk, and Small and Medium Businesses (SMBs) do not feel they have adequate tools to assess and mitigate these risks.

There are several security protocols and best practices, however, that can come in handy for situations like this. There are three security components that must form the minimum security requirements for any mobile security management. These components are hardware encryption, remote wiping and the ability to set a passcode policy[7]:

Mobile Device Encryption

The two ways mobile device encryption can be done are through application and hardware encryption.

Application Encryption

In securing mobile devices using applications, encryption protects the mobile device from attacks made on the host device, as well as across network connections end-to-end. There are many vendor solutions for this kind of encryption.

Hardware Encryption

Hardware encryption is an encryption protocol embedded into the hardware by either the original mobile hardware manufacturer like Research in Motion (RIM), the manufacturer of BlackBerry. On the BlackBerry, RIM combines strong Advanced Encryption Standard (AES) and Triple Data Encryption Standard (Triple DES) encryption with a strong mobile device management platform to provide a strong security stance for enterprise BlackBerrys. Similarly, other mobile device manufacturers like Apple, Google, Microsoft and others have corresponding embedded encryptions either in their device operating systems, embedded SIM cards or movable encryption SIM cards.

Mobile Remote Wiping

Mobile remote wiping offers the security IT managers the basic mobile device management capabilities to remotely wipe data from lost mobile device. The remote wipe and other management features are mobile device manufacturer and third-party developed. Many are cross-platform like the Google's Apps Premier and Education Edition which works for iPhones, Nokia E series devices, and Windows Mobile smartphones.

Mobile Passcode Policy

A security policy requiring a passcode tag for devices is the best deal to deal with the growing plethora of devices running different operating systems or different versions of an operating system. A complete mobile security solution should include[8]:

- A firewall to secure the device from attacks and malicious code.
- A VPN to allow flexible means to ensure secure communications for any wireless data traffic.
- An authentication mechanism to ensure that unauthorized persons are not accessing the device if it is lost or stolen.
- Data encryption on the device to ensure that information is not stolen, either physically or electronically.
- Anti-virus software to protect the device from viruses and malware.

Chapter 11

Security in the Cloud

LEARNING OBJECTIVES:

After reading this chapter, the reader should be able to:
- Understand the cloud computing infrastructure
- Learn about cloud computing models
- Learn about software models
- Understand security issues in the cloud
- Understand privacy issues in the cloud
- Learn the ethical framework most suited for the cloud

Introduction

According to the National Institute of Standards and Technology (2011),[1] cloud computing is a model for enabling ubiquitous, convenient, on-demand network access to a shared pool of configurable computing resources like networks, servers, storage, applications and services that can be rapidly provisioned and released with minimal management effort or service provider interaction. So for this chapter, we are going to focus on this model of computing and discuss its benefits and security concerns. This computing model is composed of a number of essential characteristics, three service models, and four deployment models.

Cloud Computing Infrastructure Characteristics

Historically, data center computing models have been based on a client-server model architecture and design, relying firmly on a three-tier architecture design that included access, distribution and core switches, connecting relatively few clients and meeting limited client needs compared to today's cloud services models. In most cases, each server was dedicated to either a single or limited applications and had IP addresses and media access control addresses. This static nature of the application environment worked well and lent itself to manual processes for server deployment or redeployment. According to Jim Metzler and Steve Taylor of Network World (2011), they primarily used a spanning tree protocol to avoid loops. But dramatic advances in the previous years in virtualization technology, distributed computing, rapid improvements and access to high-speed Internet have all dramatically changed the staid nature of the data center. Today's data center, providing cloud services, is anything but staid, as it is bursting with activities and services with distinctly new characteristics that differentiate it from its traditional cousin. For example, its services are now on demand, by the minute or the hour; it is elastic, that is, users can have as much or as little of a service as they want at any given time; and the service is fully managed by the provider, that is, the consumer needs nothing but a personal computer and Internet access. These characteristics are discussed below.

Ubiquitous Network Access

The advances and use of virtualization technology and the availability and access to high speed internet have all helped to change the nature of access to the computing services sought by customers and have also increased in the number of services a customer can select. With more choice also came the high specialization and quality of services that a customer can expert.

Measured Service

Because cloud services are flexible, on demand and elastic, it is important, therefore, for these services to be metered. The concept of metered services allows customers to get what they want in the required amounts at the time they want the service. As part of the metering services, cloud systems automatically control and optimize resource use based on the type of service such as storage, processing, bandwidth and active user accounts and can report these statistics as needed, thus providing transparency for both the provider and consumer.

On-Demand Self-Service

With the rapid and unprecedented use of virtualization technology and the availability and access to high speed internet, the traditional and all other models of acquisition of computing services that demanded perpetual ownership of software or computing hardware and long contracts with employees that helped to use the service, the need for redundancy and outsourcing of services, all diminished and turned into a more flexible model. Consumers of computing services were no longer restricted to having one of the rigid traditional models of either ownership, outsources or boxed services. Now, a consumer is able to not only automatically provision any computing services and capabilities as needed but also can determine the time and how long to use the provisioned services.

Rapid Elasticity

Computing service elasticity means the ability to resize and dynamically scale the virtualized resources at hand such as servers, processors, operating systems and others to meet the customer's on-demand needs. The provider makes sure that there are resources at hand that meet the elastic capabilities to ensure that end-users' requests are continually and promptly met. Amazon's EC2 and IBM ASC are good examples of web service interfaces that allow the customer to obtain and configure capacity with minimal effort.

Resource Pooling

Increased flexibility, access and ease of use usually lead to high and varied demands of services from customers. To meet these new demands, providers usually respond by offering a variety of system resources and services. As noted by Peter Mell and Timothy Grance in the NIST report (2011), the provider's computing resources are pooled to serve multiple consumers using a multi-tenant model, with different physical and virtual resources dynamically assigned and reassigned according to consumer demand.

Others

There are other characteristics common to cloud computing beyond the five discussed. Among these are:

- Massive scale—that the cloud offers the resources at a massive scale on demand.
- Virtualization—in fact this is the linchpin of the cloud technology. The cloud is possible because of virtualization of the fundamental functionalities of the physical machine.
- Free software—or near free software as needed from the cloud.

- Autonomic computing—in a sense that you scale computing resources at a time you want them on the fly.
- Multi-tenancy—because of cloud's massive scale and easy access of those resources, cloud computing can accommodate a large number of users at a time.

Cloud Computing Service Models

Infrastructure as a Service (IaaS)

The process of providing the customer with the ability and capability to manage and control, via a web-based virtual server instance API, with system resources such as starting, stopping, accessing and configuring the virtual servers, operating systems, applications, storage, processing and other fundamental computing resources, is referred to as Infrastructure as a Service (IaaS). In doing all these, however, the consumer does not have access nor control the underlying physical cloud infrastructure.

Platform as a Service (PaaS)

This is a set of software and product development tools hosted on the provider's infrastructure and accessible to the customer via a web-based virtual server instance API. Through this instance, the customer can create applications on the provider's platform over the Internet. Accessing the platform via the web-based virtual instance API protects the resources because the customer cannot manage or control the underlying physical cloud infrastructure, including network, servers, operating systems, or storage.

Software as a Service (SaaS)

Ever since the beginning of computing software, the cost of software has driven software acquisition. Trying to control the cost of software has resulted into software going through several models. The first model was the home developed software where software users developed their own software based on their needs. They owned everything and were responsible for updates and management of it. The second model, the traditional software model, was based on packaged software where the customer acquired a more general purpose software from the provider with a license held by the provider. The provider was responsible for the updates while the customer was responsible for its management. However, sometimes, software producers provide additional support services, the so-called premium support, usually for additional fees. Model three was the Open Source model led by a free software movement starting around the late '80s. By the late 1980s, free software turned into open source with the creation of the Open Source Initiative (OSI). Under the name "open source" philosophy, some for-profit "free software" started to change the model from a purely free software to some form of payment to support the updates of the software. The open source software model transformed the cost of software remarkably. Model Four consisted of Software Outsourcing.

The outsourcing model was in response to the escalating cost of software associated with software management. The component of software management in the overall cost of software was slowly surpassing all the costs of other components of software including licensing and updates. In Model Four, however, software is still licensed from the software company on a perpetual basis; support fees are still paid, but the software producer takes on the responsibility of the management of that software.

Software as a Service (SaaS) became model five. Under SaaS, there is the elimination of the upfront license fee. All software applications are retained by the provider and the customer has access to all applications of choice from the provider via various client devices through either a thin client interface, such as a web browser, a web portal or a virtual server instance API. Also here, like in the previous cloud services, the customer does not manage or control the underlying cloud infrastructure including network, servers, operating systems, storage, or even individual application capabilities, with the possible exception of limited user-specific application configuration settings.

Three Features of SaaS Applications

In particular, software as a service has the following features:

- Scalability—in that it can handle growing amounts of work in a graceful manner.
- Multi-tenancy—in that one application instance may be serving hundreds of companies. This is different from the client-server model from which the cloud computing model grew, and each customer is provisioned their own server running one instance.
- Metadata driven configurability—customers can configure their application through metadata

Cloud Computing Deployment Models

There are three cloud deployment models which are actually cloud types. These are the public, private and the hybrid models.

Public Clouds

Public clouds provide access to computing resources for the general public over the Internet, allowing customers to self-provision resources typically via a web service interface on a pay-as-you-go basis. One of the benefits of public clouds is to offer large pools of scalable resources on a temporary basis without the need for capital investment in infrastructure by the user.

Private Cloud

Unlike public clouds, private clouds give users immediate access to computing resources hosted within an organization's infrastructure and premises. Users, who are usually in some form of a relationship with the cloud owner, choose and scale collections of resources drawn from the private cloud, typically via web service interface, just as with a public cloud. Also the private cloud is deployed within and uses the organization's existing resources and is always behind the organization's firewall subject to the organization's physical, electronic, and procedural security measures. In this case, therefore, private clouds offer a higher degree of security.

Hybrid Cloud

A hybrid cloud combines the computing resources of both the public and private clouds.

Virtualization and Cloud Computing

In computing, virtualization is a process of creating computing resources in effect and performance but not in reality, hence virtual. In computing, virtual resources can be either software or hardware. Software virtualization has historically been used in operating systems where the underlying operating systems creates a number of virtual operating systems, not only clones of itself but even others, to run on the underlying machine and perform tasks at a higher performance level. In hardware, virtualization has been used to create new resources like servers, storage devices and others. The potential power of virtualization is substantially increasing the performance of computing systems such as hardware and software through division of the underlying physical computing resources into many equally powerful virtual machines, thus scaling up the performance and creating elasticity of many computing systems. With virtualization, computation and storage can be scaled up or down with ease.

Virtualization is a fundamental feature in cloud computing as it allows applications from different customers to run on different virtual machines; hence, providing separation and protection.

Benefits of Cloud Computing

Cloud computing as a model of computing is very exciting and has tremendous benefits for the computing community. It is not only exciting when you come to learn it, but it also has an array of benefits including but not limited to leveraging on a massive scale, homogeneity, virtualization, low cost software, service orientation, and advanced security technologies.

Reduced Cost

The leading benefit of cloud computing for an enterprise is in cost savings. Whether it is a small, medium or large scale manufacturing business, there are essential cost benefits in using a cloud model for most of the company's computing needs. The biggest issue is the fact that cloud computing is operated remotely off company premises except for a few devices needed for accessing the cloud resources via a web portal. This means that company personnel can do the same amount of work on fewer computers by having higher utilization, save on not housing data centers on premises, save on personnel for running the data center, and save on expenses that would normally be essential for running a data center on the premises. There are also savings on power consumption since there are few computers on premises. Currently, servers are used at only 15 percdent of their capacity in many companies, and 80 percent of enterprise software expenditure is on installation and maintenance of software. Use of cloud applications can reduce these costs from 50 percent to 90 percent.[2]

Automatic Updates

Because most businesses and personal transactions depend on software, there is a need to keep updating software for efficiency and profitability and as a changing business functionality. The cost of software updates and management has always been on the rise, usually surpassing the cost of new software. For companies to stay competitive and in many cases afloat, they must be consistently updating and changing software. The business of software updates and software management and licensing is a big drain on company resources. So having automatic updates and management from the cloud provider can be a great relief to any company. But updates are not limited to only software. Also not worrying about hardware updates is cost-effective for companies.

Green Benefits of Cloud Computing

Cloud computing energy consumption has seen a vigorous debate, pitting those claiming that cloud computing is gobbling up resources as large cloud and social networking sites need daily megawatts of power to feed insatiable computing needs versus those who claim that the computing model is indeed saving power from millions of servers left idling daily and consuming more power. We will discuss this more in the coming sections. For now, we think that there are indeed savings in power consumption by cloud computing.

Remote Access

With a web portal access to the cloud, company employees may be able to work while they are on the road, home or in the office. This is of great benefit to the company so that there is no down time because somebody is not in the office.

Disaster Relief

Many companies live in constant fear of disasters occurring when they have company vital data stored on premises. No one likes to be a victim of large-scale catastrophes such as hurricanes, earthquakes, fires or terrorist attacks. Such misfortunes can create havoc to companies' vital data and disrupt operations even if there were limited physical damage. Additionally, there are smaller disasters like computer crashes and power outages that can also wreak havoc on a company's vital data. While this is possible, there many companies, especially small ones, that may not even have a disaster recovery plan, and some that have a plan may not be able to execute it effectively. This fear can be overcome with investments in cloud technology. A company's vital backup data can be safely stored on secure data centers on the cloud instead of in the company's server room.

Self-Service Provisioning

Cloud computing allows users to deploy their own virtual sets of computing resources like servers, network, and storage as needed without the delays, competency and complications typically involved in physical resource acquisition, installation and management. The cloud owners, irrespective of their physical location, not only can provide all the computing resources an organization needs but also have the necessary capacity to monitor, manage and respond to the organization's daily and hourly infrastructure, software and platform requirements.

Scalability

Because of the minute-by-minute monitoring capability of cloud computing of an organization's computing needs and the ability to increase or reduce the required resources as the demand increases or decreases, cloud computing offer the best infrastructure, platform and software scalability that cannot be matched in any owned computing facility.

Reliability and Fault-Tolerance

Because the cloud provider, with qualified professionals and experience, monitors the computing requirements of a client company and can easily scale to demand, cloud computing offers a high degree of reliability and fault-tolerance.

Ease of Use

To attract more customers, cloud providers have and must make the use interface easy so that customers can scale into the cloud with the least effort.

Skills and Proficiency

Some of the most sought-after assets from a cloud provider are professionalism and a vast skills set for customers. Companies, especially small ones, would pay a high price to get an employee with the skills, efficiency, proficiency and experience found with cloud center staff.

Response Time

Depending on the bandwidth at the company web portal, cloud computing services normally have speed because the computing resources provided are modern and powerful to be able to accommodate a large number of users.

Mobility

Because of web portal interface to the Cloud, cloud computing essentially is a mobile computing platform, allowing the users to access their applications from anywhere.

Increased Storage

Storage is cloud computing's main function. Because of this, it is cheap and readily scalable to need.

Other Benefits

Other benefits include providing a high quality of service (QoS), providing a high quality, well-defined and stable industry standard API and on-demand availability of computing resources based on "at hand" financial contraints.

Security

We are going to discuss this more in the coming section, but cloud computing, because of its individual virtual machines created per use, has a built-in security provision. In addition to these built-in provisions due to virtualization, the cloud model also offers a strong authentication regime at the browser interface gateway, a security mechanism that is individually and quickly set up and torn down as needed, and a strong validation and verification scheme that is expensive to deploy at an individual client-server model.

Cloud Computing Security, Reliability, Availability and Compliance Issues

The cloud computing model as we know it today did not start overnight. The process has taken years, moving through seven software models beginning with in-house software, licensed software normally referred as the traditional model, open source, outsourcing, hybrid, software as a service and finally the Internet model, the last two being part of the cloud computing model. When one carefully examines the cloud servicing model, one does not fail to notice the backward compatibilities or the carryovers of many of the attributes that characterized software through all the models. While this brings the benefits of each one of those software models, also many, if not all, of the software complexity and security issues in those models were carried over into the cloud computing model. Because of this, our first thought was to discuss the security issues in the cloud computing model through the prism of these models. It is tempting but we are going to follow a different path while keeping the reader rooted into the different software models. Security is and continues to be a top issue in the cloud computing model. The other three related issues are performance, compliance and availability. We will discuss all four in this section but since security is the number one issue, we will address it first.

We want to start the discussion of cloud computing security by para-phrasing Greg Papadopoulos, CTO of Sun Microsystems, who said that cloud users normally "trust" cloud service providers with their data like they trust banks with their money. This means that they expect the three issues of secu-rity, availability and performance to be of little concern to them as they are with their banks. To give a fair discussion of the security of anything, one has to focus on two items: the actors and their roles in the process you are inter-ested in securing and the application or data in play. The application or data is thought of in relation to the state it is in at any one time. For example, the states for both data and application can be either in motion between the remote hosts and the service provider's hypervisors and servers, or in the static state when it is stored at remote hosts, usually on the customer's premises or in the service provider's servers. The kind of security needed in either one of these two states is different.

Cloud Providers and Users: Their Roles and Responsibilities

In the cloud computing model, the main players are the cloud providers, customers who are data owners and who seek cloud services from the cloud provider, and the user who may be the owner of the data stored in the cloud. The first two players have delegated responsibilities to all who work on their behalf. To fully understand these delegated responsibilities assigned to each one of these, we need to look at first the marginal security concerns resulting from the peripheral system access control that always results in the easiest breach of security for any system, usually through compromising user accounts via weak passwords. This problem is broad, affecting both local and outsourced cloud solutions. Addressing this and all other administrative and security con-cerns requires companies offering and using cloud solutions to design an access control regime. This must cover and require every user, local or remote, to abide by these access policies, including the peripheral ones like the generation and storage of user passwords. Access control administration is so important that cloud providers need to spend time and resources to design a strong access control regime.

Security of Data and Applications in the Cloud

To understand and appreciate the security of data and applications in the cloud, we need to focus first on the security and the role of the hypervisor and then the servers on which user services are based. A hypervisor, also called virtual machine manager (VMM), is one of many hardware virtualization techniques allowing multiple operating systems, termed *guests*, to run concurrently on a host computer. The hypervisor is piggybacked on a kernel program, itself running on the core physical machine running as the physical server. The hypervisor presents to the guest operating systems a virtual operating platform and manages the execution of the guest operating systems. Multiple instances of a variety of operating systems may share the virtualized hardware resources. Hypervisors are very commonly installed on server hardware, with the function of running guest operating systems that themselves act as servers. The security of the hypervisor therefore involves the security of the underlying kernel program and the underlying physical machine, the physical server and the individual virtual operating systems and their anchoring virtual machines.

Hacking the Hypervisor

In his blog "Yes, Hypervisors Are Vulnerable," Neil MacDonald, vice president of Gartner Research and a Gartner Fellow,[3] observes the following about a hypervisor and the vulnerabilities associated with it:

- The virtualization platform (hypervisor/VMM) is software written by human beings and will contain vulnerabilities. Microsoft, VMware, Citrix, and others, all of them will and have had vulnerabilities.
- Some of these vulnerabilities will result in a breakdown in isolation that the virtualization platform was supposed to enforce.
- Bad guys will target this layer with attacks. The benefits of a compromise of this layer are simply too great.
- While there have been a few disclosed attacks, it is just a matter of time before a widespread publicly disclosed enterprise breach is tied back to a hypervisor vulnerability.

Published papers have so far shown that the security of hypervisors can be undermined. As far back as 2006, Samuel T. King, Peter M. Chen, Yi-Min Wang , Chad Verbowski, Helen J. Wang and Jacob R. Lorch demonstrate this in their paper "SubVirt: Implementing Malware with Virtual Machines." In this type of malware, a virtual-machine based rootkit (VMBR) installed a virtual-machine monitor underneath an existing operating system and hoists the original operating system into a virtual machine. The malware program then started to act as its own hypervisor under Windows. According to the IBM X-Force 2010 Mid-Year Trend and Risk Report,[4] which disclosed a ten-year virtualization vulnerability trend from 1999 through 2009, there were 373 reported vulnerabilities affecting virtualization solutions during the period with a steady growth trend starting around 2002 and peaking in 2008 to 100 and falling off by 12 percent in 2009.

Securing Load Balancers

For every hypervisor, there is a load balancer, used to route traffic to different virtual machines to help spread traffic evenly across available machines. A load balancer in a hypervisor plays a vital role of ensuring a fair distribution of available load to all virtual machines, especially during high traffic and ensuring the full utilization of the cloud infrastructure. An elastic load balancer plays a central in the cloud infrastructure along the following lines[5]:

- It listens to all traffic destined for the internal network and distributes incoming traffic across the cloud infrastructure.
- It automatically scales its request handling capacity in response to incoming application traffic.
- It creates and manages security groups associated with each instance and provides additional networking and security options if and when needed.
- It can detect the health of the virtual machines and if it detects an unhealthy load-balanced virtual machine, it stops routing traffic to it and spreads the load across the remaining healthy virtual machines.
- It supports the ability to stick user sessions to specific virtual machines.
- It supports SSL termination at the Load Balancer, including offloading SSL decryption from application virtual machines, centralized management of SSL certificates, and encryption to backend virtual machines with optional public key authentication.
- It supports use of both the Internet Protocol version 4 and 6 (IPv4 and IPv6).

Due to the load balancer's ability to listen and process all traffic that is destined to the internal network of the cloud, it is a prime target for attackers. If a load balancer was compromised, an attacker could listen to traffic and could compromise secure traffic destined to outside the network. Additionally, if the load balancer is compromised along with a virtual machine, traffic could be directed to an unsecure internal server where further attacks are launched.[6] Because the load balancer is a single point in the cloud infrastructure, it is very vulnerable to denial of service attacks. Compromise can lead to cloud activity disruption.

Then what is the best way to secure the load balancer from attacks? A load balancer is normally secured through proper configuration and monitoring of the balancer's logs. This is achieved through restriction of access to administration of the balancer itself by configuring the load balancer to only accept administrative access over a specific administrative network. This administrative network should be connected to the administrative only network. Limiting access over the administrator network greatly limits the number of users with access to the load balancer.[7]

Virtual Operating Systems Security

Besides the hypervisor and load balancer, the virtualization system also hosts virtual servers each running either a guest operating system or another hypervisor. And on the peripheral of the virtual machine system are the consoles and hosts. Through each one of these resources, the virtual machine system can fall victim to security vulnerabilities.

Security of Data in Transition: Cloud Security Best Practices

With the vulnerabilities in the cloud discussed, there are several ways to protect the user of the cloud. First for the cloud customer, the key areas of concerns are unauthorized access to customer data and other resources stored or implemented in the cloud, whether the cloud provider uses strong enough encryption to safeguard customer data, secure access and use of cloud applications and secure cloud management. All these should be incorporated in the Service Level Agreements (SLAs).

Service Level Agreements (SLAs)

A service-level agreement (SLA) is a service contract between the provider of a service and the client defining the level of expected service in terms of security, availability and performance. SLAs are a series of service contracts between cloud providers and clients to define the level(s) of service based on the types of services sought by the client because the effectiveness of these contracts depends on how well maximized and tailored these services are to the particular needs of each client.

Data Encryption

Encryption of the data is also important. The moment data leaves the end-point web-cloud access point in the user's location, it travels via a public network and is stored in shared environment—the cloud. In public or in shared environments, data can be intercepted and infiltrated by intruders from within and outside the cloud and during transmission from man in the middle cryptoanalysts. To prevent these kinds of breaches, strong encryption and authentication regimes are needed. Encryption to safeguard any kinds of data breaches requires a strong access control and authentication to all web-based cloud resource interface, encryption of all administrative access to the cloud hypervisor, and all access to applications and data.

Web Access Points Security

Most cloud access instances are web-based. Most security breaches to stored data originated from Web applications. There is therefore a need for strong security controls in the cloud APIs.

Compliance

Because most clouds are either public, community or hybrids, and clients using these clouds usually are in businesses that deal with personal data, cloud providers must observe a number of compliance regulations including FISMA, HIPAA, SOX and SAS 70 11 for clouds based in the United States, and the Data Protection Directive for clouds based in the EU. In addition, providers accepting payments using credit card must comply with PCI DSS.

Chapter 12

Security and Compliance

LEARNING OBJECTIVES:

After reading this chapter, the reader should be able to:
- Understand the concepts of compliance.
- Learn about the growth of compliance regulations.
- Understand the balance between security and compliance.

Introduction

The near ubiquitous computing environment we are in, resulting from the tremendous developments in communication technologies, the convergence of computing and telecommunication technologies and the miniaturization of communication devices, has almost transformed personal privacy as we used to know it beyond recognition and made the accepted, time tested, classical security protocols and techniques questionable. These new anywhere, anytime technologies with unprecedented high bandwidth and high speed are making the movement, sharing and access of huge amounts of information possible and consequently enabling and increasing the possibility of unauthorized access and misuse of personal information.

We are in uncharted territory when it comes to availability and access to personal information. Before the advent of the current technologies, there was an accepted tenant of self-regulation as one of the pillars of good security practices. Self-regulation came about as a result of the outcry of the 1980s. The early 1980s saw a rapid rise in the "new" types of crimes increasingly committed by hackers using the brand-new computer communication technology, the Internet. In response to the public outcry, governments went on a binge of passing laws to regulate the new Internet. Privacy advocates were not amused with the growing popularity with Internet regulations. Thus, the birth of the self-regulation.

198

However, with ever-advancing computer and communication technologies, self-regulation could no longer contain the wave after wave of computer-related crimes. Along with the rising computer crime rates, there was a corresponding widespread use of computers, which led to computer communication becoming even better. The collection, storage and indexing of personal information was growing at an unprecedented rate. Once again, there were increasing calls for state and national governments to legislate civility of the communication channels to mitigate the dangers to personal information.

In response, since the early 2000s, there has been an upsurge in the number of local and indeed national governments drafting and passing laws, regulations and mandates imposing standards and obligations on institutions and businesses for handling personal information, including sensitive health and financial data. The new laws and standards are all requiring, at a minimum, disclosures to victims whenever there has been unauthorized access to personal, sensitive information. Further, these laws and mandates demanded that failure to protect and disclose to victims of unauthorized access must lead to investigations, fines, and other penalties. As a result, there are growing legal obligations faced by institutions and businesses to comply with these mandates and regulations. A good, balanced and unified approach to information security compliance consists of a good security policy that effectively balances and enforces core information security and compliance elements.

The Role of a Policy in the Security Compliance of an Organization

To any organization interested in security in general and information security in particular, a security policy is very important. For any organization system, there must be somebody to say *no* when the *no* needs to be said. The *no* must be said because the administrator wants to limit the number of network computers, resources, and capabilities people have been using to ensure the security of the system. One way of doing this in fairness to all is through the implementation of a set of policies, procedures, and guidelines that tell all employees and business partners what constitutes acceptable and unacceptable use of the organization's computer system. These form the security policy. The security policy also spells out what resources need to be protected and how organizations can protect such resources. A security policy is a living set of guidelines and procedures that impact and potentially limit the freedoms and of course levels of individual security responsibilities of all users. Such a structure is essential to an organization's security. It is important for, among other things, dictating firewall installations, user discipline, and all sorts of relevant compliancy. Any firewalls in use, and their rule-bases, must be configured in adherence to the security policy. Also, all users in the organization who connect to the organization's network must conform to the security policy. Finally, all regulations and standards binding to the organization must adhere to the security policy.

Without a strong security policy that every employee must conform to, the organization may suffer from data loss, employee time loss, non-compliance and productivity loss all because employers may spend time fixing holes, repairing vulnerabilities, and recovering lost or compromised data among other things.

A security policy covers a wide variety of topics and serves several important purposes in the system security cycle. Constructing a security policy is like building a house; it needs a lot of different components that must fit together. The security policy is built in stages, and each stage adds value to the overall product, making it unique for the organization. To be successful, a security policy must[1]:

- Have the backing of the organization's top management.
- Involve everyone in the organization by explicitly stating the role everyone will play and the responsibilities of everyone in the security of the organization.
- Precisely describe a clear vision of a secure environment, stating what needs to be protected and the reasons for it.
- Set priorities and costs of what needs to be protected.
- Be a good teacher for everyone in the organization, explaining security and what needs to be protected, and why and how it is to be protected.
- Set boundaries on what constitutes appropriate and inappropriate behavior as far as security and privacy of the organization's resources are concerned.
- Create a security clearinghouse and authority.
- Be flexible enough to adapt to new conditions.
- Be sure security is consistently implemented throughout the organization.
- Adhere to all local, state and national laws governing the handling and security of personal information.

To achieve these subgoals, a carefully chosen set of basic steps must be followed to construct a viable, implementable, and useful security policy. The following list provides an example of some items in an infrastructure of a security policy that includes compliance:

Staff

- Recruit employees who are capable and whose background has been checked for positions in the implementation and operation of the network infrastructure.
- Have all personnel involved in the implementation and support of the network infrastructure attend a security seminar for awareness.
- Instruct all employees concerned to store all backups in a dedicated locked area.

Equipment Certification

To be sure that quality equipment comply with the standards and regulations used, make every effort to ensure that[2]:

- All new equipment to be added to the infrastructure adheres to specified security requirements.
- Each site of the infrastructure decides which security features and functionalities are necessary to support the security policy.
- The following good guidelines are used:
  ° All infrastructure equipment must pass the acquisition certification process before purchase.
  ° All new images and configurations must be modeled in a test facility before deployment.
  ° All major scheduled network outages and interruptions of services must be announced to those who will be affected well ahead of time.
- Portable tools are carefully used:
  ° Since use of portable tools such as laptops always pose some security risks, develop guidelines for the kinds of data allowed to reside on hard drives of portable tools and how that data should be protected.

Audit Trails and Legal Evidence

Prepare for possible legal action by:

- Keeping logs of traffic patterns and noting any deviations from normal behavior found. Such deviations are the first clues to security problems.
- Keeping the collected data locally to the resource until an event is finished, after which it may be taken, according to established means involving encryption, to a secure location.
- Securing audit data on location and in backups.

Privacy Concerns

There are two areas of concern with audit trail logs:

- Privacy issue of the data collected on users.
- Knowledge of any intrusive behavior by others including employees of the organization.

Security Awareness Training

The strength of a security policy lies in its emphasis on both employee and user training. The policy must stress that[3]:

- Users of computers and computer networks must be made aware of the security ramifications caused by certain actions. The training should be provided to all personnel.
- Training should be focused and involve all types of security that are needed in the organization, the internal control techniques that will meet the security requirements of the organization, and ways to maintain the security attained.
- Employees with network security responsibilities must be taught security techniques probably beyond those of the general public, including methodologies for evaluating threats and vulnerabilities to be able to use them to defend the organization's security, the competencies to select and implement security controls, and a thorough understanding of the importance of what is at risk if security is not maintained.
- Before connecting to a LAN in the organization's backbone, those responsible for the organization's security must be provided with documentation on network infrastructure layout, rules, and guidelines on controlled software downloads. Pay attention to the training given to those who will be in charge of issuing passwords.
- Users of computers and computer networks must be made aware of social engineering.
- Employees must be trained not to believe anyone who calls/e-mails them to do something that might compromise security.
- Before giving any information, employees must positively identify who they are dealing with.

Incident Handling

The security of an organization's network depends on what the security plan says should be done to handle a security incident. If the response is fast and effective, the losses may be none to minimum. However, if the response is bungled and slow, the losses may be heavy. To make sure that the security plan is clear and effective[4]:

- Build an incident response team as a centralized core group, whose members are drawn from across the organization, who must be knowledgeable, and well-rounded with a correct mix of technical, communication, and political skills. The team should be the main contact point in case of a security incident and be responsible for keeping up to date with the latest threats and incidents, notifying others of the incident, assessing the damage and impact of the incident, finding out how to minimize the loss, avoiding further exploitation of the same vulnerability, and making plans and efforts to recover.
- Detect incidents by looking for signs of a security breach in the usual suspects and beyond. Look for abnormal signs from accounting reports, focus on signs of data modification and deletion, check out complaints of poor system performance, pay attention to strange traffic patterns and unusual times of system use, and take interest in large numbers of failed login attempts.
- Assess the damage by checking and analyzing all traffic logs for abnormal behavior, especially on network perimeter access points such as Internet access or dial-in access. Pay particular attention when verifying infrastructure device checksum or operating system checksum on critical servers to see whether operating system software has been compromised or if configuration changes in infrastructure devices such as servers have occurred to ensure that no one has tampered with them. Make sure to check the sensitive data to see whether it has been accessed or changed and traffic logs for unusually large traffic streams from a single source or streams going to a single destination, passwords on critical systems to ensure that they have not been modified, and any new or unknown devices on the network for abnormal activities.
- Report all alerts promptly.
- Establish a systematic approach for reporting incidents and subsequently notifying affected areas.
- Use essential communication mechanisms including a monitored central phone, e-mail, pager, or other quick communication devices.
- Establish clearly whom to alert first and who should be on the list of people to alert next.
- Decide on how much information to give each member on the list.
- Find ways to minimize negative exposure, especially where it requires working with agents to protect evidence.

- Respond to the incident to try to restore the system to its pre-incident status. Sometimes it may require shutting down the system; if this is necessary, then do so but keep accurate documentation and a log book of all activities during the incident so that this data can be used later to analyze any causes and effects.
- Try to recover from an incident as quickly as possible.
- Make a post-mortem analysis of what happened, how it happened, and what steps need to be taken to prevent similar.
- Develop a formal report with proper chronological sequence of events to be presented to management.
- Make sure not to overreact by turning your system into a fortress.

Security Compliance Management

For an institution and company to be in compliance means its total adherence to a security and compliance management framework consisting of the rules, standards and mandates. This sometimes can be not only difficult but sometimes frustrating, time-consuming, and expensive. This is because being in security compliance calls for adherence to strict access controls and regular system audit. In addition, system administrators must also[5]:

- Regularly and continuously monitor all access controls to make sure that they are fully working well.
- Automatically log all event data across the network.
- Archive event logs for easy access to complete and secure audit trails.
- Provide a centralized view of security and compliance posture.
- Enable rapid threat identification, remediation and reporting.
- Automatically send alerts for security, policy and compliance violations.
- Correlate volumes of diverse events to prioritize the true threats.
- Document all incidents with full, detailed auditable records.
- Provide all out-of-the box and customizable compliance reporting.
- Report all criminal acts to law enforcement agencies.

Most Common Information Security Laws and Regulations

In the United States, there is a long list of institutional, local, state and federal information security laws and regulations. Most of these laws and regulations are not intended to cover everyone and every type of industry. They are targeted to particular industries and services. For example, there are those governing the security and privacy of information in the financial industry, those in health, in education and so on. Let us look at a few of these.

Education Based Laws and Regulations

Family Educational Rights and Privacy Act (FERPA)

The Family Educational Rights and Privacy Act (FERPA) (20 U.S.C. § 1232g; 34 CFR Part 99) is a federal law that protects the privacy of student education records. The law applies to all schools that receive funds under an applicable program of the Department of Education.

Although FERPA gives rights to protect the privacy of a student's education record, according to the U.S. Department of Education, for children under eighteen years, these rights remain vested with the parents or guardians. When the student turns eighteen, then, these rights are transferred to the student. Students to whom the rights have transferred are "eligible students." So under FERPA, parents or eligible students have the right to[6]:

- Inspect and review the student's education record maintained by the school. As long as parents and "eligible" students are able to view the records, schools are not required to provide copies of them.
- Request that a school correct records which they believe to be inaccurate or misleading. If the school decides not to amend the record, the parent or eligible student then has the right to a formal hearing.

Generally, schools must have written permission from the parent or eligible student in order to release any information from a student's education record. However, FERPA allows schools to disclose those records, without consent, to the following parties or under the following conditions (34 CFR § 99.31)[7]:

- School officials with legitimate educational interest;
- Other schools to which a student is transferring;
- Specified officials for audit or evaluation purposes;
- Appropriate parties in connection with financial aid to a student;
- Organizations conducting certain studies for or on behalf of the school;
- Accrediting organizations;
- To comply with a judicial order or lawfully issued subpoena;
- Appropriate officials in cases of health and safety emergencies; and

- State and local authorities, within a juvenile justice system, pursuant to specific state law.

Financial Laws

Gramm-Leach-Bliley Act (GLBA)

The Gramm-Leach-Bliley Act, 15 U.S.C. §§6801–6809 or the Financial Modernization Act as it is also known, regulates the sharing of personal information of those individuals who obtain financial products or services from financial institutions.[8] Under the act, financial institutions are required to inform individuals about their privacy policies and practices, so that those individuals can make choices about their financial dealings with those institutions. However, the act gives consumers limited control over how these financial institutions can use and share the consumer's personal information. The limited control over consumer data held by these institutions is through *opt-outs*. An opt-out is an option the consumer has that prevents the institution from using or disclosing of the customer's personal data beyond the purpose it was collected for.

The Payment Card Industry Data Security Standard (PCIDSS)

The Payment Card Industry Data Security Standard (PCIDSS) is a private compliance requirement by the credit and debit card industry that requires all entities private or public that use payment cards to comply with a number of technical, physical, and administrative requirements; otherwise those entities would incur large penalties and suspension of the right to use credit cards for payment purposes.

The Sarbanes-Oxley Act (SOX) of 2002

The Sarbanes-Oxley Act (SOX) of 2002 mandates a strong corporate governance to restore investor confidence. The law came in the wake of a number of major corporate and accounting scandals by many big companies in the United States. The act established the following[9]:

- New accountability standards and criminal penalties for corporate management.
- New independence standards for external auditors.
- A Public Company Accounting Oversight Board (PCAOB) under

the Security and Exchange Commission (SEC) to oversee public accounting firms and issue accounting standards.

General Laws

Federal Information Security Management Act (FISMA)

The Federal Information Security Management Act (FISMA), 2002, focuses on federal agencies. It requires each federal agency to develop, document, and implement an agency-wide program to provide information security for the information and information systems that support the operations and assets of the agency, including those provided or managed by another agency, contractor, or other source.

According to FISMA, an effective information security program should include[10]:

- Periodic assessments of risk, including the magnitude of harm that could result from the unauthorized access, use, disclosure, disruption, modification, or destruction of information and information systems that support the operations and assets of the organization.
- Policies and procedures that are based on risk assessments and that cost-effectively reduce information security risks to an acceptable level and ensure that information security is addressed throughout the life cycle of each organizational information system.
- Subordinate plans for providing adequate information security for networks, facilities, information systems, or groups of information systems, as appropriate.
- Security awareness training to inform personnel (including contractors and other users of information systems that support the operations and assets of the organization) of the information security risks associated with their activities and their responsibilities in complying with organizational policies and procedures designed to reduce these risks.
- Periodic testing and evaluation of the effectiveness of information security policies, procedures, practices, and security controls, which should be performed with a frequency depending on risk, but no less than annually.
- A process for planning, implementing, evaluating, and documenting remedial actions to address any deficiencies in the information security policies, procedures, and practices of the organization.
- Procedures for detecting, reporting, and responding to security incidents.

- Plans and procedures to ensure continuity of operations for information systems that support the operations and assets of the organization.

Health Laws

The Health Insurance Portability and Accountability Act (HIPAA)

The Administrative Simplification provisions of the Health Insurance Portability and Accountability Act of 1996 (HIPAA) contain both security and privacy provisions.[11] HIPAA applies to covered entities that use certain electronic transactions—entities such as those most health care providers, health plans, and health care clearinghouses use. In the higher education arena, HIPAA most often applies to clinics used by both students and staff and to academic medical centers. The security regulations of HIPAA require covered entities to protect specific types of individually identifiable health information kept in electronic form, referred to as Electronic Protected Health Information (EPHI). To comply with the HIPAA security regulations, covered entities must protect systems that store, process, and transmit EPHI. Entities must conduct periodic risk analyses to determine and implement reasonable and appropriate administrative, physical, and technical safeguards. The security regulations also require the implementation of risk-management processes, including policies and procedures and other documentation and training.

Although HIPAA does not allow individuals to sue covered entities that do not comply with the law, it does provide criminal and civil penalties for noncompliance.

Other Laws

FDA Rule on Electronic Records and Electronic Signatures (21 C.F.R. Part 11)

In 1997, the U.S. Food and Drug Administration (FDA) issued 21 C.F.R. Part 11, which consists of regulations that provide criteria for the acceptance of electronic records. These criteria include specific information security and electronic signature practices.

Appendix:
Questions for Classroom Use

Teachers using this book may find the following questions helpful in classroom discussions or preparing tests on the material.

Chapter 1

    1. Discuss the risks of technology.

    2. How much trust can we put in computer technology?

    3. Is our increasing dependence on computer technology a reflection of our deepening trust in computer technology?

Chapter 2

    1. Define morality.

    2. Is morality evolutionary or revolutionary? Discuss.

    3. Happiness is human. Discuss.

    4. What is the role of education in moral behavior?

    5. Show how and why the following rules are culture-free:

        (a) The Golden Rule

        (b) The Bronze Rule

    6. If you were charged with creating a "new" human society, what moral code would you design and why?

    7. We tend to live a moral script every day. Reflect on what is in your script.

    8. Morality is time sensitive. Discuss.

    9. How does guilt influence our moral journey?

Chapter 3

1. What is an ethical theory?
2. Discuss two of the following ethical theories:
   (a) Relativism
       i. Subjective
       ii. Cultural
   (b) Divine Command
   (c) Kantianism
   (d) Utilitarianism
       i. Act utilitarianism
       ii. Rule utilitarianism
   (e) Social contract
3. Discuss implications of Internet addiction.
4. What is "an ethical point of view"?
5. Discuss the differences between morality and ethics.

Chapter 4

1. How would you define ethics to the following audiences?
   (a) Seventh-graders
   (b) College students
   (c) Members of the clergy
2. Why are acts like abortion legal in some societies and not in others?
3. Does technology bring relevant changes in ethics?
4. For a seventh-grade audience, use the traditional mode of ethics to explain the effects of technology on ethics.
5. What are the merits of computer ethics education?
6. Why should we study computer ethics?
7. There are two views on teaching computer ethics. State the views. What view do you agree with and why?

Chapter 5

1. What is a communication protocol?
2. List the major protocols for:
   i. OSI
   ii. TCP/IP
3. Discuss two LAN technologies that are *not* Ethernet or Token Ring.
4. Why is Ethernet technology more appealing to users than the rest of the LAN technologies?
5. What do you think are the weak points of TCP/IP?

6. Why do we need communication protocols?
7. List the major protocols discussed in this chapter.
8. Besides ISO and TCP/IP, what other models are there?
9. Discuss the pros and cons of four LAN technologies.
10. List four WAN technologies.

Chapter 6

1. Why is IP spoofing a basic ingredient in many cyber attacks, especially DDoS?
2. Why have Windows NT and UNIX operating systems been a prime target of cyber attacks?
3. Suggest ways to prevent e-mail attacks.
4. Why is it so difficult to apprehend cyber attackers outside a country?
5. Research reasons why it took the FBI a long time to apprehend the authors of the DDoS attacks on eBay, CNN and E*Trade.

Chapter 7

1. List five types of e-attacks.
2. In a short essay, discuss the differences between a denial of service attack and a penetration attack.
3. Which attack type is more dangerous to a computer system: a penetration attack or a denial of service attack?
4. What are the major differences between a boot virus and a macro virus? Which is more dangerous to a computer system?
5. List and briefly discuss five attack motives.
6. Why do hackers devote a substantial amount of time to their trade?
7. Why is civilizing the Internet a difficult task?
8. Comprehensively define "cyberspace."
9. How are viruses spread?
10. Discuss the most common security flaw.
11. List and discuss the elements that make a crime an e-crime.
12. Create a list of times that you think may form a basis for a model for computing e-crime costs.
13. Discuss the challenges in tracking down cyber criminals.
14. Why is it so difficult to estimate the costs of business, national, and global e-crimes?
15. What is the best way to bring about full reporting of e-crimes, including costs?
16. Why do countries worldwide have very little information to help them combat cyber crimes?

17. Why are cyber crimes on the rise?

18. In addition to monetary costs, there are ethical and social costs of e-crimes; discuss these "hidden" costs.

Chapter 8

1. Why is a security policy so important in the security of a network?

2. Discuss the advantages and disadvantages of filtering.

3. If you were a network security chief, which of the following items would you put more emphasis on? Why?
   i. Prevention
   ii. Detection
   iii. Survivability

4. How can a system security team avoid an e-attack?

5. In a short essay discuss the measures being undertaken in each of the following categories to prevent e-attacks:
   i. Prevention
   ii. Detection
   iii. Survivability

6. Discuss the merits of legislating Internet policies.

7. Why is self-regulation a viable Internet control tool?

8. Discuss the differences between a firewall and a packet filter.

9. Give reasons why firewalls do not give foolproof security.

10. Discuss the advantages of using an application-level firewall over a network-level firewall.

11. Show how data protocols such as TCP, UDP, and ICMP can be implemented in a firewall and give the type of firewall best suited for each of these protocols.

12. What are circuit-level firewalls? How are they different from network-level firewalls?

13. Discuss the limitation of firewalls. How do modern firewalls differ form the old ones in dealing with these limitations?

14. How would you design a firewall that would let Internet-based users upload files to a protected internal network server?

15. Discuss the risks to the protected internal network as a result of a DMZ.

16. What is a bastion router? How different is it from a firewall?

17. Search and discuss as many services and protocols as possible offered by a modern firewall.

18. Discuss five modern online crimes.

19. Discuss strategies that can be used to effectively eliminate online crimes?

20. If you were to write a framework to prevent cyber crimes what would be in it.

21. Is cryptography all we need to secure computer network and protect information?

22. Why is cryptography failing to protect digital systems and information? What do we need to do?

Chapter 9

1. Differentiate between a social network and an online social network.

2. Discuss the challenges faced by members of the online social networks.

3. Discuss the social and ethical implications of the growth of online social networks.

4. Is there a gender gap problem in online social network? If yes, what needs to be done?

5. How can privacy of users of online social networks be strengthened?

6. Discuss the ways privacy can be violated on online social networks.

Chapter 10

1. Discuss the steps you would take to protect your mobile device.

2. Search the Internet to find a company's security policy for its mobile devices. Suggest what you would change in that security policy to enhance security.

3. Study three remote wiping solutions and compare them.

4. Comment on the reasons for the rapid growth of the Android Operating system.

5. Recently Apple's iOS4 encryption was hacked by a Russian company. Compare, discuss the weaknesses in the iOS4 disclosed by the Russian company.

Chapter 11

1. What is cloud computing?

2. Discuss the software models predating cloud computing.

3. Discuss the major models in cloud computing.

4. What are the benefits of cloud computing over software as a service (SaaS)?

5. Define and discuss Software as a service (SaaS), Infrastructure as a service (IaaS), and storage as a service.

6. Describe the seven business models of software.

7. Discuss the services that make up cloud computing.

8. Discuss the differences between clouding computing and virtualization.

9. Discuss four business applications best suited for cloud computing.

10. To determine what business applications should go on the cloud you need to estimate the return on investment for that application. What can you consider when computing ROI?

11. List and discuss three characteristics an application must have in order to be considered suited for the cloud.

12. What is MapReduce? Describe the structure and working of MapReduce.

13. What is Hadoop? Describe the three subprojects of Hadoop.

Chapter 12

1. What is an audit trail? Why is it so important in the security of an organization?

2. Why is security awareness training so important in enforcing a security policy in an organization?

3. What is security compliance? Why is it necessary in security enforcement? What form must it take?

4. Discuss two security compliance laws that you consider effective.

5. Suggest changes, if any, to those laws that you deem necessary for their effectiveness.

6. Discuss other areas of the security matrix that still need compliance laws and why.

Chapter Notes

Chapter 1

1. Lawrence A. Gordon, Martin P. Loeb, William Lucyshyn and Robert Richardson, "2005 CSI/FBI Computer Crime and Security Survey," http://i.cmpnet.com/gocsi/db_area/pdfs/fbi/FBI2005.pdf.

2. Consumers Union, "Another Week, Another Identity Theft Scandal: Recent Data Security Breaches Underscore Need for Stronger Identity Theft Protections," www.consumersunion.org/campaigns/learn_more/002232indiv.html.

3. http://www.canberra.edu.au/cis/storage/Cyber%20Crime%20and%20Security%20Survey%20Report%202012.pdf.

4. ICS-CERT: Cyber Threat Source Descriptions, http://ics-cert.us-cert.gov/content/cyber-threat-source-descriptions.

5. "Infosecurity 2012: Survey Proves Value of Security Awareness Program," http://www.computerweekly.com/news/2240149227/Infosecurity-2012-Survey-proves-value-of-security-awareness-programme.

6. "Government Launches Cyber Crime Reduction Partnership," http://www.bcs.org/content/conWebDoc/50154.

7. "Defending Against Cybercriminal," http://www.dhs.gov/defending-against-cyber criminals.

8. "Cyber Crime," http://www.fbi.gov/about-us/investigate/cyber/cyber.

Chapter 2

1. Chris MacDonald, "Moral Decision Making: An Analysis," www.ethics.web.ca/guide/moral-decision.html.

2. "Moral Relativism," Internet Encyclopedia of Philosophy, www.utm.edu/research/iep/ni/m-ration.html.

3. Carl Sagan, "A New Way to Think About Rules to Live By," *Parade Magazine,* November 28, 1993, p. 12.

4. Lee Bohannon, "The Need for a Moral Code," www.abortionessay.com/files/moral-code.html.

5. Austin Fagothey, *Rights and Reason,* 2d ed. (Rockford, IL: Tan, 1959).

6. Michael Miller, "The Good Life," www.quackgrass.com/goodlife.html.

Chapter 3

1. Robert C. Solomon, *Morality and the Good Life: An Introduction to Ethics Through Classical Sources,* 2d ed. (New York: McGraw-Hill, 1992).

2. *Ibid.*

3. D. J. Johnson. *Computer Ethics,* 2d ed. (Upper Saddle River, NJ: Prentice Hall, 1994).

4. *Internet Encyclopedia of Philosophy,* www.utm.edu/research/lep/ni.

5. Austin Fagothey, *Rights and Reason,* 2d ed. (Rockford, IL: Tan, 1959).

6. Richard T. Hull, "The Varieties of Ethical Theories," www.richard-t-hull.com/publications/varieties.pdf.

7. *Ibid.*

8. *Ibid.*

9. Joseph M. Kizza, *Computer Network Security* (New York: Springer, 2005).

10. Johnson.

11. *Ibid.*

12. "The Purpose of Ethics," www.sympatico.ca/saburns/pg0401.htm.

Chapter 4

1. Ken Funk, "Technology and Christian Values," http://web.engr.oregonstate.edu/~funkk/Technology.

2. Joseph M. Kizza, *Ethical and Social Issues in the Information Age,* 2d ed. (New York: Springer, 2002).

3. *Ibid.*

4. *Ibid.*

Chapter 5

1. William Stallings, *Local and Metropolitan Area Networks,* 6th ed. (Upper Saddle River, NJ: Prentice Hall, 2000).

2. *Ibid.*

3. Douglas Comer, *Computer Networks and Intranets* (Upper Saddle River, NJ: Prentice Hall, 1997).

4. Douglas Comer, *Internetworking with TCP/IP: Principles, Protocols, and Architecture,* 4th ed. (Upper Saddle River, NJ: Prentice Hall, 2000).

5. James F. Kurose and Keith W. Ross, *Computer Networking: A Top-Down Approach Featuring the Internet* (Boston: Addison-Wesley, 2000).

Chapter 6

1. Netscape, "'Love Bug' Computer Virus Wreaks Fresh Havoc," www.mynetscape.com/news; CNN, "Canadian Juvenile Charged in Connection with February 'Denial of Service' Attacks," http://cnn.com/2000/TECH/computing/04/15/hacker.arrest.01.html.

2. Merike Kaeo, *Designing Network Security: A Practical Guide to Creating a Secure Network Infrastructure* (Indianapolis, IN: Cisco, 1999).

3. *Ibid.*

4. "CERT/CC Statistics 1988–2005," CERT Coordination Center, Carnegie Mellon Software Engineering Institute. www.cert.org/stats/cert_stats.html.

5. *Ibid.*

6. "Online and Out of Line: Why Is Cybercrime on the Rise, and Who Is Responsible?" ABC, www.ABCNews.com/sections/us/DailyNews/cybercrime_000117.html.

7. "Security in Cyberspace." U.S. Senate Permanent Subcommittee on Investigations, June 5, 1996. www.fas.org/irp/congress/1996_hr/s960605t.htm.

8. *Ibid.*

9. *Ibid.*

10. "Online and Out of Line."

Chapter 7

1. "Section A: The Nature and Definition of Critical Infrastructure," The National Infrastructure Protection Center, www.nipc.gov/nipcfaq.htm.

2. William Stallings, *Cryptography and Network Security: Principles and Practice,* 2d ed. (Upper Saddle River, NJ: Prentice Hall, 1998).

3. Peter J. Denning, ed., *Computers Under Attack: Intruders, Worms and Viruses* (New York: ACM, 1990).

4. Karen Forcht, *Computer Security Management* (Danvers, MA: Boyd and Fraser, 1994).

5. *Ibid.*

6. Denning.

7. *Ibid.*

8. T. Fiserberg, David Gries, Juris Hartmanis, Don Holcomb, M. Stuart Lynn, and Thomas Santoro, "The Cornell Commission: On Morris and the Worm," in *Computers Under Attack: Intruders, Worms and Viruses*, ed. Peter J. Denning (New York: ACM, 1990).

9. Denning.

10. P. Stephenson, "Preventive Medicine," *LAN Magazine,* November 1993.

11. Andrew Grosso, "The Economic Espionage Act: Touring the Minefields," *Communications of the ACM,* vol. 43, no. 8 (August 2000): 15–18.

12. Don Seely, "Password Cracking: A Game of Wits," in *Computers Under Attack: Intruders, Worms and Viruses,* ed. Peter J. Denning (New York: ACM, 1990).

13. F. Grampp and R. Morris, "UNIX Operating System Security," Part 2, *AT&T Bell Laboratories Tech Journal,* vol. 63, no. 8 (October 1984): 1649.

14. *Ibid.*

15. Peter G. Neumann, "Risks of Insiders," *Communications of the ACM,* vol. 42, no. 12 (December 1999): 160.

16. Wally Bock, "The Cost of Laptop Theft," www.bockinfo.com/docs/laptheft.htm.

17. Steven Levy, *Hackers: Heroes of the Computer Revolution* (Garden City, NY: Anchor Press/Doubleday, 1984).

18. Clifford Stoll, "Stalking the Wily Hacker," in *Computers Under Attack: Intruders, Worms and Viruses,* ed. Peter J. Denning (New York: ACM, 1990).

19. *Ibid.*

20. Jonathan Calof, "Increasing Your CIQ: The Competitive Intelligence Edge," www.edco.on.ca/journal/item22.htm.

21. http://www.gfi.com/blog/the-most-vulnerable-operating-systems-and-applications-in–2011/#sthash.PPHmEajK.dpuf.

22. http://www.gfi.com/blog/the-most-vulnerable-operating-systems-and-applications-in-2011/#sthash.PPHmEajK.dpuf.

23. "SCO SNMPd Default Writeable Community String," www.securiteam.com/unixfocus/SCO_SNMPd_default_writeable_community_string.html.

24. http://www.esecurityplanet.com/network-security/6-emerging-security-threats-and-how-to-fight-them.html.

25. http://www.esecurityplanet.com/network-security/6-emerging-security-threats-and-how-to-fight-them.html.

26. "CERT/CC Statistics 1998–2005," CERT Coordination Center, Carnegie Mellon Software Engineering Institute, www.cert.org/stats/cert_stats.html.

27. John Christensen, "Bracing for Guerilla Warfare in Cyberspace," CNN, April 6, 1999.

28. "Computer Attacks: What They Are and How to Defend Against Them," www.bluemud.org/article/11438.

29. CNN Headline News, May 28, 2000.

30. "The 2012 Cost of Cyber Crime Report Says Successful Attacks Doubled," = http://www.infosecurity-magazine.com/view/28664/the-2012-cost-of-cyber-crime-report-says-successful-attacks-doubled-/.

31. David S. Alberts, "Information Warfare and Deterrence—Appendix D: Defensive War: Problem Formation and Solution Approach," www.ndu.edu/inns/books/ind/appd.htm.

32. Mary Mosquera, "Computer Attacks Spreading," TechWeb, November 18, 1999, www.techweb.com/wire/story/TWB19991118S0003.

33. *Ibid.*

Chapter 8

1. Joseph M. Kizza, *Computer Network Security* (New York: Springer, 2005).

2. Mani Subramanian, *Network Management: Principles and Practice* (Boston: Addison-Wesley, 2000).

3. Merike Kaeo, *Designing Network Security: A Practical Guide to Creating a Secure Network Infrastructure* (Indianapolis, IN: Cisco, 1999).

4. Kizza, *Computer Network Security;* Mick Bauer, "Paranoid Penguin: Practical Threat Analysis and Risk Management," *Linux Journal* 93 (March 2003).

5. R. Smith, *Internet Cryptography* (Boston: Addison-Wesley, 1997).

6. William Stallings, *Cryptography and Network Security: Principles and Practice,* 2d ed. (Upper Saddle River, NJ: Prentice Hall, 1998).

7. "Nmap—The Network Mapper," www.insecure.org/nmap.

8. *Ibid.*

9. Lincoln Stein, *Web Security: A Step-by-Step Reference Guide* (Boston: Addison-Wesley, 1998).

10. "Computer Attacks: What They Are and How to Defend Against Them," Computer Security Resource Center, National Institute of Standards and Technology, May 1999, http://csrc.nist.gov/publications/nistbul/html-archive/may-99.html.

11. Mick Bauer, "Paranoid Penguin: Practical Threat Analysis and Risk Management," *Linux Journal* 93 (March 2003).

12. Janet Kornblum. "Federal Unit to Fight Hacking," CNET News.com, http://news.com.com/2100–1023–208562.html.

13. Stein.

14. Kornblum.

15. Kizza.

16. Marcus J. Tanum, "Network Forensics: Network Traffic Monitoring," www.nfr.net/forum/publications/monitor.html.

17. *Ibid.*

18. Stein.

19. *Ibid.*

20. Tanum.

21. Stallings.

22. *Ibid.*

23. James F. Kurose and Keith W. Ross, *Computer Networking: A Top-Down Approach*

Featuring the Internet (Boston: Addison-Wesley, 2000).

24. M. Mullins, "Implementing a Network Intrusion Detection System," May 16, 2002, http://www.zdnet.com.au/itmanager/technology/story/0,2000029587,20265285,00.htm.

25. *Ibid.*

26. "Central Texas LAN Association Network vs. Host Based Intrusion Detection." http://www.ctla.org/newsletter/1999/0999nl.pdf.

27. M. Handley, V. Paxson and C. Kreibich, "Network Intrusion Detection: Evasion, Traffic Normalization, and End-to-End Protocol Semantics." http://www.icir.org/vern/papers/norm-usenix-sec-01-html/norm.html.

28. Mullins.

29. "Central Texas LAN."

30. "Evolving the High Performance Computing and Communications Initiative to Support the Nation's Information Infrastructure." http://www.nap.edu/readingroom/books/hpcc/contents.html.

31. "Information Technology for the Twenty-First Century: A Bold Investment in America's Future." http://www.ccic.gov/pubs/it2-ip/.

Chapter 9

1. "Social Network Service." Wikipedia. http://en.wikipedia.org/wiki/Social_Network_Service.

2. BITNET History, http://www.livinginternet.com/u/ui_bitnet.htm.

3. *Ibid.*

4. *Ibid.*

5. Janet F. Asteroff, "Electronic Bulletin Boards, A Case Study: The Columbia University Center for Computing Activities," http://www.columbia.edu/acis/history/bboard.html.

6. Mailing Lists: Listserv History, http://www.livinginternet.com/l/lli.htm.

7. *Ibid.*

8. "Social Network Service."

9. *Ibid.*

10. *Ibid.*

11. *Ibid.*

12. *Ibid.*

13. Monica Chew, Dirk Balfanz and Ben Laurie, "(Under)mining Privacy in Social Networks," http://w2spconf.com/2008/papers/s3p2.pdf.

14. Balachander Krishnamurthy and Craig E. Wills, "Privacy Leakage in Mobile Online Social Networks," http://web.cs.wpi.edu/~cew/papers/wosn09.pdf.

15. *Ibid.*

16. *Ibid.*

17. *Ibid.*

18. Chew, et al.

Chapter 10

1. "Everything You Need to Know About Each Mobile OS (Operating System), Parts 1–4," http://www.fusedblog.com/everything-you-need-to-know-about-each-mobile-os-operating-system-part-1-of-4-series-40-symbian/; and Mark Komisky, "Mobile Device Security II: Handheld Operating Systems," http://www.datamation.com/mowi/article.php/3575316/Mobile-Device-Security-II-Handheld-Operating-Systems.htm.

2. http://esec-lab.sogeti.com/post/Analysis-of-the-jailbreakme-v3-font-exploit.

3. C-Skills, http://c-skills.blogspot.com/search?q=exploit, July 23, 2010; C-Skills, http://c-skills.blogspot.com/, July 15, 2010; and "Android Malware DroidDream: How it Works," Lookout Mobile Security Blog, http://blog.mylookout.com/2011/03/android-malware-droiddream-how-it-works, March 2011.

4. "Types of Bluetooth Hacks and Its Security Issues," http://hassam.hubpages.com/hub/Types-Of-Bluetooth-Hacks-And-Its-Security-Issues.

5. http://trifinite.org/trifinite_stuff_bluedump.html.

6. Ibid.

7. Wikipedia, http://en.wikipedia.org/wiki/Mobile_device_management.

8. Komisky, "Mobile Device Security II."

Chapter 11

1. Peter Mell and Timothy Grance, "The NIST Definition of Cloud Computing, NIST Special Publication 800–145," http://csrc.nist.gov/publications/nistpubs/800-145/SP800-145.pdf, 2011.

2. Greenpeace. "Make IT Green: Cloud Computing and its Contribution to Climate

Change," Greenpeace USA, http://www.greenpeace.org/usa/en/media-center/reports/make-it-green-cloud-computing/.

3. Neil MacDonald, "Yes, Hypervisors Are Vulnerable," http://blogs.gartner.com/neil_macdonald/2011/01/26/yes-hypervisors-are-vulnerable/, January 26, 2011.

4. IBM X-Force 2010 Mid-Year Trend and Risk Report, http://www-05.ibm.com/fr/pdf/IBM_X-Force2010_Mid-Year_Trend_and_Risk_Report.pdf.

5. "Elastic Load Balancing," AWS, http://aws.amazon.com/elasticloadbalancing/.

6. http://it-audit.sans.org/community/papers/ids-load-balancer-security-audit-administratorsperspective_119.

7. Ibid.

Chapter 12

1. Joseph M. Kizza, *A Guide to Computer Network Security* (London: Springer-Verlag, 2009).

2. *Ibid.*

3. Kizza.

4. *Ibid.*

5. "Security Compliance Management," NetForensics, http://www.netforensics.com/compliance/.

6. Family Educational Rights and Privacy Act (FERPA), http://www2.ed.gov/policy/gen/guid/fpco/ferpa/index.html.

7. *Ibid.*

8. Financial Modernization Act (Gramm-Leach-Bliley Act), http://www.consumerprivacyguide.org/law/glb.shtml.

9. Sarbanes-Oxley. http://www.soxlaw.com/.

10. FISMA, Detailed Overview, http://csrc.nist.gov/groups/SMA/fisma/overview.html.

11. Health Insurance Portability and Accountability Act (HIPAA), Centers for Medicare and Medical Aid Services. http://www.cms.gov/hipaageninfo/.

Bibliography

Acohido, Byron. http://www.enterprise-security-today.com/news/Mobile-Devices-Vulnerable-to-Attack/story.xhtml?story_id=0010003FAI65, April 10, 2012.

Alberts, David S. "Information Warfare and Deterrence—Appendix D: Defensive War: Problem Formation and Solution Approach." www.ndu.edu/inns/books/ind/appd.htm.

"AOL Charged with Blocking Opponents' E-Mail." ZDNet News, April 13, 2006. Retrieved on July 10, 2006.Asteroff, Janet F. "Electronic Bulletin Boards, A Case Study: The Columbia University Center for Computing Activities." http://www.columbia.edu/acis/history/bboard.html.

Bauer, Mick. "Paranoid Penguin: Practical Threat Analysis and Risk Management." *Linux Journal* 93 (March 2003).

"BITNET History." http://www.livinginternet.com/u/ui_bitnet.htm.

Bock, Wally. "The Cost of Laptop Theft." www.bockinfo.com/docs/laptheft.htm.

Bohannon, Lee. "The Need for a Moral Code." www.abortionessay.com/files/moralcode.html.

"Bylaws for Internet Corporation for Assigned Names and Numbers." ICANN, April 8, 2005. www.icann.org/general/bylaws.htm

Calof, Jonathan. "Increasing Your CIQ: The Competitive Intelligence Edge." www.edco.on.ca/journal/item22.htm.

"CERT/CC Statistics 1998–2005." CERT Coordination Center, Carnegie Mellon Software Engineering Institute. www.cert.org/stats/cert_stats.html.

Chew, Monica, Dirk Balfanz and Ben Laurie. "(Under)mining Privacy in Social Networks." http://w2spconf.com/2008/papers/s3p2.pdf.

Christensen, John. "Bracing for Guerilla Warfare in Cyberspace." CNN Interactive, April 6, 1999.

Chronicle of Higher Education, July 17, 1998. http://chronicle.com.

CNN. "Canadian Juvenile Charged in Connection with February 'Denial of Service' Attacks." http://cnn.com/2000/TECH/computing/04/15/hacker.arrest.01.html.

CNN. "Mitnick Schools Feds on Hacking 101." http://cnn.com/2000/TECH/computing/03/03/mitnick.the.prof/mitnick.the.prof.html.

CNN Headline News, May 28, 2000.

Comer, Douglas. *Computer Networks and Intranets*. Upper Saddle River, NJ: Prentice Hall, 1997.

_____. *Internetworking with TCP/IP: Principles, Protocols, and Architecture*, 4th ed. Upper Saddle River, NJ: Prentice Hall, 2000.

Common Vulnerabilities and Exposures. www.cve.mitre.org/cve/downloads/full-cve.html

"Communication from the Commission to the Council and the European Parliament." Commission of the European Communities (Com2000), 2002. www.europa.eu.int/eurlex/en/com/pdf/2000/com2000_0202en01.pdf.

"Computer Attacks: What They Are and How to Defend Against Them." Computer Security Resource Center, National Institute of Standards and Technology, May 1999. http://csrc.nist.gov/publications/nistbul/html-archive/may–99.html

Consumers Union. "Another Week, Another Identity Theft Scandal: Recent Data Security Breaches Underscore Need for Stronger Identity Theft Protections." www.consumersunion.org/campaigns/learn_more/002232indiv.html.

CSI. Press Release. www.gocsi.com/prelea_000321.htm.

CSI Computer Crime and Security Survey 2009. http://gocsi.com/survey.

Denning, Peter J., ed. *Computers Under Attack: Intruders, Worms and Viruses.* New York: ACM, 1990.

"Evidence Mounts that Comcast Is Targeting Bittorrent Traffic." ARS Technica. http://arstechnica.com/old/content/2007/10/evidence-mounts-that-comcast-is-targeting-bittorrent-traffic.ars.

"Evolving the High Performance Computing and Communications Initiative to Support the Nation's Information Infrastructure—Executive Summary." www.nap.edu/readingroom/books/hpcc/exec.html.

Fagothey, Austin. *Rights and Reason*, 2nd ed. Rockford, IL: Tan, 1959.

"Falling Through the Net: Toward Digital Inclusion." NTIA 2000. www.ntia.doc.gov/ntiahome/digitaldivide/execsumfttn00.htm.

Family Educational Rights and Privacy Act (FERPA). http://www2.ed.gov/policy/gen/guid/fpco/ferpa/index.html.

Federal Communications Commission Policy Statement, August 5, 2005. http://fjallfoss.fcc.gov/edocs_public/attachmatch/FCC-05-151A1.pdf.

"Federal Cybersleuth Armed with First Ever Wiretap Order Nets International Hacker Charged with Illegally Entering Harvard and U.S. Military Computers." U.S. Department of Justice, March 1996. www.usdoj.gov/opa/pr/1996/March96/146.txt.

Financial Modernization Act (Gramm-Leach-Bliley Act). http://www.consumerprivacyguide.org/law/glb.shtml.

Fiserberg, T., David Gries, Juris Hartmanis, Don Holcomb, M. Stuart Lynn, and Thomas Santoro. "The Cornell Commission: On Morris and the Worm." In *Computers Under Attack: Intruders, Worms and Viruses*, ed. Peter J. Denning. New York: ACM, 1990.

FISMA, Detailed Overview. http://csrc.nist.gov/groups/SMA/fisma/overview.html.

Forcht, Karen. *Computer Security Management.* Danvers, MA: Boyd and Fraser, 1994.

Fox, Robert. "News Track: Age and Sex." *Communications of the ACM*, vol. 43, no. 9 (September 2000).

Funk, Ken. "Technology and Christian 'Values.'" http://web.engr.oregonstate.edu/~funkk/Technology.

Gady, Franz-Stefan. "Statistics and the 'Cyber Crime Epidemic,' 2011," http://www.ewi.info/statistics-and-cyber-crime-epidemic.

Grampp, F., and R. Morris. "UNIX Operating System Security," Part 2. *AT&T Bell Laboratories Tech Journal*, vol. 63, no. 8 (October 1984).

Grosso, Andrew. "The Economic Espionage Act: Touring the Minefields." *Communications of the ACM*, vol. 43, no. 8 (August 2000).

Handley, M., V. Paxson and C. Kreibich C. "Network Intrusion Detection: Evasion, Traffic Normalization, and End-to-End Protocol Semantics." http://www.icir.org/vern/papers/norm-usenix-sec-01-html/norm.html.

Health Insurance Portability and Accountability Act (HIPAA). Centers for Medicare and Medical Aid Services. http://www.cms.gov/hipaageninfo/.

"How Viruses Work: Some Common Viruses." ZDNet. www.zdnet.com/pcmay/pctech/content/18/03/tn1003.06.html.

Hull, Richard T. "The Varieties of Ethical Theories." www.richard-t-hull.com/publications/varieties.pdf.

"Information Age Haves and Have-Nots." www.library.wustl.edu/~listmgr/devel-1/august1998/00058.html.

"Information Technology for the Twenty-First Century: A Bold Investment in America's Future." www.ccic.gov/pubs/it2-ip.

"Internet2 Initiatives." www.internet2.edu/initiatives.

"Israel Citizen Arrested in Israel for Hacking U.S. and Israel Government Computers." U.S. Department of Justice, March 1, 1998. www.usdoj.gov/opa/pr/1998/march/125.htm.html.

Jackson, Steve. "ESM NetRecon: Ultrascan." www.si.com.au/Appendix/NetRecon%20Ultrascan%20technology.html.

Johnson, D. J. *Computer Ethics,* 2nd ed. Upper Saddle River, NJ: Prentice Hall, 1994.

Kaeo, Merike. *Designing Network Security: A Practical Guide to Creating a Secure Network Infrastructure.* Indianapolis, IN: Cisco, 1999.

Kessler, Andy. "Give Me Bandwidth..." *The Weekly Standard.* http://www.weeklystandard.com/Content/Public/Articles/000/000/012/348yjwfo.asp, retrieved July 9, 2006.

King, Samuel T., Peter M. Chen, Yi-Min Wang, Chad Verbowski, Helen J. Wang and Jacob R. Lorch. "SubVirt: Implementing Malware with Virtual Machines." http://web.eecs.umich.edu/~pmchen/papers/king06.pdf, 2006.

Kizza, Joseph M. *Civilizing the Internet: Global Concerns and Efforts Toward Regulation.* Jefferson, NC: McFarland, 1998.

_____. *Computer Network Security.* New York: Springer, 2005.

_____. *Ethical and Social Issues in the Information Age.* New York: Springer, 1999.

_____. *Ethical and Social Issues in the Information Age,* 2nd ed. New York: Springer, 2002.

_____. *A Guide to Computer Network Security.* London: Springer-Verlag, 2009.

Kornblum, Janet. "Federal Unit to Fight Hacking." CNET News.com. http://news.com.com/2100–1023–208562.html.

Krishnamurthy, Balachander, and Craig E. Wills. "Privacy Leakage in Mobile Online Social Networks." http://web.cs.wpi.edu/~cew/papers/wosn09.pdf.

Kurose, James, F., and Keith W. Ross. *Computer Networking: A Top-Down Approach Featuring the Internet.* Boston: Addison-Wesley, 2000.

Laxton, William G., Jr. "The End of Net Neutrality." *Duke Law and Technology Review,* 2006, http://www.law.duke.edu/journals/dltr/articles/2006dltr0015.html.

Levy, Elias. "Trends in Computer Attacks." USENIX. www.usenix.org/publications/login/1998-5/levy.html.

Levy, Steven. *Hackers: Heroes of the Computer Revolution.* Garden City, NY: Anchor/Doubleday, 1984.

MacDonald, Chris. "Moral Decision Making: An Analysis." www.ethicsweb.ca/guide/moral-decision.html.

Mailing Lists: Listserv History. http://www.livinginternet.com/l/lli.htm.

McAfee Virus Information Center. "Virus Alerts." www.vil.nai.com/villib/alpha.asp

"Melissa Virus Writer Pleads Guilty." Sophas. www.sophas.com/virusinfo/articles/melissa.htm.

Mell, Peter, and Tim Grance. "Effectively and Securely Using the Cloud Computing Paradigm." *http://www.scribd.com/doc/13427395/,* 2011.

Metzler, Jim, and Steve Taylor. "The Data Center Network Transition: Wide Area Networking Alert." *Network World,* http://www.networkworld.com/newsletters/frame/2011/080811wan1.html?source=nww_rss, 2011.

Miller, Michael. "The Good Life." http://www.quackgrass.com/goodlife.html.

"Moral Relativism." Internet Encyclopedia of Philosophy. www.utm.edu/research/iep/ni/m-ration.html.

Mosquera, Mary. "Computer Attacks Spreading." *TechWeb,* November 18, 1999. www.techweb.com/wire/story/TWB19991118S0003.

_____. "Most Computer Attacks Come from Organizations." *TechWeb,* September 14, 1999. www.techweb.com/wire/story/TWB19990914S0014.

Mullins, M. "Implementing a Network Intrusion Detection System." May 16, 2002. http://www.zdnet.com.au/itmanager/technology/story/0,2000029587,20265285,00.htm.

"Net Neutrality Alternative Proposed." http://www.pcmag.com/article2/0,2817,1970356,00.asp.

Netscape. "'Love Bug' Computer Virus Wreaks Fresh Havoc." www.mynetscape.com/news.

"Network Neutrality." Wikipedia. http://en.wikipedia.org/wiki/Network_neutrality.

Neumann, Peter G. "Risks of Insiders." *Communications of the ACM*, vol. 42, no. 12 (December 1999).

"News and Events: Web Surpasses One Billion Documents." *Inktomi*. www.inktomi.com/news/press/billion.html.

"Nmap—The Network Mapper." www.insecure.org/nmap.

"Online and Out of Line: Why Is Cybercrime on the Rise, and Who Is Responsible?" ABC News. www.ABCNews.com/sections/us/DailyNews/cybercrime_000117. html.

"The Purpose of Ethics." www.sympatico.ca/saburns/pg0401.htm.

Rubens, Paul. "Apple Security Isn't a Sure Bet," http://www.enterprisenetworkingplanet.com/netsecur/article.php/3883946/Apple-Security-Isnt-a-Sure-Bet.htm.

Sagan, Carl. "A New Way to Think About Rules to Live By." *Parade Magazine*, November 28, 1993.

SANS. "The Twenty Most Critical Internet Security Vulnerabilities (Updated) : The Experts Consensus." www.sans.org/top20.

Sarbanes-Oxley. http://www.soxlaw.com/.

"SCO SNMPd Default Writeable Community String." www.securiteam.com/unixfocus/SCO_SNMPd_default_writeable_community_string.html.

"Section A: The Nature and Definition of Critical Infrastructure." The National Infrastructure Protection Center. www.nipc.gov/nipcfaq.htm.

"Security Compliance Management." NetForensics, http://www.netforensics.com/compliance/.

"Security in Cyberspace." U.S. Senate Permanent Subcommittee on Investigations, June 5, 1996. www.fas.org/irp/congress/1996_hr/s960605t.htm.

Seely, Don. "Password Cracking: A Game of Wits." In *Computers Under Attack: Intruders, Worms and Viruses*, ed. Peter J. Denning. New York: ACM, 1990.

Smith, R. *Internet Cryptography*. Boston: Addison-Wesley, 1997.

"Social Network Service." Wikipedia. http://en.wikipedia.org/wiki/Social_Network_Service.

Solomon, Robert C. *Morality and the Good Life: An Introduction to Ethics Through Classical Sources,* 2d ed. New York: McGraw-Hill, 1992.

Stallings, William. *Cryptography and Network Security: Principles and Practice*, 2nd ed. Upper Saddle River, NJ: Prentice Hall, 1998.

_____. *Local and Metropolitan Area Networks*, 6th ed. Upper Saddle River, NJ: Prentice Hall, 2000.

Stein, Lincoln. *Web Security: A Step-by-Step Reference Guide*. Boston: Addison-Wesley, 1998.

Stephenson, P. "Preventive Medicine." *LAN Magazine*, November 1993.

Stoll, Clifford. "Stalking the Wily Hacker." In *Computers Under Attack: Intruders, Worms and Viruses*, ed. Peter J. Denning. New York: ACM, 1990.

Stoller, Matt. "Craigslist Blocked by Cox for Three Months." MyDD Direct Democracy. http://www.mydd.com/story/2006/6/8/144357/7525.

Subramanian, Mani. *Network Management: Principles and Practice*. Boston: Addison-Wesley, 2000.

Tanum, Marcus J. "Network Forensics: Network Traffic Monitoring." www.nfr.net/forum/publications/monitor.html.

"2011 Mobile Threat Report." https://www.mylookout.com/mobile-threat-report.

"Verizon Rejects Text Messages for Abortion Rights Group." *New York Times,* September 27, 2007.

Whitehats. "Risk Assessment." www.whitehats.com/tools/vuln.html.

Wu, Tim. "Network Neutrality, Broadband Discrimination." *Journal of Telecommunications and High Technology Law* 2 (2003): 141. doi: 10.2139/ssrn.388863.

Index